RESTLESS BONES

By the same author

Ritualism and Politics in Victorian Britain
Martin Niemöller
Oberammergau and the Passion Play
Secrets of Mount Sinai
A Guide to the Dordogne
Between Marx and Christ
A Children's Bible
Our Christian Heritage
(with Warwick Rodwell)
The Life and Teaching of Jesus
(with Audrey W. Bentley)

James Bentley

RESTLESS BONES:
THE STORY OF RELICS

Constable · London

First published in Great Britain 1985
by Constable and Company Limited
10 Orange Street London WC2H 7EG

Set in Linotron Plantin 11pt by
Rowland Phototypesetting Limited
Bury St Edmunds, Suffolk
Printed in Great Britain by
St Edmundsbury Press
Bury St Edmunds, Suffolk

British Library CIP data
Bentley, James, *1937–*
Restless bones: the story of relics
1. Relics and reliquaries
I. Title
231.7'3 BV890

ISBN 0 09 465850 1

For St Etheldreda

Contents

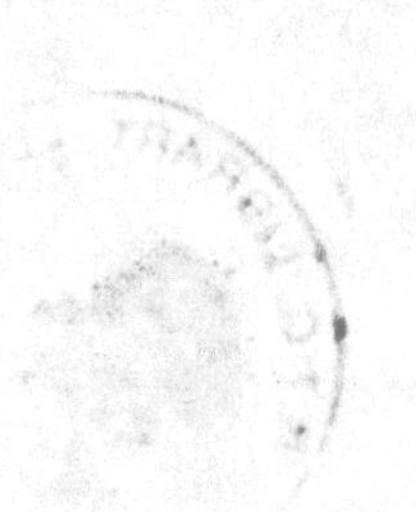

Illustrations

Between pages 60 and 61

Between pages 156 and 157

St Edmund's Head (*Richard Burn*)

Cromwell's Head (*The British Library and the Brometrika Trustees*)

Jeremy Bentham (*University College, London*)

A ninth-century Irish reliquary (*National Museum, Copenhagen photographer Niels Elswing*)

Mr Jinnah's shoes (*Department of Archaeology, Government of Pakistan*)

The Sainte-Chapelle (*French Government Tourist Office*)

Three saints, depicted on a reliquary carrying their severed heads (*Musée de Cluny*)

Riemenschneider's Holy Blood Altar (*Tourist Office, Rothenburg ob der Tauber*)

Acknowledgements

For helping me in various ways as I was writing this book I should like to thank Miss Helen Alexander, Mr Andrew Best, Dr Michael Clanchy, Mr Stephen Dykes Bower, the Revd Paul Hawkins, the Revd Leslie Mitchell and Mrs Anne Shortland-Jones.

JAMES BENTLEY.

I say that time is at the doors
When you may worship me without reproach;
For I will leave my relics in your land,
And you may carve a shrine about my dust,
And burn a fragrant lamp before my bones,
When I am gathered to the glorious saints.

St Simeon Stylites
(Alfred Lord Tennyson)

Introduction

In the view of the Romantic poet Samuel Taylor Coleridge, Cologne was a city of stenches and stinks and 'of monks and bones'. A hundred and fifty years later the odious smells have gone, the monks are fewer, but the bones remain in all their astonishing profusion.

This book is about such bones: the remains of the saintly (and not so saintly) dead. More than any other city in western Europe, Cologne exults in its countless relics, housed and proudly displayed in twelve majestic Romanesque churches and the mightiest cathedral on the river Rhine. To examine a few of them is an enticing introduction to this enquiry into some of the many thousands of others dispersed throughout the world.

Cologne is the resting place, for instance, of a British queen and her eleven thousand companions. St Ursula was the daughter of King Deonotus. Legend has it that a 'most ferocious tyrant' sought to marry her, threatening to lay waste her father's lands should she refuse. Ursula consented, provided that the tyrant become a Christian and she were granted as companions eleven noble virgins, each with a thousand attendant virgins, along with eleven ships. The women sailed to Cologne, travelled on foot to meet the Pope in Rome, and returning to Cologne were massacred by the Huns in the year A.D. 238.

The martyrs were buried in a Roman cemetery, where today stands St Ursula's church. An ancient stone let into the chancel wall of the church records that a certain Clematius built a church over the virgins' graves in the fourth century. But the cult of these bones was enormously boosted in 1106, when excavators building a new city wall dug many of them up. Amongst those fired by this discovery was Archbishop Reinald of Cologne. By great good fortune his agent discovered a headless corpse with a label identifying Queen Ursula. Soon countless more relics were found in the cemetery, all neatly labelled as bishops, cardinals, even a Pope.

Clematius's church was deemed too mean for the newly discovered relics, and so the present exquisite building was founded. Today you can sit in St Ursula's church, gazing behind the high altar where the saint's remains (or most of them) lie in a jewelled shrine. On either side are busts of two of her virgins, sweetly smiling in the joy of their swift passage by martyrdom from earth to Heaven (for, as Seneca observed, what was grievous to endure can be sweet to remember). The busts of these maidens are pierced, so that the faithful may gaze on their bones inside. Similar busts and bones stare down from high on either side of the church. The worshipper is carried, so to speak, by the saintly dead beyond the high altar and up into Heaven.

Ursula's corpse is present here only in part, first because her head was chopped off by the Huns and secondly because so many Christians longed to own a piece of her that many bits were parcelled out throughout Europe. In the fourteenth century Pope Boniface IX deemed this a scandal and forbade it. Even so the Jesuits managed a spectacular translation of parts of St Ursula to Lisbon in 1588.

And as if this were not enough, the church of St Ursula in Cologne possesses a yet greater wonder: the so-called Golden

Chamber, a square chapel built on the south side in the seventeenth century. Here is a riot of relics. On all four sides busts bearing bones are ranged on shelves, all looking happy, even prim in death. Many have the tops of their heads sliced through, so that you can lift off the corona and look down on the skull. In between the rows of shelves rise glass cupboards containing more saintly skulls, wrapped in red embroidered cloths. A piece of St Ursula herself is inside a baroque bust that depicts her hands wide in ecstasy, as she rejoices among the remains of her virgins. As Byron wonderingly put it:

Eleven thousand maidenheads of bone,
The greatest number flesh has ever known.

And above the shelves, on all four walls, thousands and thousands more bones are arranged in brilliantly inventive patterns, protected by wire-netting. This, however, is no macabre art; this is a holy cult. And on the altar itself, in a glass container, is the little skull of Queen Ursula.

Though it seems scarcely possible, Archbishop Reinald of Cologne soon laid his hands on a set of ancient bones even worthier than those of St Ursula and her eleven thousand virgins. To honour these new relics he decided to rebuild his already superb cathedral. Today the enormous Gothic building still houses Cologne's greatest treasure: the crowned corpses of the Magi, the three kings who brought to the infant Jesus gifts of gold, frankincense and myrrh.

The story of these three kings developed over Christian history since the time St Matthew first wrote them into the Gospel. Matthew does not even record that they were kings. No-one in the early church thought they were – though the church father Tertullian says they were 'nearly kings'. Today scholars surmise that the devout, reading in the Book of Psalms that 'the Kings of Tharsis and the Isles shall offer gifts,' assumed that this text could refer only to the wise men – so they dubbed them kings.

Again, Matthew never says how many wise men actually

visited Jesus. Early catacomb paintings depict sometimes fewer, sometimes more than three of them. Eventually Christians agreed that they must have brought one present each – and so there were three.

Finally Christians began assigning them names: Zarvanades, Gusnaphus, Assuerus, Kagba, Badalima and Bithisaria are a few of those suggested until finally most believers settled on Caspar, Melchior and Balthasar. Eventually legend hardened into fact. By the early eighth century the Venerable Bede could describe with total confidence Melchior as 'old and white-haired, hairy with a long beard and long locks'. Melchior, Bede asserted, gave the gold to Jesus. Caspar, who was 'a beardless youth', brought frankincense. And Balthasar, 'olive-complexioned, with a goodish beard,' gave the infant Saviour myrrh.

If the legend of the three wise men could be thus embroidered over eight centuries, need we be surprised that devout men and women began to tell how their bones had been discovered by the mother of the Emperor Constantine on her visit to the Holy Land, how she sent them to Constantinople, whence in the sixth century they were transferred to the church of San Eustorgio in Milan? There they were treasured until 1164, when the Emperor Frederick Barbarossa defeated the Milanese and gave them to his chaplain and counsellor, Reinald of Cologne.

Frederick Barbarossa specially needed the bones of these three kings. Longing to restore the empire to the Christian glories of his predecessor Charlemagne, he was unfortunately at odds with the papacy which could have confirmed that glory. Now he possessed relics symbolically more potent than the papacy itself. Had not these same magi been the first to acknowledge Christ the King? Their presence in Cologne now divinely acknowledged the reign of Frederick Barbarossa.

Their presence remains potent today. They lie behind the high altar of Cologne cathedral in a fantastic golden shrine made between 1220 and 1230 by the most skilled craftsmen of Aachen. A removable panel enables holy men to reach into the shrine and touch the bones, while the people rejoicing may venerate them, open to human sight. The shrine was damaged during the Second World War and restored in 1973 under the direction of the goldsmith Peter Bolg. In that year the Archbishop of Cologne magnanimously gave a fragment of the three wise men back to the church of San Eustorgio, Milan. Twenty thousand twentieth-century pilgrims visited the shrine when it was venerated at the feast of the Epiphany in 1974; and during the three days of the feast the following year the number venerating these relics rose to one hundred thousand.

The magi came a long way to see Jesus. Their alleged bones have travelled much further since then. Sometimes much travelled relics seem to have arrived in two places at once, making it difficult for the believer to judge which are the authentic ones. Legend has it that Jesus's apostle Thomas, for example, was chosen by the other apostles to missionise India. He converted many to Christianity and worked several miracles, but eventually he annoyed King Mazdai by persuading his son to embrace the new faith. Mazdai ordered his soldiers to take Thomas to the summit of a hill and there slay him.

Today many Indian Christians claim to derive their church from the work of the Apostle Thomas. We learn from the *Anglo-Saxon Chronicle* that King Alfred the Great sent offerings to the shrine of Thomas in India. Marco Polo actually visited his tomb in 1293, recording that even the Saracens revered the saint as a holy man. 'As for pilgrims from Christian lands, they take the earth from the place where the saint was killed and give a portion of it to anyone who is sick; and by the power of God and the Apostle Thomas, the sick one is immediately cured.'

Portuguese missionaries arrived in India in the early sixteenth century and found the apostle's relics still there. Today you drive along the beautiful shore of the Bay of Bombay to a suburb of Madras named Mylapore and find the bones they discovered honoured in the cathedral of San Thomé. Only one question hangs over this long tradition identifying these as the relics of St Thomas. Other reputable early Christian historians state that his corpse was not in India but at Edessa in the early fourth century. From there *someone's* bones purporting to be Thomas's were taken to the Aegean island of Khios. From there they were translated yet again, to the Italian town of Ortona in the Abruzzi. And there today they are venerated.

Such difficult questions continually tax the historian of the relic, as this book will show. But questions of authenticity have always exercised the minds of those who came across them. Not every medieval Christian was credulous. Sometimes chauvinism played its part too in leading a man to doubt whether the bones of a dead foreigner deserved veneration. The French churchman Lanfranc, who became Archbishop of Canterbury after the Normans overcame the English, was tempted to throw the bones of the Anglo-Saxon saint Alphege out of Canterbury cathedral. Alphege, a former archbishop, had been kidnapped by the Danes in 1011. He had refused to pay an enormous ransom of £3,000, and he also forbade the poor Anglo-Saxons to pay it on his behalf. Alphege further enraged his captors by preaching sermons to them while they feasted. Eventually the goaded Danes smashed him to the ground with the great bones left over from their feasting, and one of Alphege's converts, a youth named Thrum, mercifully finished him off with an axe.

Lanfranc suggested that Alphege did not die so much as a martyr than as one who failed to keep his promise to pay a ransom. He appealed to the philosopher-statesman Anselm. Anselm replied that just as St John the Baptist, himself slain by the impious, was a martyr for truth, so St Alphege was a martyr for justice. Lanfranc repented of his prejudice and confirmed the cult of the Anglo-Saxon.

Curiously enough, a century later the relics of this Anglo-Saxon were decisively to inspire another Norman, St Thomas Becket. (Though born in Britain, Becket was the son of a Rouen merchant.) Knowing that his violent death was rapidly approaching, Thomas Becket in the last sermon of his life described Alphege as Canterbury's first martyr. As he himself was about to die he commended his soul to Almighty God and to St Alphege. Within two years Becket had been canonised and the cult of his bones soon far outshone that of the relics of Alphege.

Thus one relic generated another. If the bones of St Ursula and her eleven thousand virgins initially simply startle us by the bizarreness of the cult of relics, they – like Alphege and Becket – also remind us that the blood of the martyrs is the seed of the church. If the bones of the magi in Cologne take us far from the simple Gospel story into the realms of legend and historical fancies, the relics of St Thomas, in Ortona or Mylapore, remain as visual reminders of Jesus's parting words to his followers: 'Go therefore and make disciples of all the nations.'

These often restless bones are thus far more than mere clay, 'dead sinners revised and edited,' as Ambrose Bierce expressed it, to bemuse the simple-minded. Many of them still exercise a powerful fascination for sophisticated men and women of the twentieth century as well as for the supposedly simple believer. They may tax our credulity. They cannot be lightly dismissed. It is time to look more closely at some of the more extraordinary among them.

I

Relics still potent

For over four hundred years Naples cathedral has guarded two glass phials of thick, almost black, coagulated liquid. The faithful believe it to be the blood of St Januarius, martyred nearly 1,700 years ago.

Januarius, a son of Naples, had been converted to Christianity and consecrated Bishop of Benevento when the Emperor Diocletian began to persecute the faithful. After the governor of Campania, on Diocletian's orders, arrested three Christian friends of the bishop, Januarius made a secret visit to comfort them. Discovered, he was arrested and after humiliation by the governor (Januarius was forced to run in front of the governor's chariot, carrying huge iron bars), was condemned to death. The punishment was savage: Januarius and his fellow-Christians were to be torn to pieces in the arena of Pozzuoli by wild beasts. Strangely, according to later legend, none of these beasts would lay a single claw on these good people. The governor accordingly sentenced them to be beheaded. The sentence was carried out outside Pozzuoli, and there Januarius and his fellow-sufferers were buried.

All this took place around the year A.D. 305. About a hundred years later Christians dug up what they took to be Januarius's bones and put them in a small church, San Gennaro, dedicated to the martyr, near the Solfatara. But the holy corpse did not rest there. During the wars with the Normans St Januarius was removed for safe keeping first back to Benevento and then to the monastery of Montevergine on the Via Avellino (a monastery so-called because it possesses a picture of the Virgin Mary allegedly painted by St Luke himself).

But the Neapolitans did not forget Januarius, now regarded as their patron and protector. In 1294 they began building a superb cathedral in the French Gothic style, dedicated to the saint. In 1497 the body of Januarius was transported in triumph from Montevergine to this new cathedral, where it remains to this day.

Death by execution left the saint's corpse in two parts. To honour the trunk the brilliant architect Tommaso Malvito was commissioned to create a richly decorated crypt under the cathedral. Today this masterpiece of Neapolitan renaissance architecture, with its two great bronze doors, shelters Januarius's remains – apart from his head and the phials of his congealed blood. The head, in a silver-gilt bust, flanked by the phials of blood, lies in a tabernacle behind the chief altar of a sumptuous baroque chapel off the south aisle of the cathedral. Six lesser altars honour the altar of the blood. The Roman artist Domenichino was employed to paint the interior of this chapel. The Lombard sculptor Cosimo Fanzago built an enormous grille of gilded bronze to protect the whole chapel and a balustrade to protect Januarius's altar itself.

As if by way of recompense to their Saviour, who was buried in a borrowed tomb, Christians have often placed their illustrious dead in fine surroundings. But the last resting place of St Januarius surpasses most others. Not surprisingly: for St Januarius has continued to display his favour to the city of Naples by an extraordinary miracle. Legend has it that when his corpse was first transferred to that city from Pozzuoli, the bishop who carried him was astounded when the dead saint's congealed blood began to flow again. Before the blood congealed a second time, a quantity was saved, and this now flanks the bust containing Januarius's head. And since that time, no fewer than eighteen times a year, the thick opaque liquid has continued to liquefy itself again.

No-one can be sure that St Januarius's blood will liquefy at the requisite time. The faithful believe that the speed with which it liquefies indicates the degree of prosperity Januarius will grant to Naples in that year. Should the blood fail to liquefy, the omens are truly bad.

The eighteen occasions on which vast crowds gather in Naples cathedral to pray for the liquefaction occur around three specific dates each year: the Saturday before the first Sunday in May (the anniversary of the translation of Januarius's bones to Naples); September 19th (the anniversary of the saint's martyrdom); and December 16th (on which day in 1631 Januarius is credited with preventing a threatened eruption of Vesuvius).

On each occasion the ceremony is the same. The martyr's head is exposed on its altar. Then a priest brings the blood close to this sacred relic, while the people pray. These prayers are led by privileged women – poor but spiritually wealthy – who are known as St Januarius's aunts (*zie di San Gennaro*). As if to display the saint's complete control over the miracle, the process of liquefaction is erratic. If nothing happens the anxious priests will turn the glass phials upside down for a while. But if all goes well, the thick black liquid ceases to congeal to the sides of the glass. It turns red. Sometimes it froths. At other times it increases in volume. The priest proclaims, 'The miracle has occurred.' The people sing 'We praise Thee, O God,' and those allowed inside the chapel reverently kiss the phial.

This is the miracle described in the sixteenth century by St Aloysius Gonzaga, who testified that on eight successive days around September 19th, while low mass was being said in Naples cathedral, 'the previously solid, dark brown mass, during an interval of no more than twenty-five minutes, became perfectly liquid and at the same time ruby red in colour, like freshly shed blood.' And in our own century the British observer Ian Rheidhaven Grant saw the blood liquefy several times, noting that the liquefied blood on those occasions did not increase in volume ('had it done so to any appreciable extent,' he commented, 'the already almost completely filled vessel must have blown out the stopper, or, more probably, have burst like a shrapnel shell').

So easy is it for the twentieth-century secular mind to mock the cult of relics that even something as startling as the liquefactions in Naples may fail to give the sceptic pause for thought. The monks of Peterborough Abbey in the twelfth century proudly claimed to possess, along with the right arm of St Oswald, the swaddling clothes in which the infant Jesus was wrapped, some wood from his manger, and even a fragment of the five loaves with which he allegedly fed 5,000 people. Today even a believing Christian is likely to doubt the authenticity of such relics, just as a believer might nowadays look askance at those holy places claiming to own, say, the Saviour's holy navel or the thirty pieces of silver for which Judas betrayed his Master. But that *something* actually happened and still happens to the alleged relics of St Januarius can scarcely be denied. In the words of a distinguished Jesuit scholar, Fr Herbert Thurston, who – though a devout Christian – did not in the end believe that the blood at Naples was truly that of the martyred saint, 'Few, if any, alleged miracles have been examined more carefully, more often, or by people of more divergent views than this of the blood of St Januarius, and it may be safely affirmed that no expert inquirer, however rationalist in temper he may be, now denies that what is said to take place *does* take place.'

As the historian Norman H. Baynes warned, writing about the relics that once protected the city of Constantinople, 'belief in miracle is a fact of history which the student ignores at his peril'. St Januarius in Naples reminds us to find some alternative explanation for his repeatedly liquefying blood or to continue to believe in the possibility of miracles today.

And the liquefying blood points towards a proper understanding of the relic as something far more than a gruesomely preserved corpse. In the eyes of the faithful, Januarius's blood liquefies as a sign that the martyr is not dead but alive in Heaven.

In the past believers were equally aware as we are of the horror of death. A relic of a saint transformed that horror into hope. In the fourth century A.D. St Gregory of Nyssa, revelling in this paradox, pointed out how the mould and dust from the martyred body of St Theodore was carried away as if it were gold. To touch the corpse of such a saint was a matter for huge gratification. Again, he noted how the ashes of forty Christian martyrs who had been burned to death were prized by their followers. 'I myself have a portion of this holy gift,' he wrote, 'and I have laid the bodies of my parents beside the relics of these warriors for Christ, that in the hour of the resurrection they might be awakened alongside these privileged comrades.'

Self-evidently, unless a saint whose relic is preserved and reverenced on earth is also alive in Heaven, in no way can he or she protect and assist those who seek such aid. Once accept that their souls live in Heaven, and their withered bodies seem transformed. For Gregory of Nyssa, the actual state of the saints on earth was beautiful and magnificent. 'Their souls have been carried to Heaven and there live in their own proper place. Their bodies, venerable and immaculate servants of those souls, whose incorruptibility they respected in life, keeping them far from vices and passions, are now honoured in their holy places,' he declared.

So the historian Peter Brown, writing of St Gregory of Tours who died in A.D. 594, notes that 'Gregory's world is full of tombs. They stood in the shady corners of the great basilicas, in crypts, scattered in the great dormitory suburbs of the dead outside the town, or they lay hidden in the brambles of some deserted village.' But the corpse of a saint transformed such a tomb from a place of gloom and sorrow into a source of hope and spiritual power. As Gregory of Tours himself declared of a saint, 'What sort of reward he has in Heaven is shown at his grave; the power coming out of his tomb declares him to be living in Paradise.'

Such beliefs are to be found today. In Corfu the body of St Spiridon lies for most of the year in a silver sarcophagus in the church of Agios Spiridon. Like Januarius, Spiridon was a bishop martyred during the Diocletian persecution of the church. His corpse was brought to Corfu in 1489.

Four times a year, on Palm Sunday, the Saturday of Holy Week, August 11th and the first Sunday in November, the citizens take the body out of the church and parade the saint round the old town and the Esplanade, seeking his blessing on all they do. 'So popular is the saint,' observes one guide, 'that nearly half the boys in the island are named after him.' If the islanders supposed they were dealing merely with a corpse, the parades would be no more than a grisly tourist charade. But just as the Neapolitans remember that their saint is alive and powerful by recalling how he averted an explosion of Vesuvius, so the relics of St Spiridon are paraded round Corfu on anniversaries of the times he delivered the island from the Turks, from the plague (twice) and from famine.

Basically, then, it is foolish to assume that the attitudes of our forefathers to the bones of saints are 'old-fashioned', or 'out-of-date' notions that no-one these days could countenance. While a twentieth-century Anglican Bishop of London (Dr Graham Leonard) can walk about with a bone of St Philip Neri in his pocket, we are very far from a totally secular age. In Graham Leonard's own view, 'this bone is a part of that saint in which he lived for God, not something to be discarded; and we must now treat it with reverence and respect and thankfulness, that in this piece of bone a man actually walked and lived and loved God.'

In my experience some people actually revere relics in the face of strong opposition from the official church authorities. Some thirty kilometres south of Calais is the town of Saint-Omer, a spot that countless British tourists must have driven heedlessly past on their drive to the sun and the south. Saint-Omer in fact possesses a fine late-medieval church of Notre-Dame, in which, inside a plain stone tomb, lie the bones of the seventh-century Bishop of Thérouanne from whom the city takes its name. A notice tells how the saint's bones were removed and scattered by impious hands at the time of the French Revolution and how the faithful gathered him together again and brought him back to this resting place. Another notice begs the 'superstitious' not to place objects of clothing on St Omer's tomb. The faithful pay no attention to it. The last time I was there, amongst other touching objects, a child's bloodstained vest had been placed on the tomb. To it was pinned a note from the child's parents begging the saint to intercede to cure their baby.

Rich and poor, strong and weak, sophisticated and simple, cruel and gentle all alike in the twentieth century can still call on the relic of a holy saint for aid. General Franco of Spain obtained an arm of St Theresa of Avila in 1937. Thereafter it accompanied him everywhere. He died clutching it, no doubt believing that through the saint's efforts he had remained the only European dictator of the Thirties to retain power after the Second World War and also hoping through her intercessions to gain a heavenly crown.

Once we have appreciated the power of such contemporary faith, then – and only then – can we also rejoice at the absurdity of some aspects of the cult of the relic. We can without blasphemy enjoy the fruits of the prodigious researches of Mme Nicole Hermann-Mansard, the leading French expert on the legal attitude to relics throughout the centuries, who discovered according to ancient inventories from churches the world over that if all surviving relics were authentic Saint Mary Magdalen must have had six bodies and St Gregory the Great two whole bodies and four heads.

We can also then take a properly historical view of relics through the ages. That urbane and graceful scholar Sir Steven Runciman has observed that 'Christian relics have never received their due attention in history'. Historians, he explains, 'justly suspecting the authenticity of the more eminent of them, have tended therefore to put them all to one side, forgetting even a forgery can have its historical value; and only the theologians have taken notice of them, in their relations to the apocryphal improvements on Christian thought and virtue'. Sir

Steven's conclusion is that this neglect of relics is undeserved, 'for there are some of them that not only throw important sidelights on the history of their times, but even have played an active part in the moulding of that history'.

Only then can we fully enjoy the fun, not to say the frequent idiocy that has surrounded the cult of relics down the ages: how people would dream about relics and how relics would punish those who mocked them; how relics were bought and sold, cut into little pieces, fought over, lost and found, stolen and given away as presents without price; how in times of dire distress men would physically punish and humiliate a relic. Only when one acknowledges the fervour excited in men and women by the cult of relics can one understand the passion with which others have attacked the cult.

It is instructive too to see how the secular philosophies of the west have failed to extirpate relics. As a news correspondent in Moscow in the early Thirties Malcolm Muggeridge would visit the Anti-God museum which occupied what had been a church in Red Square. Most of the exhibits, he recalled, 'purported to be exposures of clerical chicanery – for instance, the belief fostered by the Russian Orthodox Church that saints do not decay and stink when they die, but pass on intact to Heaven'. To show this, Muggeridge remembered, the fossilised remains of buried saints were dug up and put on display. At the same time he noted that, ironically, 'another demonstration of the indestructibility of particular flesh had been mounted in Lenin's mausoleum across the way. There, Lenin has lain in state since his death, to be stared at by an endless procession of visitors and local inhabitants.' As Muggeridge aptly commented, 'Truly God is not mocked.'

The study of history in truth shows that the secularists need their relics quite as much as the religious. In the following pages I shall write about the severed head of Oliver Cromwell, the curious history of the relics that Napoleon's chaplain snipped off his body after his death, the pathetic relics that lovers have kept of each other's persons and the sad fate of the corpse of Charlie Chaplin. I shall remind those theologians (such as the

Dean of Emmanuel College, Cambridge, the Revd Don Cupitt) who hold that Buddhism reveals how religion can dispense entirely with dogma and any belief that is not derived from earthly experience alone, that relics of the Buddha have survived and been reverenced for their spiritual value for over two and a half millenia.

Small wonder, if relics permeate the secular as well as the religious consciousness and emerge among godless Soviets, that they also survive and even prosper in other cultures overtly hostile to them. In present-day Yugoslavia, whatever the current religous attitudes of the political authorities, St Blaise remains the patron saint of Dubrovnik. As Bishop of Sebaste in Armenia in the fourth century, Blaise saved the life of a child choking on a fish-bone – hence his reputation for curing any throat ailment. He also has long been credited with the ability to cure sick cattle. People still suffer from sore throats, and cattle still fall ill in contemporary Yugoslavia. Today bits of St Blaise continue to adorn an altar in the treasury of the baroque cathedral of Dubrovnik – his skull in a silver and enamel reliquary of beautiful filigree design; an arm in a silver-gilt reliquary fashioned in the thirteenth century; and a leg in another reliquary made of silver filigree work in the seventeenth century.

And on the feast of St Blaise, which falls on February 3rd, these three precious bones, along with over a hundred other relics, are carried in procession through the streets of Dubrovnik, to evoke God's blessing on the city, to cure sick cattle and soothe sore throats.

We in Britain at our Reformation lost many of our most celebrated relics, even though – I hasten to add – we retain enough to make a goodly show both in Christendom and amongst the secularists. I am myself particularly pained at the many Celtic saints whose bones lie abroad. St Gobhan rests over the high altar in the village of Saint-Gobain near Laon in the north of France. The relics of St Fursey lie in a most remarkable state in a shrine at the Mont de Cignes also in northern France. (At the Revolution the saint's head was saved from the impious, only to be bombarded by the Prussians in 1870. From the ashes of the church the face was recovered, though melted by the heat and forming its own impression in the crystal reliquary.) St Columban rests in a white marble sarcophagus in Bobbio in Italy. In Germany the remains of St Boniface are in the ruined old Cathedral of Fulda, lying alongside the dagger with which the Frisians martyred him in A.D. 754. And St Willibrord of Northumbria has been divided into three: part rests at his monastery of Epternach near Luxembourg; part rests at Aichstadt in Germany; and part succours the faithful in a shrine at Furnes in Flanders.

To bring back these saints to their native land would be for me something of a minor miracle. And I accept that their relics, situated where they now are, mutely proclaim the fame of British missionaries of the early middle ages. Other British saints whose relics lie abroad testify to the lure of Rome. One such is a 'Saint Richard, King of England' whose relics lie in the church of San Frediano, Lucca, in Tuscany. Some say he was a king of Mercia, born in Devonshire; others allege he was a Hampshire farmer's son. In 1645 John Evelyn copied down an inscription – since disappeared – on his sarcophagus: 'REX FUIT ANGLORUM'. Whoever he was, history relates that he abdicated to devote his life to Christ, and died on a pilgrimage to Rome.

To bring these relics home would do much to replace those lost to us at the Reformation. It is a futile hope – though patriotism over relics has a long history: the church historians Rosalind and Christopher Brooke tell of the devotees of the Welsh St Teilo who, well aware that more than one community claimed his relics, asserted that the saint, 'to prevent bloodshed after his death . . . miraculously provided three bodies of himself by a singular, and perhaps unique, act of celestial diplomacy'. This unusual technique of allowing someone else to possess the relic of one's favourite saint whilst holding onto it oneself did not catch on elsewhere in the middle ages.

Yet, as I shall argue, some of our native relics ought to be brought home. One such is the body of St Edmund, King of East Anglia, who was murdered by the Danes in the ninth century. Another is the corpse of Thomas Becket (with or without his brain); though as will also become apparent, the precise whereabouts of this saint's bones alas still eludes us.

Not everyone would agree. An American scholar, Paul Alonzo Brown, has written that 'The bones of Thomas Becket, if discovered now, could be of no more service in bringing the medieval hero closer to us, or of throwing light upon the turbulent but heroic life, than can the lock of Milton's hair displayed in a showcase in the cottage at Chalfont St Giles help us to understand the motive of the sublime Puritan or aid us in interpreting *Paradise Lost.*'

I cannot concur. For me to gaze on the hand of St Catherine of Alexandria, now on Mount Sinai; to kneel before a shoulder-blade of St Andrew, now in Edinburgh; to contemplate the 'Auto-Icon' of Jeremy Bentham in London; to revere the corpses of St Francis and St Clare, reverently displayed in Assisi; to observe these relics is to be movingly reminded that (as G. M. Trevelyan once put it) these were men and women who lived and breathed like us and now are gone, like ghosts at cockcrow. Unless, that is, they are today alive in Heaven.

2

The golden age of the relic

The earliest Christian martyrs died splendidly. St Stephen, the protomartyr, powerfully insulted his enemies, crying, 'You stiff necked and uncircumcised in hearts and ears; you continually resist the Holy Spirit. As your fathers did, so have you done.' Understandably perhaps (since they regarded themselves as God's chosen people), they stoned him to death. Then his friends took away the martyr's body and buried it.

Nearly four centuries later, in December A.D. 415, a Christian priest named Lucian claimed to have been told in a dream exactly where the body lay. At Kafr Gamala in Palestine he dug up not only what purported to be Stephen's remains, but also those of the wise Jew Gamaliel (who had urged his fellows to tolerate the Christians), along with the bones of Jesus's secret admirer Nicodemus. St Stephen's body eventually reached Constantinople, where it was joined by stones said to be the ones that killed him. From Constantinople the corpse was taken to Rome. But by this time the fame of Stephen's relics was so great that many bits had been pulled off to adorn other Christian centres throughout the world. Eventually relics of St

Stephen ended up in no fewer than three great French cathedrals: Bourges, Sens and Toulouse, all of which were dedicated to him.

Even as the saint's bones were being exhumed by Lucian they revealed remarkable powers: 'the earth trembled,' reports the earliest account, 'and a smell of sweet perfume came from that place such as no-one had ever known'. The onlookers imagined it was the scent of the Garden of Eden. 'And from the smell of that perfume,' we are told, 'seventy-three sick persons were healed.' St Stephen's relics were especially kind to women. When a high-born lady of Carthage visited a shrine containing part of his corpse, we are told that as she prayed for healing she beat her head against the shrine so forcibly that the grille in the front swung open. Overjoyed the lady thrust her head through the opening and laid her chin on the relics, drowning them with her tears.

In the four centuries between St Stephen's relatively sober burial and his exhumation by Lucian, the Christian attitude to the relics of the holy dead had been completely transformed. The development of the cult of relics represents a totally unexpected change in the way Christian men and women treated the dead.

In Jewish law, to come into contact with a corpse made a man or woman instantly impure. 'He that touches the body of a dead man shall be unclean for seven days,' says the Book of Numbers. 'Whosoever touches the body of any man that is dead and purifies not himself, defiles the tabernacle of the Lord; and that soul shall be cut off from Israel.' Simply to walk into a tent containing a dead body made a person impure for seven days. In the fields to touch even a dead man's bone or stumble on a grave similarly made a person impure. Solemn ritual sprinkling for seven days was prescribed – and also for the tent in which a person had died. No Jew could possibly have behaved like the well-born lady of Carthage.

At the same time the children of Israel always showed deep respect for the bones of their fathers and forefathers. When Moses led them out of Egypt, he took the bones of the patriarch

Joseph with him. According to the Book of Joshua, 'the bones of Joseph which the children of Israel brought out of Egypt, buried they in Shechem, in the parcel of ground which Jacob bought of the sons of Hamor the father of Shechem for a hundred pieces of money: and they became the inheritance of the children of Joseph'. No doubt Joseph's body had been embalmed in the manner of the Egyptians. Similar care was taken to bury the bodies of King Saul and his son Jonathan in well-remembered spots. In Jesus's time the Pharisees were still 'building the sepulchres of the prophets and garnishing the tombs of the righteous'. Jesus himself never condemned anyone for this practice, but only those who did so without listening to the words of living prophets. Nonetheless Jesus's own words show that the tradition of impurity connected with the dead was still strong in his own time, when he observed of hypocrites that they were 'like whitened sepulchres, which outwardly appear beautiful but inwardly are full of dead men's bones and of all uncleanness'.

In short, while the ancient Jews certainly revered their famous dead, they made no cult of their relics. A German scholar (Joachim Jeremias) has identified forty-nine tombs, chiefly in Judaea, held in some sense sacred by the Jews. Eight of these were tombs of the patriarchs. Twenty-one others belonged to leading figures in Jewish history. Nineteen were tombs of prophets, two of whom had also been martyrs. Only one was the tomb of a man whose claim to fame was simply martyrdom. By contrast, in the later Christian cult those supremely cherished as relics were the holy martyrs.

Occasionally we read of the Jews praying at their historic tombs. At funerals, they would have a wake beside them. And that is the sum total of Old Testament attitudes to the dead. The Christian religion arose out of Judaism. But Christians learned from the Jews only to revere the memories and occasionally the graves of pious men and women, not to revere their corpses. In this respect Jesus as a Jew took over the attitudes of his own people and handed these attitudes on to his followers.

Some eighty years after the crucifixion of Jesus and the

stoning of Stephen, a Bishop of Antioch named Ignatius was martyred in Rome. Ignatius faced his tormentors (in this case led by the Emperor Trajan) with rhetoric as splendid as St Stephen's. Learning in prison that he was shortly to be torn to pieces by wild beasts, he refused to let his influential Roman friends try to save him. His body, he said, was 'the wheat of God; and I must be ground by the teeth of wild beasts to become the pure bread of Christ'. So the saint was taken to the arena and there torn to pieces.

Up to this point the story of his martyrdom bears a marked resemblance to that of St Stephen, both men resolute in the face of death, both forgiving their persecutors, both envisaging a future glory after death. The difference appears in the behaviour of the friends of the two saints. In the case of St Stephen, the Acts of the Apostles simply notes that 'devout men buried him and made great lamentation over him'. His body was of no further significance to them. Not so with Ignatius – even though there was less of him left after death. 'Only the hardest bits of his holy remains had escaped the jaws of the beasts,' we are told. 'These pieces were carried off and put into a coffin. Because of the grace remaining in the martyr they were an inestimable treasure for the holy congregation of the faithful.' In short, the corpse of St Ignatius became a relic.

The same honour was soon to be bestowed on Ignatius's friend Bishop Polycarp of Smyrna. We still possess from that distant age a letter written by Ignatius to Polycarp. And the two men had met and strengthened each other's faith when Ignatius was being taken under armed guard to Rome. (St Polycarp had reverently kissed his friend's chains.) Some time during the reign of Marcus Aurelius in the late second century A.D. (or, some scholars think, a little earlier), Polycarp fell foul of the authorities by refusing to take part in a pagan festival. He was now eighty-six years old. He could have saved himself by renouncing his Lord. But with a valour in death comparable to that of Stephen and Ignatius, he replied: 'Fourscore and six years have I served him and he has done me no wrong. How then shall I blaspheme my king and Saviour?'

By now it seems that the authorities suspected that the Christians might have some bizarre use for the bones of their illustrious dead. It was decided to reduce Polycarp's body to ashes. As the martyr took off his clothes and shoes by the stake, his followers pushed forward to touch his wrinkled body. Polycarp refused to be nailed to the stake and so bravely perished in the flames.

If the authorities hoped to destroy his relics completely, they failed. It is scarcely possible to cremate a person without trace. The Christians of Smyrna wrote a panegyric on the martyrdom of their revered bishop. It describes how they revered perhaps more than his living body what was left of him after death. 'Taking up his bones,' they wrote, 'more precious than the richest jewels and tried above gold, we placed them in a spot worthy of them'. But their aim was more than merely to give him a decent burial. 'There,' they continued, 'assembled as we shall have opportunity, with joy and gladness we shall be permitted by the Lord to celebrate the anniversary of his martyrdom.' The relics of St Polycarp were now the basis of a permanent cult.

Later legend alleges that the murderers of St Polycarp actually pleaded with the magistrates not to hand over his remains to his followers. We certainly have evidence from shortly after his martyrdom that the authorities were finding the love of relics extremely annoying. In the year A.D. 177 Christians in Lyons had to bribe corrupt judges to prevent the relics of their martyred saints from being thrown into the Rhône.

Paradoxically, the more Christians were persecuted, the more relics were available. The stories of martyrdoms, no doubt sometimes embroidered for the edification of the faithful, contain many tales of the wiles of the faithful in getting hold of holy bones. During the persecutions under the Emperor Maximian, Flaccus, Governor of Umbria, arrived at Spoleto with orders to kill any Christian unwilling to recant. A crowd, sensing sport, assembled in the forum of the town. One of the magistrates told Flaccus that a certain Gregory had been tiresomely active in throwing down pagan images, so soldiers were despatched to bring the Christian for trial. Flaccus asked him, 'Who is your God?' Gregory answered, 'He who made man in his own image and likeness, who is all-powerful and immortal, who will render to all men and women according to their works.' Flaccus replied that Gregory talked too much, adding, 'If you wish to save your skin, go and sacrifice in the Temple to Jove, Minerva and Aesculapius. Then you will be our friend and receive much favour from our invincible Emperor.'

In the now venerable tradition of Ignatius and Polycarp (for this was the year A.D. 304) Gregory replied, 'I do not want such friendship, nor shall I sacrifice to devils but only to my God, Jesus Christ.' At this the magistrate angrily commanded that Gregory be beaten in the face and then roasted to death. The chronicle of these events records, however, that at that moment an earthquake diverted the people. Gregory was spared the roasting, but the following day he was tortured and then beheaded.

The question arose who should have his remains. The chronicle goes on: 'The corpse lay in the middle of the amphitheatre, till a Christian lady name Abundantia went to find Tircanus the magistrate and demanded the right to take it away. Tircanus answered, "Give me thirty-five *aurei* and take it." Abundantia replied, "Willingly I give it you, but make sure I have the body right away." Tircanus said, "Give me the cash and be off with it." She counted out thirty-five *aurei* and received the cadaver in exchange.'

Such tales abound in the early Christian world. The desire for the relics of martyred saints occasioned considerable bravery. Often women seem to have been far braver than men – a point expressly noted by the chronicler who describes how two Christian women in the year 257 courageously carried off the bleeding corpse of St Saturnin of Toulouse, martyred by being tied to the tail of a wild bull.

Now it must be conceded that the reluctance of the authorities to sanction Christians taking away the relics of the dead was not mere cussedness. Roman law was precise about the disposal of the dead – whether Christian or pagan. According to the Imperial code, even those executed by crucifixion could be given an honourable burial. So Joseph of Arimathea was able to go to Pontius Pilate after the death of Jesus and ask for the corpse. 'Then Pilate commanded it to be given up,' says St Matthew's Gospel. 'And Joseph took the body and wrapped it in a clean linen cloth and laid it in his own new tomb, which he had hewn in the rock: and he rolled a great stone to the door of the tomb, and departed.' Roman law provided severe penalties for those who violated such tombs or bodies.

This was now precisely what Christians seemed to be doing in their lust for relics. A law of Valentinian III describes bishops and priests as grave-robbers.

What made them do it? Were these Christians, as they drew further away from the Jewish background that would have abhorred such behaviour, increasingly influenced by the pagan cult of heroes? There are undoubted analogies between the legendary exploits of the pagan heroes and the legends of the saints. In the ancient world cities competed for the tombs of heroes, and if one died abroad his remains would be brought home in great triumph. According to Herodotus the Lacodaemonians believed that until they had brought the body of Orestes from the land of the Tegeans, they should fail in battle. During a plague at Orchomenos, the priestess declared that it would not cease till the body of Hesiod were brought back from Naupactus. The Athenians, despite their reputation for logic and reason, were careful to get back the body of Theseus from Scyros.

If by some chance a whole body was not available, the pagans, like the Christians, eagerly sought such parts as remained. Orpheus's head was buried at Smyrna, where Christians were later to cherish the remnants of the incinerated Bishop Polycarp. The shoulder-blade of Pelops lay in a tomb of bronze at Elis and another bronze coffin housed the bones of Tantalus in Argos. Sometimes a kind of chapel was built over the hero's tomb; sometimes the body rested in the temple of Zeus. But all were shown what Christians would no doubt have described as superstitious reverence – even though the reverence increasingly offered to Christian relics was dangerously akin to it.

And just as a dream had revealed to Lucian the whereabouts of St Stephen's bones, so oracles or dreams frequently pointed to the burial places of pagan heroes. One Cimon saw an eagle trying to dig up the ground with its beak and talons. He chased it away, dug there himself, and discovered the body of Theseus. Similarly the body of Hesiod rested hidden in a cave till a crow perched above it and revealed the spot to the citizens of Orchomenos.

In the middle of the fifth century the Christian apologist Bishop Theodoret of Cyrrhus explicitly compared the two sorts of cult. God, he wrote, had replaced heroes with martyrs; and precisely as the pagans built temples over their heroes' tombs, the Christians now built churches over the relics of the saints. Theodoret would never have conceded that any true comparison existed between the *powers* of Christian and pagan relics. For the pagan relics were worthless delusions – even though many legendary stories of their ability to heal the sick, guard against the plague and so on were current in the ancient world.

Whatever the precise relationship between pagan practices and the Christian cult of relics, the latter soon took on a momentum of its own, a momentum so powerful that in many parts of Christendom it has lasted to this day. By the end of the third and the beginning of the fourth century A.D., throughout many parts of the Christian world the bodies of saints and martyrs were ceasing to be given decent burial. Instead the greater honour of preservation as a relic overrode the old objections to trafficking in corpses. To celebrate the Eucharist over the tomb of a saint was now commonplace. St Jerome describes the Bishop of Rome doing so over the alleged bodies of St Peter and St Paul. Soon men and women began to look upon a piece of a saint as something they could carry around as a permanent talisman and as their own possession. At the beginning of the fourth century the Archdeacon of Carthage angrily rebuked a woman called Lucilla, who had got hold of the bone of a martyr and used to kiss it before she received the sacrament of Holy Communion. But such rebukes became rarer and then disappeared altogether.

Soon the Christians were carrying their relics about in triumph on feast days. A few pagan cults had done this. In Crete, at the festival of Europa, her alleged bones, crowned in myrtle leaves, were paraded about the streets. But such pagan practices were rare, whereas the Christians increasingly exulted in them – to the scorn of the Emperor Julian the Apostate, who found the practice disgusting and mockingly asked how days so contaminated with death could be considered lucky.

As the thirst for relics grew, the supply seemed unable to slake it. Fortunately a remedy was at hand. The saints after all had worn clothing. They had used seats and worn rings. They had been beaten with chains or rods. Surely, it was argued, these objects, by their very contact with a saint or martyr became themselves holy. 'The virtue of saints is so great,' declared St John Chrysostom, Bishop of Constantinople and Doctor of the Church, 'that Christians venerate not only their words and bodies but also their garments'. In support of this Chrysostom could appeal to the New Testament itself. The Acts of the Apostles asserts that God wrought many special miracles by the hands of St Paul, adding that 'unto the sick were carried away from his body handkerchiefs and aprons, and the diseases departed from them and the evil spirits went out'. Elsewhere in Acts we learn that so great was the healing power of St Peter that people carried out the sick into the streets and laid them on beds and couches in the hope that as he went by at least his shadow might pass over some of them. If, argued Chrysostom, handkerchiefs, aprons and even the shadow of a saint could heal, then to touch something that had belonged to one of these holy men and women would surely bring a blessing.

Chrysostom means 'golden-mouthed', and this great Christian orator used all his powers of rhetoric here. A relic, he preached, was like an overflowing spring that never runs dry and blesses everything it waters; again, it is like a light that never goes out but illuminates everything it passes over.

So the supply of relics did not run out. Instruments of

torture, crosses, chains, nails, iron claws, pincers, whips, stakes, gridirons, were all imbued with the merits of those who had suffered from them. Pope St Sixtus was beheaded in A.D. 258 sitting on his episcopal chair, so it was taken to the catacomb of St Callistus with his corpse. When St Germain of Auxerre died in the fifth century, Bishop Peter of that city took his hair shirt and six priests divided up the rest of his clothing. When St Honoratus, the Archbishop of Arles, died in 429, so keen were the people to obtain secondary relics that his body was stripped almost naked. The gridiron on which St Laurence fried to death was kept in Rome – though most scholars believe he was really beheaded and not grilled.

Pagan antiquity again affords parallels with these secondary relics, as they came to be called. Achilles' lance was kept in the temple of Athene at Phaselis. Several temples claimed to guard Orpheus' lyre. Agamemnon's sceptre was at Chaeronaea. The temple of Athene at Iapygia claimed the sandal of Helen. Other cities boasted of the egg of Leda and what was left of the clay from which Prometheus made man. And these secondary relics were credited with the same powers as primary relics (namely, the actual bones of the pagan heroes): they cured the sick, guaranteed fertility, protected cities in times of plague and famine, and gave victory in war.

Yet the secondary relics of the pagan world can compete neither in their abundance nor in their complexity with those of the Christians. Christians were in a sense fortunate that their relics initially derived mostly from martyrs, whereas those of the pagans were the relics of heroic figures of history; for martyrs usually shed blood, and soon their devotees would catch the blood as it was shed, in napkins and sponges, or mop it up from the ground with a cloth, thus creating an instant relic. Christians in their insatiable search for a relic soon learned to neglect nothing connected with a saint. When in 821 a vision revealed to Pope Pascal I that the bones of the third century martyr St Cecilia were in the catacomb of Praetextatus, he moved her sacred body to a church bearing her name inside the city of Rome. He was delighted to find also, rolled up at the saint's feet, the linen and napkins that had wiped her wounds, and these too he reverently took away.

Christians by now were assiduously visiting the tombs of the saints in order to create new, secondary relics. At best the visitor's own faith, his own powers of devotion and determined fasting also had some bearing on the successful outcome of the quest. A sixth century account of how to visit the alleged tomb of St Peter, over which Constantine had built a basilica in Rome, tells the supplicant to open the barriers around the saint's tomb, open a little window, lean through it and ask for what he or she needed. The instructions continue: 'If he would like to have a holy relic, he should leave a small cloth there.' The pilgrim must now pray, fast and wait. 'And then – by an amazing wonder, the cloth which he draws up from the tomb will be rich with divine power.' One way of recognising this, the visitor is informed, is to weigh the cloth beforehand, for the divine power will surely make it heavier after contact with St Peter.

Repeatedly accounts of the martyrdom of the saints of the early church refer back to the death of St Cyprian in 258, when his followers eagerly mopped up the blood as it flowed from the neck of their beheaded bishop. St Cyprian died at Nicomedia. Sixty years later the first Spanish martyr, St Vincent was murdered, and his followers – inspired by the followers of Cyprian – dipped their vests in his blood. Their hope was to protect their homes from all future evil. Thus by degrees the notion of a relic's power, flowing through secondary relics, was elaborated, until the sixth century visitor to St Peter's basilica could be convinced that this power was actually ponderable.

Akin to this notion was the widespread belief that overflowing oil from a lamp or vessel close by the relics of a saint had somehow been infused with a tangible virtue. Throughout the middle ages, the most famous such oil came from St Catherine's monastery on Mount Sinai.

St Catherine's was initially dedicated to the Blessed Virgin Mary and the Transfiguration of Jesus. It had no connection with the saint. The rich daughter of a pagan king, she lived in

Alexandria in the early fourth century, and is said to have criticised the emperor for persecuting Christians. The emperor brought fifty learned men to convert her back to paganism. To his dismay, she converted them. So she was condemned to death and sentenced to be broken on a wheel. Unfortunately, according to the legend, the spiked wheels on which she was to be broken broke themselves. This did not enable her to escape martyrdom. She was beheaded. It is recorded that milk flowed from her headless body instead of blood.

Five hundred years after her death the monks of Mount Sinai found what they decided was St Catherine's body, lying on the mountainside. They concluded that the precious relic must have mysteriously flown there from Alexandria. And her bones were oozing oil. The monks took the body back to their monastery and began to collect this oil, which soon became enormously prized by pilgrims. In the thirteenth century a German visitor named Magister Thietmar saw the saint's body in the monastery, still oozing oil. He was delighted to be given a few drops of this precious sign of the saint's virtue. A hundred years later Henry II of Brunswick visited Mount Sinai, and he also came back with some of Catherine's holy liquid.

About this time too an English poet, John Capgrave, wrote a long and famous work in her honour. As he rightly observed, writing of Catherine's miraculous flight to Sinai, 'It is fro Alisaundre of lond ful grete distauns.' He had been told by pilgrims that the relic oozed oil (or that the monks scraped it from her bones), 'whiche oyle of soores all grevauns, whiche men suffre, it will be hooled anon.' Capgrave was perfectly prepared to believe this – evidence, incidentally, that such oozings were fairly commonplace in the history of relics. He had also heard that a lamp filled with this oil would burn a whole man's lifetime; but about the truth of that, he was prepared to suspend judgment.

Such reverent agnosticism was rare. Initially, as the cult of relics got under way, some theologians warned against excess. In particular, St Augustine was angry that the credulous did not enquire more carefully whether they were dealing with fakes or genuine relics. But he was equally vehement that those saintly bodies that the Holy Spirit had used for great wonders should be respected. 'The clothing or the ring of a saint,' he asserted, ought to be dearer to us than those of our own parents.'

At the same time Augustine is one of a number of distinguished fathers of the church who were absolutely clear that the saints were not to be worshipped as Gods. 'Christians surround the memorials of the martyrs with a holy solemnity in order to excite imitation, to associate themselves with their merits and to be aided by their prayers,' he wrote. He added immediately, 'Although we erect altars for them in our churches, we do not sacrifice to them i.e. offer the sacrifice of the Eucharist. No bishop has ever at the altar, in any holy place which contained the relics of the martyrs, said, "Peter, or Paul, or Cyprian, we offer you this sacrifice." It is to God, who crowns these martyrs, that the sacrifice is offered.'

St Jerome was similarly firm about what is and what is not legitimate in the veneration of saints and their relics. 'We do not worship, we do not adore, for fear that we should bow down to the creature rather than to the Creator,' he insisted; 'but we venerate the relics of the martyrs in order the better to adore him whose martyrs they are.' St Cyril of Alexandria agreed. 'We by no means consider the holy martyrs to be Gods,' he wrote, 'nor do we habitually bow down before them adoringly, but only relatively and reverentially.'

That most practical of Popes, Gregory the Great, well aware that the cult of relics could be abused, was nonetheless securely certain that properly deployed, a relic could be used to drive out superstition. So, commissioning Augustine of Canterbury to convert pagan England, he equipped the saint and his followers not only with Gospels, books of liturgy and vestments but also with holy relics. These last, in the Pope's view, would specifically counter the pagan, superstitious rites of the English. Gregory's instructions were clear. 'Because the English have been used to slaughtering many oxen as sacrifices to devils,' he told Augustine, 'some solemnity must be put in place of this. So on the feast days or birthdays of the holy martyrs whose relics are there deposited, close by those churches which were once pagan temples they may build themselves huts of the boughs of trees and hold a religious feast. Instead of offering beasts to the devil, they shall kill cattle and in eating them praise God, giving thanks to the giver of all things needful for food.' For Gregory the distinction between the one God and his virtuous, revered saints was perfectly clear.

Had the great church fathers not given their sanction to the cult of relics – albeit with such careful distinctions between worshipping God and revering the holy saints and martyrs – it is doubtful whether popular practice in the church could have flourished as it did. Neither St Jerome nor St Augustine of Hippo was lax over what they held to be heretical behaviour or belief. But these church fathers, instead of checking the growth of the cult of the relic, gave the theological green light to its golden age.

But the Christian church by no means consists principally of theologians or even bishops and priests; and the great popular movements of Christianity, such as the cult of relics, have never been totally under the control or inspiration of such men. Far greater relics than any we have so far spoken of were introduced to Christendom in the century before St Augustine, by a lowly-born laywoman, whose life was one of both exaltation and suffering and who died greatly acclaimed by all who knew her.

So humble was the birth of St Helena that historians cannot say for certain where it took place. She may well have been the daughter of an inn-keeper of Drepanum in Bithynia. Despite her lowly origins, her manner and character entranced the Roman general Constantine Chlorus. In the year 274 she bore him a son, whom they also named Constantine.

In 292 Helena was cruelly thrust aside, when her husband became Caesar and for reasons of politics decided to marry the stepdaughter of the Emperor Maximian. For fourteen years Helena remained out of favour, until in 306 her former husband died and the troops which her son was commanding at York proclaimed him Caesar in his father's place. Two years later

Constantine was proclaimed Emperor, and in 312, after the battle of the Milvian Bridge, entered Rome.

Out of love for his mother, the Emperor now renamed the place of her birth Helenopolis and bestowed on her the name 'Most Noble Lady'. She, however, about this time embraced Christianity and with it a remarkable humility. Aware that for many years she had remained ignorant of her new creed, Helena resolved to make amends, devoting herself to prayers and good works, dressing humbly, relieving the poor. Then in the year 326, at an advanced age, she determined to make a pilgrimage to the Holy Land, to see for herself those places made sacred by the presence of her Saviour.

Later chroniclers insisted that she had another reason for this journey: the quest for relics of the Saviour himself. And that she found them.

The aged empress reached Palestine and persuaded a knowledgeable Jew to take her to Golgotha where Jesus was crucified. There she is said to have ordered excavations which revealed three crosses, one with the superscription of Pontius Pilate describing Jesus as the king of the Jews. There too were nails which had fastened Jesus's body to the cross. Nearby was a temple of Venus built by the Emperor Hadrian over the tomb where Joseph of Arimathea laid the body of the dead Jesus. When this was removed, Helena discovered the crown of thorns which had been thrust on his head during the tortures leading up to his crucifixion.

Now all this information must be recognised as historically unprovable. Contemporary evidence for the discovery of the cross simply does not exist. After the pagan temple of Venus had been demolished, the Emperor Constantine wrote to the Bishop of Jerusalem ordering him to replace it with a splendid church; and this same letter tells the bishop to look for the true cross. No early evidence unassailably connects its discovery with St Helena. One legend recounts that no-one could decide which of three crosses discovered by Helena was the one on which Jesus died. The matter was settled when the true cross healed a sick woman. But the earliest extant reference to Helena discovering the cross occurs in a sermon preached by St Ambrose seventy years later, when he observed that even after its discovery she worshipped not the wood but the king who hung on it. And it is only around this time that others, such as the historian Sulpicius Severus, and a translator named Rufinus, who visited Jerusalem in the 370s, begin to say the same.

Writing half a century before these men the famous church historian Eusebius describes Helena's visit to the Holy Land without specifically connecting it with these momentous discoveries. Eusebius was more concerned to praise her Christian humility, recounting how she built two basilicas in Palestine, one on the Mount of Olives and the other at Bethlehem. He contrasts the extreme humility with which she dressed and the way she would richly adorn churches and chapels, as well as caring for the old, the imprisoned and the poor. 'Though Empress of the world and mistress of the empire,' he exclaimed, 'she saw herself as the servant of the handmaidens of Christ.'

But he never says that this fine woman discovered the greatest of all the relics. Nevertheless the tradition became established that it was Helena who had excavated the true cross, the nails and the crown of thorns. Of the true cross, half remained behind in Jerusalem. The other half, along with the nails, was sent to Constantinople, the city set up in A.D. 330 as Constantine's capital, on the site of the old Greek city of Byzantium.

The fifth-century Bishop of Nola once observed that however much wood of the true cross was cut away, the rest would renew itself; but he was a poet and perhaps spoke metaphorically of the way in which the virtues of Jesus's crucifixion were seen by Christians as inexhaustible. A later chapter will tell of the vicissitudes of the two pieces of the cross, as well as the wanderings of the holy nails and the crown of thorns. Suffice it here to record that at this time sophisticated Christians found no difficulty in the notion that somehow fragments of the true cross filled the whole world. St Cyril of Jerusalem (who had been a boy when the cross was discovered) said so in as many words. Only later, when the age of scepticism had dawned, did this become a matter for mockery. To my mind the time expanded on the mathematics of this matter is something of a waste of the human spirit. (Thus M. G. Rehault de Fleury maintained that whereas the whole cross would have contained 178 million cubic millimetres of wood, all the existing relics of it put together amounted to no more than 5 million cubic millimetres, whereas J. C. Wall held that the true figure for all the bits combined was no more than 3,942,000 cubic millimetres.) One can as fruitlessly speculate as to how the body of St Helena herself managed by the seventh century to reach the French Benedictine abbey of Hautvillers, near Reims (an abbey which today houses also the body of the celebrated Dom Pérignon who is said to have invented champagne).

For relics were now proliferating everywhere throughout the Christian world. Constantinople was naturally rich in them, and its fame drew yet more. A monk named Sergius decided, for instance, that the body of St Stephen there needed to wear the belt of St Simeon Stylites, so he obtained it and gave it as a present to the Emperor Leo, and Leo placed it round St Stephen. One relic enhanced another. St John the Baptist's head revealed to the leaders of the city that it too would like to be venerated there; so to Constantinople it came.

Constantinople, as one historian observed, 'became one enormous reliquary.' Alongside relics of Jesus and St Stephen could be found the belt and head-dress of the prophet Elijah. Somehow the city obtained the column to which Jesus was bound for his flagellation. Here were relics of St Luke and St Andrew, and of Paul's disciple St Timothy. Here were the chains of St Peter.

In the year 1200 Antony, Archbishop of Novgorod, visited Constantinople and left us a list of the relics in the great church of St Sophia. He kissed what he took to be two slabs from Christ's tomb. He saw the blood of the holy martyr St Pantaleon. There was a table on which, men claimed, Jesus had celebrated his Last Supper in Jerusalem. An oddity among relics was a curious chart which, it was said, had been used to measure Jesus's height when he lived on earth.

If the Jews had eschewed relic worship, the Christians of Constantinople, according to Antony's letter, seem to have made up for this. He saw there not only the clothing of Elijah but also the tablets of the Law, which God had given to Moses long before, along with the Ark of the Covenant and some of the mysterious manna which had fed the children of Israel on their journey from Egypt through the desert. He saw with wonder the trumpet Joshua blew outside Jericho.

Some relics at St Sophia were evidently displayed only at certain times throughout the Christian year. Archbishop Antony saw what he called 'the column of St Gregory the Miracle-Worker, all covered with bronze plates'. Apparently St Gregory had once appeared near this column, with the result that, Antony observed, 'the people kiss it, and rub their breasts and shoulders against it to be cured of their pains'. He noted that, 'On St Gregory's feast day the Patriarch of Constantinople brings his relics to this column.' And of course he saw 'the wood of the cross which Christ's neck touched, inserted in a reliquary in the form of a cross', close by 'the hammer, the gimlet and the saw with which the cross was made'.

But other towns and cities were rich in relics too. Almost from the very start of the relic cult the question had been posed whether one needed the whole of a saint's corpse in order to gain the full value from the relic. Clearly the answer must be no, in view of the fact that such notable martyrs as Ignatius and Polycarp survived only in bits. The theologians were soon ready to give authoritative answers. In the fourth century the Cappadocian father St Gregory of Nazianzus declared that even a drop of blood from a saint or martyr was quite as efficacious a relic as the whole corpse. A finger was as good as a foot.

So the way was opened for men and women to cherish any part of a saint. Later on nit-picking theologians would attempt to classify relics according to their wholeness. A relic which included if not the whole corpse at least its head, arms and legs (or most of them) would be classed among the *reliquae insignes*. Relics consisting of less than this were *reliquae non insignes*; and the pedantic divided these further into *notabiles* such as hands and feet and mere *exiguae* such as fingers and teeth. But the faithful for the most part cared little for such niceties.

In any case relics had a habit of turning up unexpectedly when necessary. Northern Italy, unlike Rome, was relatively short of the bones of the saints; but this did not trouble St Ambrose who conveniently discovered the bodies of two saints in his cathedral city Milan. Later he discovered the relics of two more saints, Victor and Agricola, who had apparently been mistakenly interred in the Jewish cemetery at Bologna. This happy find soon adorned the basilica of Florence. Another happy miracle took place at Sebaste, which possessed at least part of the body of John the Baptist (notwithstanding the presence of his head at Constantinople). His tomb was violated, and the Christians feared that his bones had been burned and thrown to the winds. Even so, they continued to pray around the tomb, as if the relics were still there – and an unknown messenger brought the corpse back, whole.

There is much scope for mockery here. 'The fame of the apostles, and of the holy men who had imitated their virtues,' according to the arch-sceptic Edward Gibbon, was at this time 'darkened by religious fiction'. In Gibbon's view, the veneration of relics was a superstition that tended to extinguish the light of reason in the Christian world.

To sympathetic historians these tales of holy relics triumphing over violation signify more than mere credulity and idiocy. They point to a faith that those holy men and women, who in life and in martyrdom were not defeated by the powers of evil, had left behind visible remains as a reminder that evil could be conquered by the power of the Saviour. By extension these visible relics themselves seemed able wondrously to overcome the wiles of evil ones. Why should not such a relic be able to take care of itself?

These tales also indicate the immense importance that our Christian forefathers placed on holding onto their relics. In times of persecution, when Christians often had to flee for their lives, they frequently refused to leave their relics behind. These relics after all offered them hope of victory over pain, persecution and death. The Venerable Bede, writing in Northumbria when much of Christendom lay in dark ruins, describes in his life of St Cuthbert some of the miracles performed not simply by the power of the relics of that saint but even by dirt from the spot where the water had been thrown that had washed his corpse. Thus, Bede tells us, 'a boy who lived in the territory of Lindisfarne was so terribly vexed by an evil spirit that he totally lost his reason and shouted and cried aloud, trying to tear into pieces with his teeth his own limbs and whatever else came in his way.' No-one could expel or exorcise this evil spirit. The lad's father put him into a cart and drove him to the monastery of Lindisfarne 'to pray to God on his behalf before the relics of the holy saints there'. But, says Bede, 'the holy saints, to show how high a place Cuthbert occupied amongst them, refused to heal him as he desired.' Then a priest went quietly to the place where the water had been thrown after Cuthbert's body had been washed. 'He took from there a small portion of the dirt. He mixed it with some water and carrying it to the sufferer, poured it into his open mouth, from which he was uttering the most horrible and lamentable cries.' Immediately the boy fell into a profound sleep. And next morning he was cured.

Bede tells of other amazing cures wrought by the relics of St Cuthbert. One young inhabitant of the monastery suffered a paralysis which had begun in his feet. He cured it by putting on the shoes of the dead Cuthbert. Not surprisingly, when Bishop Eadbert of Lindisfarne died, he arranged for his own body to be laid in the same grave as Cuthbert's, underneath the saint's coffin. Eadbert had given the monks permission, nine years after Cuthbert's death, to open the saint's tomb, when, as Bede relates, they 'found his body entire, as if he were still alive, and his joints were still flexible, as if he were not dead but sleeping'. Bede adds that his clothes too were undecayed and still retained their original freshness and colour. 'When the brethren saw this,' he records, 'they were so astonished that they could scarcely speak, or look on the miracle which lay before them. They hardly knew what they were doing.'

Such a relic was too precious to be lost or abandoned – which is why it is no longer in Lindisfarne. When Cuthbert had died in 687 he had left specific instructions that if the monks ever left Lindisfarne they should take his corpse with them. About two hundred years later Danish invaders drove them out. Taking Cuthbert's body with them, they wandered for a century or so, till they founded a new shrine for the saint on the site of what is now Durham cathedral. In all this time the saint's corpse did not decay. By strangely fitting chance, the Venerable Bede's body shared his tomb until the year 1370. (Today it lies in Durham by a sumptuous Bede Altar designed by Stephen Dykes Bower in 1935.)

Cuthbert's tomb, alas, was destroyed in 1540, after being revered by countless medieval pilgrims. He now lies in the cathedral, under a plain slab of marble, inscribed CVBERTHVS. The twentieth century has made some amends to the holy relic; four fine candlesticks designed by Sir Ninian Comper now guard each corner of his tomb, still a reminder (as Bede put it) that the Most High can work through humble men and that his 'mighty miracles never cease to show themselves forth to mankind'.

Bede himself both revered relics and firmly believed that they had no power to help men and women still alive save for the power of God working through them. Still more famous than his life of St Cuthbert was his *Ecclesiastical History of the English Nation*, completed a mere four years before he died in 735. There we read, for instance, of King Oswald, killed by the pagan Mercians, whose bones cured the ague, cast out devils and brought men and women from the brink of death. 'Small wonder,' observed Bede, 'that the prayers of this king, now reigning in Heaven should be most efficacious with our Lord, since he never ceased to pray and care for the eternal when he lived in his temporal kingdom.' A relic was an object of power, Bede believed, because the saint who once inhabited it now interceded for us in Heaven.

And although in his lifetime Bede was 'unknown save to his brethren and to a few of the local magnates', as David Knowles observed, Bede's pupils became the great missionaries of eighth-century Europe. As a result, 'He was the only native Englishman to join the small band of indispensable authors to be found in every great collection of manuscripts in north-western Europe,' declared David Knowles, 'and among them he ranks in popularity only below the great doctors of the Church and a few Latin classical writers.' His pupils spread his beliefs. One became Archbishop of Mainz in Germany. Another, when Archbishop of York built up the library of which Bede was spiritual father. And from this library, half a century after Bede's death, the great English scholar Alcuin came to Europe as the counsellor and tutor of that fanatic promoter of relics, the Emperor Charlemagne.

Charlemagne not only learned to love and cherish relics himself. He also made them the instruments of his policy in the church. A relic, for Charlemagne, represented power; and he used relics to bestow power on others. He seems somehow to have gained access to a vast number, and remarkable ones at that.

Today he is himself a relic. It is not quite certain whether or not he is a saint. Crowned Holy Roman Emperor by Pope Leo III in 800, he became the protector of Christianity in the west, dividing his empire into twenty-one provinces, each under the jurisdiction of a bishop. He never learned to write, but (with Alcuin at his side) fostered the arts, learning and music. After his death, Pope Paschal III canonised him – though unfortunately Paschal turned out to be an anti-Pope and the canonisation remains doubtful. In 1475 the French government made devotion to the memory of the Blessed Charlemagne compulsory, and this, lesser honour was confirmed by Pope Benedict IV.

Today Charlemagne lies in the cathedral of Aachen (Aix-la-Chapelle), once the chapel of his palace, an amazing octagonal building consecrated by Leo III in 805, a house of God in which altogether thirty-three German Emperors have been crowned. As one might expect, it is filled with the rarest and most precious relics and its treasury remains to this day the most important of any north of the Alps.

The loveliest of the shrines of Aachen cathedral, a masterpiece of Rhineland silverware, houses the four greatest of these relics: the swaddling-clothes of the infant Jesus; the loincloth he wore on the Cross; one of his mother's dresses; and the cloth laid out by those who decapitated John the Baptist in order to catch his head and his blood. Elsewhere in the cathedral are part of Jesus's winding sheet, a thorn from the crown of thorns, a fragment of cord from the thongs with which Jesus was beaten; his leather belt; the sponge which, dipped in vinegar, gave him drink as he was dying; and a belt which once encircled the waist of Our Lady.

These holy relics served to confirm Charlemagne's status as co-protector, with the Pope, of Christendom. Throughout his empire he utilised other relics in the same way. In showering them on the humble and great, on his monastic foundations, on cathedrals and great churches throughout Europe, the Holy Roman Emperor enhanced the status of those he honoured and confirmed them in their loyalty and gratitude to him.

And whatever an eighteenth-century sceptic like Gibbon might assert, the Emperor Charlemagne, far from indulging in superstition, believed himself to be using relics to drive out the superstitious. One of the first tasks he set his educated clergy was to root out the false reverence of paganism. The *Admonitio Generalis* of March 789 declared that 'there must be no more enchanters or weavers of spells or weather magicians'. Having thus condemned false holy men and women, the *Admonitio* attacked their holy places and objects: 'Where there are trees or rocks or springs where idiots are in the habit of carrying lights and holding other rites, such evil customs must be altogether removed and destroyed.'

How were these to be driven out of the minds and hearts of newly-Christianised pagans? They were to be driven out by substituting a godly relic for a meaningless superstition. A Gibbon might have observed: Superstition was employed to extirpate superstition; but Charlemagne thought otherwise.

You come across his benefactions in what are often today

exquisite, sometimes out-of-the-way towns and villages throughout Europe. In Périgord, south-west France, Charlemagne founded the Benedictine abbey of Brantôme. He presented the monks with the body of one of the holy infants murdered at the orders of King Herod. There today is a delicate thirteenth-century bas-relief of the martyrdom of the Holy Innocents. Further south in Périgord is the contemporary tourist paradise of Sarlat. Here Charlemagne gave to the Benedictines the bones of St Sacerdos (a bishop of Limoges who had been born close by Sarlat in the village of Calviac), a piece of the true cross and a spine from the crown of thorns. He was equally generous to the diocese of Périgueux, giving the see one of baby Jesus's vests.

In the east and the middle east, in Carthage, Smyrna, Constantinople, on Mount Sinai, in Jerusalem itself, in remote Britain, in France, Italy, Spain and Germany, wherever a Christian journeyed he walked amongst relics and was constantly aware of their power and presence. If great princes such as Constantine and Charlemagne profited from this golden age of the relic by utilising the sanctity of martyred bones to enhance their own power, princes of the church did not lag far behind them.

One such was Gregory, Bishop of Tours from 573 to 594. Gregory assiduously promoted the relics of his illustrious predecessor, the soldier-saint Martin.

Martin's life had already been glamorised by the Aquitaine publicist Sulpicius Severus nearly two centuries earlier. This 'largely fictitious biography', as Professor Henry Chadwick has described it, 'was designed to show that Gaul could produce a saint superior even to the Egyptian ascetics. Martin was credited with extraordinary miracles and prodigies,' Professor Chadwick continues, 'and thanks to Sulpicius's historical novel became one of the most popular saints in the barbarian West.' His most famous action, however, was not a miracle at all but simply a fine act of charity. While still a pagan and soldier Martin was riding with his regiment through snow into the city of Amiens when he saw an almost naked beggar holding out his hands for bread. Martin dismounted, drew his sword and sliced his military cloak in two, giving one half to the beggar.

This spontaneous act, in the account of Sulpicius Severus, seems to have convinced Martin that he was a natural Christian. He was baptised; and before he could return to his native Hungary to inform his mother of all this, Bishop Hilary of Poitiers ordained him as a Christian exorcist. Similarly, almost without his own consent, Martin was consecrated Bishop of Tours, and ruled there from 371 till his death in 397.

He seems to have been a deeply pious Christian and extremely kind. He established what was probably the first French monastery (at Ligugé, eight kilometres south of Poitiers). He abhorred persecution. When Priscillian, Bishop of Avila, confessed under torture that he and his companions had prayed naked at night with depraved women, Martin strongly condemned their execution. Two centuries after Martin's death, Bishop Gregory of Tours found it entirely convenient to use his relics to bolster his own prestige.

Some of Martin's legendary miracles were extremely congenial to a successor such as Gregory, anxious about his own standing in an uncertain world, where power was often in dispute. Once (Sulpicius Severus relates) the Emperor Valentinian refused to stand up when Martin entered the room. The startled Valentinian suddenly discovered that his throne was on fire and his bottom burning. The relics of a man of such superiority to the secular powers were so assiduously and successfully promoted by Gregory that today almost 4,000 French parishes are named after Martin (not to speak of several churches in Britain, the oldest being St Martin's in Canterbury, and the best-known St Martin-in-the-Fields, London). In Tours the relics of the saint were translated to a splendid basilica, to the glory of Martin – and of Gregory!

Unfortunately, neither the basilica nor the relics remain. Just as the bones of St Cuthbert, threatened by invaders, were trundled about Britain for safety, so St Martin of Tours was continually carried from place to place when the Normans invaded Aquitaine. Having survived this danger, his relics were partly dispersed by the Protestants during the French Wars of Religion and then totally disposed of by godless Revolutionaries in 1793.

St Martin's Church in Tours survived the Revolution and then was sadly demolished as redundant and too expensive to maintain. Next in 1861 a rock-hewn tomb which once held the saint's bones was discovered under a house built on the site of the former high altar of the church. The French now began to build again. A new basilica – the costliest and most imposing to date, apart from Sacré Coeur de Montmartre in Paris – arose on the spot. The English architecturual historian and romantic, T. Francis Bumpus, visited it eighty years ago. 'Right and left of the steps leading up the transepts from the nave is a short flight conducting down to the crypt, whose roof is sustained by thick red granite piers,' he reported. 'Here is the great object of veneration – the tomb of St Martin. The shrine, a species of twin-gable temple, with two rows of four columns, is raised on a lofty plinth inlaid with mosaics in bands, gratings at the north and south ends giving a view of the tomb before which a lamp is burning.' Bumpus judged that 'Altogether, new St Martin's is a superb piece of work, and one that atones, in some measure, for the loss of the medieval abbey.'

To my mind a lamp burning before an empty shrine is a melancholy sight, especially when that tomb once contained the most famous relics in France. If today we wish to see and admire relics used by princes of the church to assert their own spiritual (and secular) authority, we should best visit Rome, and particularly the Basilica of St John in the Lateran.

Roman law forbidding burials within the city itself was relaxed only in the seventh century A.D. Before then the Bishops of Rome, anxious to venerate the relics of the martyrs, would journey on their feast days to celebrate the eucharist in the catacombs. The first translation of relics into the city took place as late as the year 648, when the bodies of St Prime and St Felicien were taken from the Nomentane Way to the church of San Stefano Rotunda. (Pope Urban VIII discovered these bones under a side altar in the early seventeenth century, and put them in a new, finer shrine.)

Thereafter translations were swift. Pope Paul I (757 to 767) decided to speed up the process, ostensibly because dogs and other creatures had taken up homes in the catacombs and were gnawing sacred relics as tasty snacks. But Paul had another reason for translating these dry bones: his own prestige and status. The golden age of relics was not a time in which a spiritual prince would leave such tokens of divine favour buried outside his holy city. Altogether Paul I moved more than a hundred relics inside the walls of Rome. The papacy enhanced relics. Relics also enhanced the papacy.

At this time and indeed until the Popes returned from Avignon in the later middle ages, the Lateran palace and the basilica of St John in the Lateran were regarded as the centre of western Christendom. Even today the chapter of St John in the Lateran takes precedence over that of St Peter's in Rome. St John's still glories in the weight of relics it houses – even though some, such as the Ark of the Covenant (containing, we are told, golden haemorrhoids and golden mice) have long since disappeared. There you can still see the Gothic ciborium over the high altar which Urban V built in the late-fourteenth century to house the reliquary chamber of the heads of St Peter and St Paul; and those two heads still rest there behind a bronze lattice. When the French troops ransacked Rome in 1799 they stole the bejewelled figures in which these skulls had been encased: but they left the skulls behind as valueless. The Popes knew better. Pius VII discovered that even though not much bone remained, the seals of Pope Urban V were still intact, and so these most precious relics were encased in new shrines.

No other prince, sacred or secular, was blessed with relics such as these. Saints Peter and Paul outclassed the Magi. Christians scarcely remembered that St James the Great, whose body was now at Compostela in Spain, had chaired the first synod of the church and not Peter nor Paul. Since the body of Christ himself was generally held to be in Heaven, nothing of his – not even the seamless robe he once wore, which

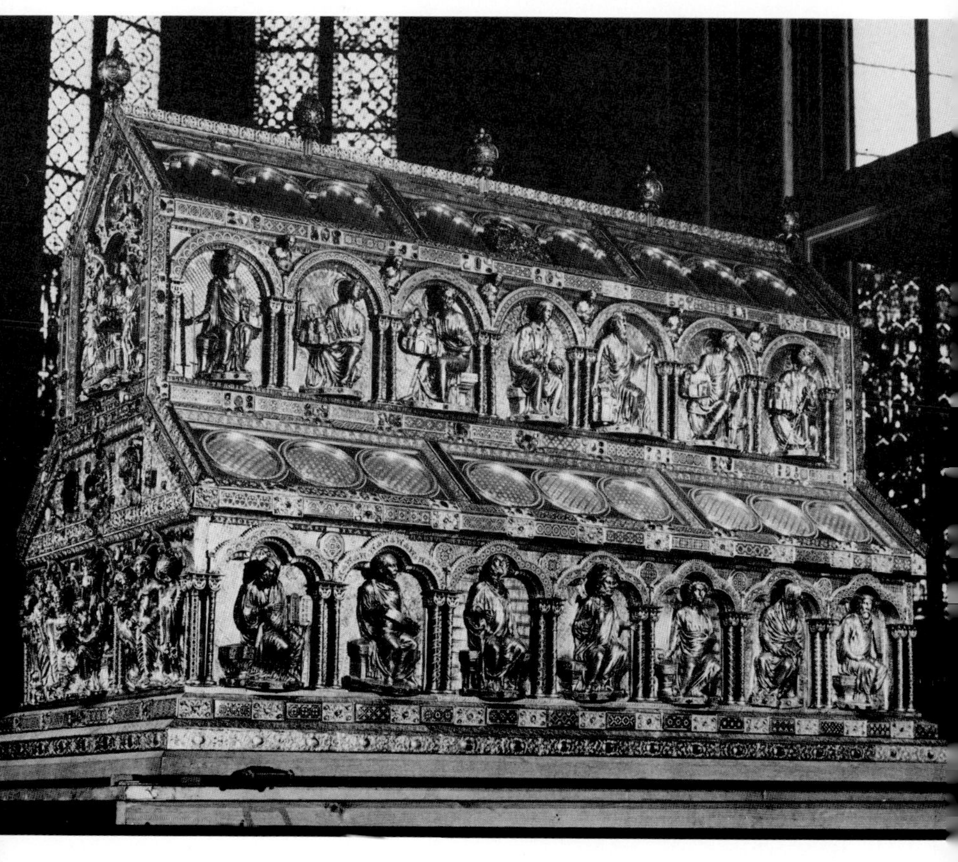

The shrine of the Magi in Cologne
Made between 1220 and 1230, this golden shrine houses the bones of the three wise men and stands behind the high altar of Cologne cathedral

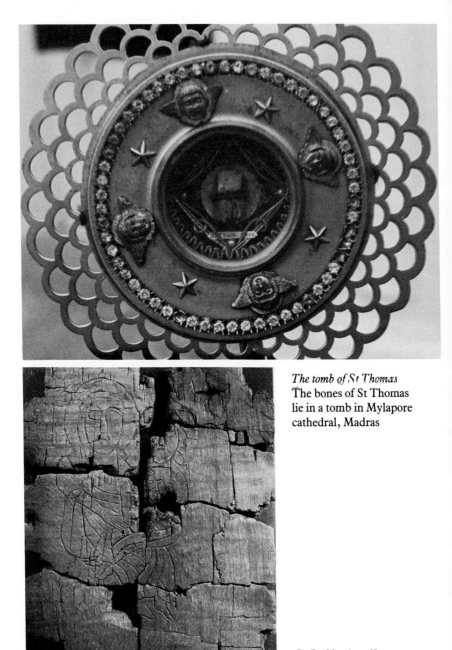

The tomb of St Thomas
The bones of St Thomas lie in a tomb in Mylapore cathedral, Madras

St Cuthbert's coffin
Fragments of the coffin of St Cuthbert, made in the late seventh century

The Scala Sancta

The Scala Sancta, once the steps of the house of Pontius Pilate, and now in Rome

St Remi's basilica, Reims
The Romanesque basilica which houses the bones of St Remi in Reims

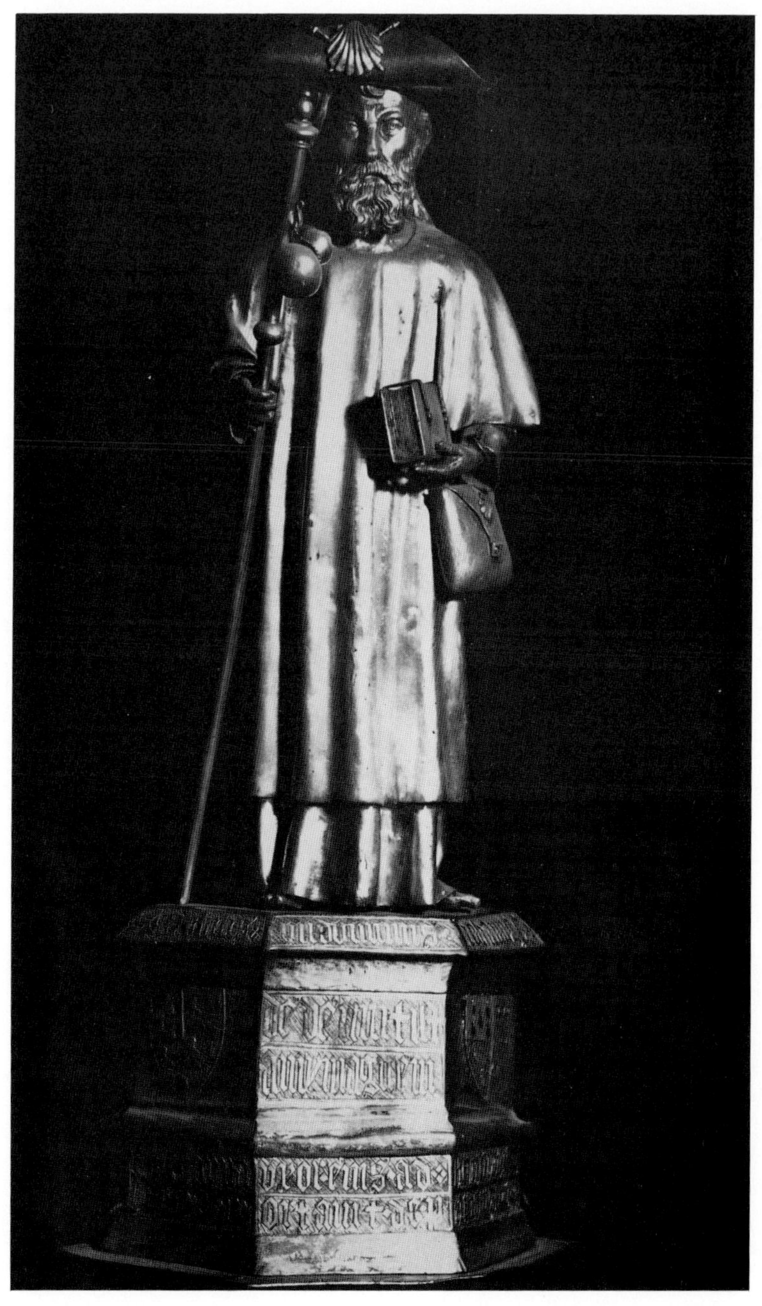

St James in Compostela

A statue of St James the Great, dressed as a pilgrim, in the reliquary chapel at Compostela

St Francis of Assisi
Giotto's picture of St Francis, receiving the stigmata

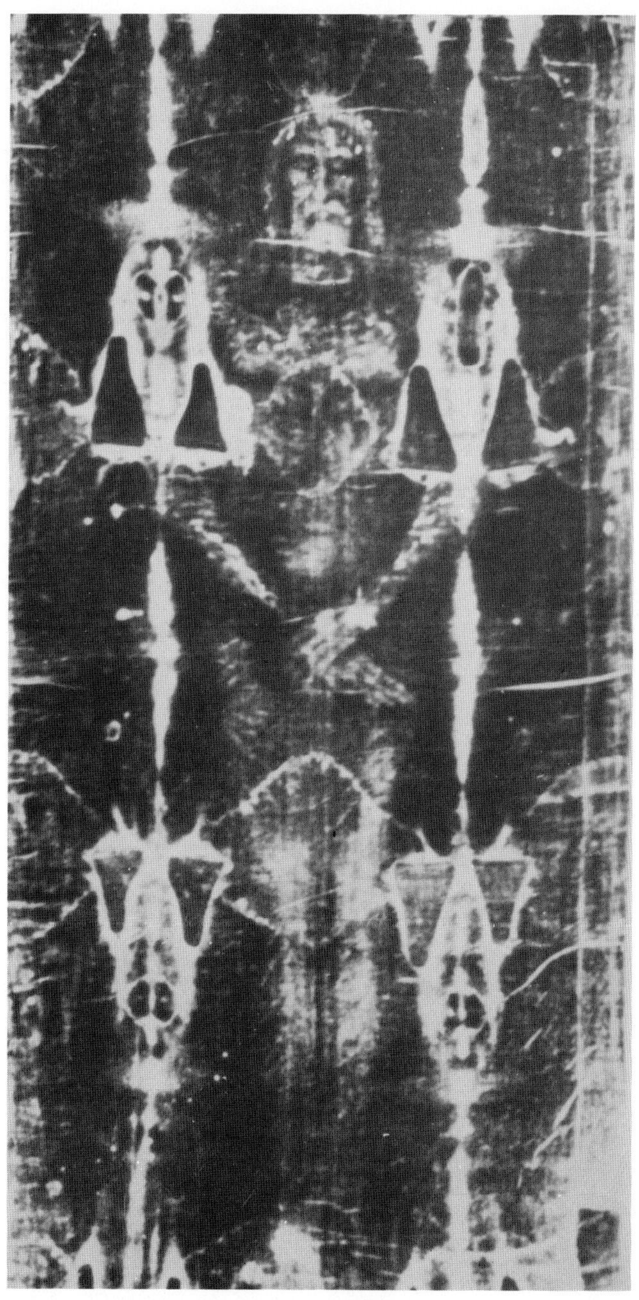

The Turin Shroud
The image on the Turin Shroud

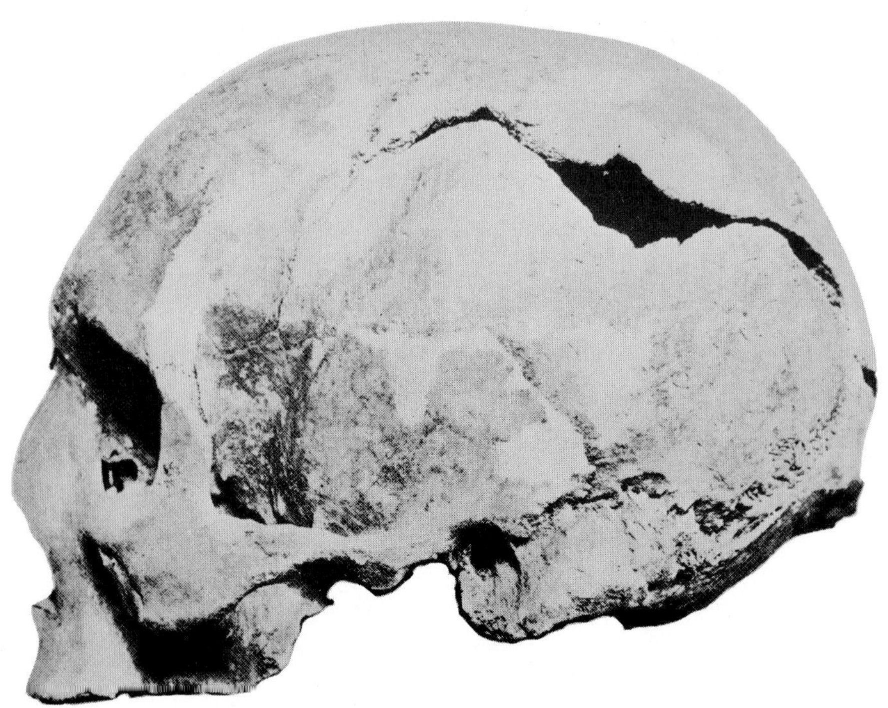

The skull of St Magnus
St Magnus's skull reveals the blow that killed him

arrived at Trier cathedral in the twelfth century – could be said to outrank in honour the Apostle to the Gentiles and St Peter, to whom, according to St Matthew's Gospel, Jesus had given the keys of the Kingdom of Heaven. And the relics of these men, and especially of Peter, were the property of the Bishop of Rome.

This sublime possession, more than anything else in the middle ages, confirmed in the eyes of the faithful the claims of the Bishop of Rome to be supreme pontiff of Christendom. In the words of Sir Richard Southern, 'the Pope, whatever theoretical claims were made for him, in practice owed most of his authority to the fact that he was the guardian of the body of St Peter. This brought men to Rome and made them listen to the voice of St Peter mediated through his representative on earth.' The relic authenticated the papacy.

Not that the Popes neglected their other relics or failed to utilise them in time of need. Elsewhere in the basilica of St John Lateran can still be seen the head of the child-martyr St Pancras. (The rest of his body, mostly reduced to ashes, was kept in the church of San Pancrazio on the Via Aurelia, but French soldiery scattered the ashes to the winds.) Amongst the countless other relics still sheltering in the Lateran church is a porphyry slab on which the soldiers guarding the crucified Jesus arc said to have diced for his seamless robe. And almost opposite the chief doors of the basilica is one of the largest secondary relics in the world: twenty-eight marble steps said once to have belonged to the palace of Pontius Pilate in Jerusalem. Pious legend (on little enough evidence) credits St Helena with bringing them from Jerusalem in 326. Pope Sergius II had them repaired in the mid-ninth century, and today the marble is protected with wood.

The glory of this *Scala Sancta* is not of course that Pontius Pilate once owned it but that Jesus himself may well have climbed and descended the stairs. And in this belief Christians have sought a blessing or a miracle by devoutly following in their Saviour's footsteps, humbly climbing the *Scala Sancta* on their knees. The Popes themselves have not ceased to demonstrate their own respect for the spiritual ability of such relics and their practical usefulness in time of need. Thus in September 1870, as Victor Emmanuel II prepared to invade Rome in his quest for Italian unity, Pope Pius IX at the age of seventy-eight hastened to the *Scala Sancta* and climbed its twenty-eight steps on his knees. It must be acknowledged even by the sceptic that the Vatican subsequently escaped incorporation into a united Italy.

3

Relics in action

A few days before the annual feast-day of any one of the great monasteries on Mount Athos, the celebration monks from other monasteries and laymen from the surrounding islands begin to arrive. On the eve of the saint's day there is an all-night service. Dawn reveals the shapes of the monastery church, and the worshippers in their stalls.

'While the liturgy is in progress a row of benches is set up outside the church and covered with richly embroidered purple and golden cloth,' writes the Byzantine scholar Philip Sherrard: 'on the benches are laid the monastery's most treasured possessions – miraculous icons, the skull and bones of saint and martyr. The service over, pilgrims crowd round to worship them with kisses and prostrations to the ground, offering them also their humble gifts. Then the treasures are carried round the court of the monastery, while barefoot workmen, black-clad monks and surpliced priests chant the last hymns of the long office.'

In some respects little that is wondrous takes place. After the liturgy, Sherrard continues, 'the feast begins. Refectory, private cells and cellars are thrown open. Food and wine are given freely to all. The talk flows. The sun burns. The monastery and its guests rejoice all day long in the saint's honour.' Such could be a secular paradise, without the aid of divine legacies of holy men and women. But to the Orthodox the relics of the saints have once again brought to pass a great mystery. Through them the unseen world has come closer. Their bodies, which were taken over and sanctified by the Holy Spirit to an awesome degree, have been venerated by worshippers who themselves seek such a transformation and hold that by that day's devotion they and the relic have brought paradise nearer.

Mount Athos is the home of some of the most revered relics in Christendom: the left hands of both Mary Magdalen and St John Chrysostom; the skull of St Basil the Great; the gifts of gold, frankincense and myrrh presented by the Magi to the infant Jesus; part of the crown of thorns; the sponge used by the soldiers to moisten the lips of the dying Jesus (notwithstanding the similar sponge in Charlemagne's cathedral at Aachen).

These relics are seen not principally as wonderworking talismans, but first of all as evidence of a world unseen, of the saints in Heaven, of the continuity of Christian people, past, present and future, of what the historic creeds call the communion of saints.

That they can work miracles in time of need is taken for granted. One of the Blessed Virgin's precious girdles has been divided into three for safe-keeping at the monastery of Vatopedi on Mount Athos. Made of camel's hair, it was given (tradition holds) by the dying Virgin to Jesus's disciple Thomas. Eventually, in the fourteenth century it reached Vatopedi. It is renowned for its miraculous powers. In 1872, sent at the Sultan's request to Constantinople, part of this girdle is said to have halted a cholera epidemic. In 1884 it was on the island of Chios, cleansing the orange and lemon trees from blight.

God, averred Francis Bacon, never wrought a miracle to convert an atheist. Jesus himself observed that some people would not believe even though a person rose from the dead. The problem with miracles is that many people don't accept them. After all, there is no necessary connection between Pope Pius

IX climbing the *Scala Sancta* in 1870 and the subsequent history of the Vatican State. Pius IX simply chose to believe there was one. Others prefer to doubt. In a sceptical age, wonderworking relics inevitably have difficulty in proving their credentials.

In the ages of faith, by contrast, the miraculous was precisely what convinced people that a particular set of bones were those of a genuine saint. Thus St Etheldreda was and is still honoured as a virgin in spite of having twice been married. The Venerable Bede, recounting this, says he was convinced that she never slept with either husband, because the Bishop of Ripon told him that several years after her death 'her grave was opened and her body, being brought into sight was found as free from corruption as if she had died and been buried on that very day'. And as if that were not enough to prove her perpetual virginity, Wilfrid further testified that the neck of the saint, once disfigured by a noxious swelling, proved to have healed completely, *after her death*.

Bede was an historian anxious to believe the best about the English saints. But he was here also careful to obtain first-hand testimony to the miracle of St Etheldreda's incorruptible corpse.

Others might still doubt. A corpse entombed or buried in certain conditions could remain in good order without the intervention of the miraculous. In August 1984 a peat-cutting machine sliced through the body of a man who had lain in Lindow Moss, Wilmslow, ever since being garrotted with a cord and dumped there naked 2,500 years previously. So well preserved was the bog man that his perfectly manicured finger-nails, his mousy-coloured balding hair and his red moustache, beard and sideburns were still intact. Was the incorruptible Etheldreda simply the result of a similar quirk of nature? Or was it a new corpse?

We could ask such questions about other alleged miracles connected with holy relics. St Gregory of Tours, as we have noticed, was a man ardently willing to believe in their efficacy. He also suffered from migraine – a sickness said to be partly psychosomatic. Since then (as now) doctors were frequently baffled by this ailment, Gregory sought the help of a secondary relic connected with one of the most famous Gaulish martyrs, St Julian of Brioude. Julian, a former soldier turned Christian, withdrew to the Auvergne when the governor of Vienne, one Crispin, began persecuting the followers of Jesus. Crispin's servants pursued the saint, who cried, 'I have been too long in this evil world. I want to be with Jesus.' He was beheaded; and the church at Brioude near Clermont-Ferrand, built for his relics, soon became a famous pilgrimage centre.

One of Gregory's terrible headaches was cured, it seems, through the intercessions of St Julian of Brioude. Peter Brown amusingly describes the occasion, observing that 'Many of the cures which Gregory experienced himself were connected with a precise and congruent moment of suffering in the martyr.' He continues: 'At Brioude he was cured of a splitting headache caused by sunstroke after dousing his head in the fountain of St Julian – that is, in the water where the martyr's own head had been washed clean after the ultimate headache of decapitation.' We may legitimately ask how far Gregory's cure derived from the psychological effects of a deep emotional experience. Similar questions could be asked about the many allegedly miraculous cures at those moments in the liturgy when the accounts of the sufferings of particular saints were read. The occasions were highly charged. The saint's sufferings often seemed closely akin to the sufferings of the supplicants gathered around his or her bones. Since the saint had triumphed over these sufferings, a deep sense of emotional well-being could certainly overwhelm those who needed such a victory themselves.

But such naturalistic, psychological or physiological explanations can in no way account for or explain away the vast number of miracles Christians soon began to attribute to relics. St Augustine of Hippo tells us that he knew some seventy accounts of miracles connected with the relics of St Stephen alone. Blindness, fistula and gout, even raising the dead to life, none of these nonplussed the remains of the protomartyr. Augustine showed not the slightest surprise at these miracles. They seem to have been part of his environment.

Certainly men and women believed themselves cured miraculously, whether or not we today want to take these claims at their face-value. From the fifth century to the present day they have hung beside the shrines of saints model legs and arms as a sign of thankfulness because the relic has driven away arthritis or healed a troublesome fracture. The citizens of Constantinople looked to their relics to repel their enemies, and when John Curcuas brought that city a famous portrait of Jesus said to have been drawn from life (or even marvellously transferred to the cloth/canvas by Christ's own touch) he did so, he declared, 'for the glory of the faithful, for the safety of the emperors, for the preservation of the entire city'. Sure enough this portrait, and the other superb relics of Constantinople, inspired and helped the inhabitants to repel the Persians, the Avars and especially the Arabs and Slavs in the seventh century. In the ninth century they repelled a huge Russian fleet. They were to repel the Muslims in 1322. Alas they failed before the Turks in 1453.

Even if a relic failed to defend those who cherished it, that never seemed sufficient reason to abandon the bones. After the defeat of the English by William the Conqueror, the new abbot of Evesham mocked the relics of the English saints Egwin, Odulf, Wystan and Credan. If they were as good as the English supposed, he jibed, how had the English been beaten? But all he did then was set fire to part of the bones ('testing them by fire', to check their authenticity) before retaining them for his own future use.

What we can often see, with the insights of modern history, is the continual embroidering of fact. For instance the late Denis Bethell analysed the new cult of St Ithamar (Bishop of Rochester in the mid-seventh century), which arose five hundred years after most people had forgotten him. 'Few English saints can be as little known as St Ithamar,' Bethell rightly observed, even though he was the first native Englishman to become a Christian bishop and to have a reputation for sanctity. Yet in the twelfth century he became the subject of a cult at Rochester and his bones were translated to a new imposing shrine. Why? Denis

Bethell suggests the reason was injured patriotism: the nostalgic English monks of Rochester were reacting against the Norman conquest and the Normanisation of the English church under their French masters, by creating a cult around the corpse of an obscure Englishman. To do so they needed to write a treatise recounting his alleged miracles. No matter that these miracles were almost entirely inventions: Ithamar's relics restored injured English pride.

The closer the writing of the saint's life to the time he or she actually lived, the more likely we are to have some genuine reminiscences, miraculous or otherwise, of what actually went on. But in fact the most entertaining tales of miracle-working relics are usually those that few of us could take seriously today. Even so, they are of fascinating historical interest.

The legends of St Osyth of Essex and St Osyth of Aylesbury are such. Again it was Denis Bethell who excavated from history the stories of their relics, which were frequently confused in medieval memories. Osyth of Essex was the daughter of King Frithewald of Mercia and his Queen Wilburga. As many another saint of the time, she swore an oath of chastity. Pagan pirates apparently failed to overcome this oath, nor could they make Osyth worship idols. Enraged, the pirates' captain decided to have her beheaded. A stick was used to twist her hair back and her throat was slit.

This took place in 635 and some of it, possibly, is authentic history. But next we are told that a fountain sprang up where she died, curing many. And instead of lying there dead, Osyth is said to have picked up her head and walked with it to the church of St Peter and St Paul three leagues away. As she entered the porch, she placed her hand on the church door, leaving a bloodstain that lasted 450 years. In the sanctuary she offered her martyred head to God, and finally expired near the entry to the choir. There she was buried, being translated many miracles later to the middle of the choir in 1076.

Some of St Osyth's miracles seem simple acts of kindness – straightening a hump-backed woman, making the lame walk. But we can also read in her miracles the dominant anxieties of late-medieval life. After St Osyth's relics had cured a young woman's withered arm, the girl vowed perpetual virginity. When she married, St Osyth bound her feet with an invisible chain till she repented. Another woman, healed by St Osyth, decided to be a servant of her sanctuary. Unfortunately a man named Godwin enticed her to bed. The affronted relics twisted the woman's feet into the shape of the cross – no doubt rendering impossible any repetition of the sin. Godwin begged the clergy to intercede with the relics; but in vain. Only on the day of his death did St Osyth appear before the woman and unlock her feet.

Clearly, as well as healing the sick, St Osyth's relics and their like had a role of reinforcing the social mores of contemporary society. The function of a relic was certainly to heal; but relics tended to heal those who also desired to lead a better life. By all means beg a personal favour of a relic; but stern theologians insisted that help was available only to those who wished to imitate the lives of the saints before whose bones they were pleading. Relics liked to act only for the good and holy.

In the sixth century Pope Gregory the Great had explicitly said that miracles were truly found at the shrines of holy martyrs but only by those who sought them with a pure soul. And in any case, quite apart from the injunctions of a Pope or the terrifying prospect of the wrath of a saint like Osyth, these countless corpses on show throughout Christendom each exerting supernatural powers, could provoke a numinous dread in the most hardened sinner. Even St Jerome confessed: 'Whenever I have been angry or had some bad thought on my mind, or some evil fantasy has disturbed my sleep, I do not dare enter the shrines of the martyrs. I quake in body and soul.' While healing the sick, averting plagues, defending cities and saving crops, relics were also promoting morality.

They still do. The relics of the Venerable Matt Talbot lie in the church of Our Lady of Lourdes, Sean McDermott Street, Dublin. From all over the world tens of thousands flock there, seeking favours. Many of them are alcoholics; and many such leave reformed.

Matthew Talbot's earthly remains are specially suited to reforming alcoholics, for Matt himself was sent on the way to becoming one when (after a single year's schooling) he went to work in a wine store. 'He wanted only one thing – the drink,' recalled a friend. By the age of sixteen he was a chronic drunkard. He sold his clothes and boots to pay for drink. He became desperate enough to steal money from a blind beggar in order to satisfy his craving. By the time he was twenty-eight and too drunk to earn a penny, Matt was reduced to soliciting drinks from his friends outside O'Meara's bar.

Their contemptuous refusal hurt him deeply. He looked into his soul and was deeply ashamed. He resolved to amend his life, and signed the pledge. Every Saturday after work and all Sunday he would kneel before the Blessed Sacrament in church, fighting his burning thirst for alcohol. Sometimes his resolve almost broke. But Matt reached extraordinary heights of austerity and devotion in fighting his particular devil. He rose each morning at 2 a.m. and prayed for two hours with outstretched arms. Then he prepared for Mass. He would slit his trouser legs to admit the cold, and would try to arrive at church before the priest had unlocked the doors so that he might have an excuse to pray outside. After Mass and daily devotion to the Stations of the Cross, Matt would return home for a breakfast of dry bread and a mixture of cold tea and cocoa (without sugar or milk).

He had taken work in a timber yard, where his workmates recognised Matt's extraordinary piety. They eschewed bad language; they watched with awe as he prayed between the timber-stacks during breaks; they admired his support for the poor during the Dublin Dock Strike of 1900 and the General Strike of 1913, respecting equally his determination to avoid all violence during these grievous disputes. Matt had learned to read and write, and he mastered countless spiritual books without ever becoming vain or self-righteous. ('The Kingdom of Heaven was promised not to the sensible or the educated,' he wrote, 'but to such as have the spirit of little children.') Increasingly his workmates sought his advice. After the death of his mother, he spent most of the time at home on his knees in prayer, rising only to greet a visitor or to eat. (He always ate standing up.) Then in June 1925, on the way to Mass, he collapsed and, dying, was taken to Jervis Street Hospital. Today a shrine in Granby Lane marks the spot where he fell. The hospital attendants were astonished to discover Matt Talbot's secret mortifications: he had tied a chain round his body, two others round an arm and a leg, and a rope was tightly drawn round the other arm.

Matt Talbot had become a lay member of the Third Order of the Franciscans. He was buried in the brown habit of the order, his bonds lying alongside him in the coffin. Six years later the Archbishop of Dublin submitted the arguments for Matt's sanctity to Rome and in 1972 this led to his translation to a new shrine of Wicklow granite in the church in Sean McDermott Street. In 1975 the Pope made him the 'Venerable' Matt Talbot. Today in the church of Our Lady of Lourdes his relics are still in action.

Yet remarkable as the doings of Matt Talbot's relics undoubtedly are, they fall far short of what was expected of many a medieval relic. No-one today, for example, thinks of using dead Matt in the legal processes of the Republic of Ireland. Yet in the middle ages relics had a leading role in the maintenance and the administration of justice.

One well-tried technique for bringing a miscreant to heel was actually to stop a relic doing anything at all until the villain relented. Thus in the first half of the sixth century St Eloi of Paris was much put out by King Chilperic I, who had stolen the ornaments of the tabernacle of the church of Sainte-Colombe. Eloi therefore forbade completely the cult of St Colombe, thus depriving the citizens and the city itself of the benefits of a most powerful relic. Chilperic I was brought to heel. He restored the precious ornaments, and the cult of the relic was once again allowed.

Some relics were equal in strength to the most powerful rulers of the middle ages. Martin of Tours, for example, was more than a match for the terrifying Fulk Nerra, Count of Anjou, even though the saint had been dead for six centuries when Fulk was building up his powerful sway in the Valley of the Loire. Fulk was in some respects a devout man. He not only constructed fortresses; he also built, for instance, a Romanesque abbey at Beaulieu on the River Indre. But when Fulk captured the city of Tours, his military ardour overcame his piety and he dared to march, fully armed, into the collegiate church of St Martin. This invasion of sanctuary and insult to a house of God horrified the canons. They determined to force an apology out of the count. Taking the saint's relics out of their shrine, the canons placed them on the ground by the cross. Then they gathered thorns and placed these over the famous bones. They closed the doors of the church, barring countless pilgrims from access to St Martin. Anger spread throughout Fulk's domain. The canons refused all appeals to restore the relics to their former dignity until the chastened Count Fulk begged forgiveness for his act of impiety and promised never to behave so wickedly again.

For my own part even today I cannot go into the basilica at Tours without feeling a tremendous *frisson* at the thought of the great and overpowering Fulk Nerra, barefoot before the clergy and the common people, prostrating himself before the long-dead body of St Martin, then solemnly and in humiliation being led to the bones of other saints and martyrs before making offerings to the church and begging absolution. The relic, fighting with spiritual powers on behalf of the church, had triumphed.

We in Britain can point to a victory of a martyr's bones over a ruler who in life had been his enemy. King Henry II, at Argentan in Normandy, learned on New Year's Day, 1171, that Thomas Becket had been murdered in Canterbury Cathedral. During Becket's lifetime the king had longed to be rid of the archbishop. Now the dead saint threw him into a state of total dismay. Arnulf, Bishop of Lisieux, was present and described the king's misery in a letter to Pope Alexander III. 'At the first words of the messenger,' wrote Arnulf, 'the king burst into loud lamentation and exchanged his royal robes for sackcloth and ashes.' For three days Henry remained shut up in his room, eating nothing, refusing to be comforted, till men began to fear for his life. 'At times,' Arnulf continued, 'he fell into a stupor, after which he would utter cries and groans louder and more bitter than before.'

The saint was already avenging his own death. And the Pope was not slow to take advantage of the enormous power put into his hands by the transformation of an English archbishop at odds with his king into a relic so patently superior to him. For some time Alexander III simply refused to see Henry's envoys. Finally, after negotiations lasting a year and a half, the king totally capitulated to the Pope's demands. He agreed to do any penance imposed on him by the papal legates. He promised to annul church legislation offensive to Alexander. Those who had been penalised for supporting Becket against the king were to be recompensed. Canterbury cathedral was to be given back its sequestered estates. Henry promised to equip and pay for two hundred knights to fight for a year in the Holy Land. He himself promised to be ready at the Pope's command to fight in Spain against the Muslim invaders.

But this was not enough. It was also necessary to demonstrate before the Christian world the superiority of the martyr's bones over the great ones of this world. Alexander III lost no time in recognising the stature of the dead archbishop and thus enhancing the prestige of Becket's bones. On 21 February 1173 Becket was canonised as St Thomas of Canterbury. On 12 July the following year, Henry II did penance before his tomb. Voluntarily he allowed the monks of Christ Church to scourge him, and he spent a whole day and night in prayer before the saint's holy remains.

In the middle ages there seems to have been little a ruler could do when faced with a determined churchman deploying a powerful relic. Undoubtedly the clergy in charge of sacred bones soon perceived their capacity for disconcerting the laity. Different methods for deploying this capacity were developed. Sometimes a relic was 'humiliated' only in a minor fashion – taken out of the reliquary at night, to the accompaniment of lamentations and psalms of woe, before being replaced in the shrine the next morning. At other times, when more important issues were at stake, the ritual humiliation was a great public act. Thorns, sackcloth, briars and ashes could be laid on the saint's bones. Then the great doors were shut against a clamouring people, and all were denied access to the solace of the relic.

Some scholars have seen such 'humiliation' as a kind of punishment of the relic itself, for allowing some heinous crime to take place instead of using its supernatural powers to prevent this in the first place. I do not personally accept this theory. Symbolically to crown a relic with thorns would exalt the bones rather than punish them, for it aligned the holy saint or martyr with the crucified Jesus himself, with the judge of all, whose transcend-power was the ultimate basis of the relic's own power.

Against such forces even the most powerful layman or woman must have felt helpless. However, one ruler did try to fight back. In 1220 King Henry III watched the bones of St Thomas Becket honoured yet more: an enormous procession of bishops and clergy, led by the papal legate and the archbishops of Canterbury and of Reims, transferred Becket's bones from the crypt of Christ Church, Canterbury, to a new, costly shrine east of the high altar in the Trinity chapel. Henry III conceived of the brilliant scheme of fighting the cult of this saint whose relics had so decisively humiliated his grandfather. He would set up a rival cult. This time the cult would be in London. And the relics would be those of an English monarch. Henry III set one relic to fight another.

The relic he enlisted was the corpse of King Edward the Confessor. Edward had been canonised by the same Pope as canonised Becket. His sanctity was undoubted, since – though married at the age of forty or so – he had never slept with his wife. (She, it is said, though crowned as his consort, lived with him and served him as a beloved daughter.) Certainly Edward's queen bore him no children. And his virginity was confirmed after death by the time-honoured method: in 1102 Abbot Gilbert Crispin opened his coffin, along with many of Edward the Confessor's contemporaries who longed to see his face again, and discovered the body incorrupt in the tomb. An unbelieving age might attribute this to some good embalming, especially as his shroud too remained intact. In 1102, by contrast, the undecayed shroud was also seen as evidence of the Confessor's sanctity, preserved by contact with the holy bones. This conclusion was confirmed fifty-eight years later when the coffin was again opened and both corpse and shroud were still intact. The following year Alexander II declared Edward a saint.

Already two persons had written glowing accounts of his life. Ailred of Rievaulx's was the first, followed by one written by Osbert, prior of Westminster, in 1123. Osbert had been born in Claire, Suffolk, in 1138. He conceived two tremendous passions: to promote the cult of the immaculate conception of the mother of Jesus, and to promote the canonisation of King Edward the Confessor. On the first translation of the relics of the newly-canonised king, Osbert offered his life of the saint to King Henry of England and Abbot Laurence of Westminster.

It must be noticed that Osbert of Clare's life of Edward the Confessor lays much more emphasis than Ailred of Rievaulx's biography on the saint's alleged virginity. Osbert was also suspiciously anxious to insist that the whole of Edward's body was still in the abbey's possession. (He tells, for instance, how the Bishop of Rochester, about to pluck out somc hairs of the king's beard, changed his mind.) And successive editions of this hagiography of the last Anglo-Saxon king interpolated even more miracles, attributed to Edward's relics, than even Osbert was prepared to vouch for.

Nevertheless here was the ideal royal saint to offset the irritatingly anti-monarchist relics of Thomas Becket. Henry III decided to build a completely new abbey church for the Confessor's bones, notwithstanding the fact that Edward himself had rebuilt Westminster Abbey sumptuously, seeing it consecrated one week before his own death. Henry demolished the Romanesque building, and in July 1245 the foundation stone of the new abbey was laid. He employed an architect from

Reims, Henry de Reyns, to build the tallest church in his realm, utilising the skills and soaring dreams of contemporary French Gothic. The west front was modelled on the deeply recessed porches of Amiens cathedral. From Reims came the pattern of much of the apse, with its superb arcades and the passage extending round the whole of the abbey. The astonishing rose windows and the flying buttresses owe a huge debt to French architecture at its finest; England knew scarcely anything like them.

The glory was for St Edward. In the triforium was carved the legend of the Confessor giving his ring to a pilgrim who turned out to be St John (one of the miracles later interpolated into Osbert's life). And Edward was given a superb new shrine.

The work was finished quickly. On 13 October 1269 Henry watched the bones of Edward the Confessor translated to their new home. Today his relics are among the comparatively few in England still in their medieval shrine. But the king's purposes were not fulfilled. Relics, it seems, do not fight against each other. Though Westminster Abbey is where kings and queens are crowned, the cult of the Confessor totally failed to eclipse that of St Thomas Becket. The ways of relics do not always coincide with the wishes of rulers.

Sometimes indeed comparatively humble relics, such as St Osyth of Essex, could show a certain viciousness in protecting the rights of the godly. In the twelfth century St Osyth's bones were moved to a new abbey erected in her honour by Augustinian canons. There for the most part she rested content with performing miracles profitable both to the canons and to the Essex seafarers, promising for example favourable winds in return for a gift to the abbey. When however the powerful Bishop of London unjustly took away some of the monks' rights along with certain of their lands, the canons took Osyth's relics out of their shrine and covered them with a cloth. This ordinarily ought to have brought any miscreant to heel; but to make doubly certain that Bishop Richard repented, Osyth's bones struck him in addition with a deadly paralysis until he restored both rights and lands to her benefactors.

So the notion that to humiliate a relic could bring low an overweening scoundrel grew enormously popular in the west from the sixth century onwards. Theft, injustice, physical wrongdoing could be indulged in with considerable insouciance by the powerful. But the saintly dead were more powerful still. The technique of humiliating a relic played on the evildoer's fears that his or her sins were displeasing even the all-powerful one, the Judge Eternal, to whom those godly men and women whose bones were on earth had access in Heaven. This displeasure was reflected in the displeasure of the clergy, who forbade penitents and supplicants to light candles or sing hymns at the shrines of the holy dead. The impression was thus given that the relic too must be displeased – especially when the clergy, and sometimes laypeople too, would physically 'hurt' the saintly corpse by scattering thorns and brambles over it. As they did so, clergy and people would weep, before the priests firmly and solemnly shut the doors of the reliquary. Then they would wait for the relic to bring about justice.

The clergy did not use their relics in this fashion simply to right wrongs done to themselves. Relics were also humiliated in response to some secular evil. In 1105 St Geoffrey of Amiens, incensed that Germundus of Pécquigny had unjustly imprisoned Adamus, Lord of Saint-Omer, decided to humiliate the most treasured relic in his possession, that of St Firmin, the fourth-century martyr who had converted the Belgic tribe of Ambiani (from whom Amiens takes its name). Adamus was speedily released.

But in spite of the solicitude that clergy could show to laymen and women who had been wronged, naturally enough the men of God mostly humiliated their relics to set right injustices which directly affected themselves. And sometimes to humiliate a precious relic could succeed when all other appeals to justice failed.

Thus in the year 1061 the monks of the abbey of Stavelot in Belgium found themselves at odds with Archbishop Anno of Cologne and King Henry IV. Anno had persuaded the king, who was still a minor, that the famous convent of Malmédy, a dependency of Stavelot, should be assigned to himself. For ten years the matter was disputed. Many of the monks of Stavelot deeply resented Anno's action, arguing that their convent had always belonged to the diocese of Liège, never to Cologne. The monks sought justice of Henry IV at the Imperial Diet at Goslar. Henry did nothing. The following year the monks appeared at the Diet of Aachen. This time the king promised action, and again did nothing. Now the monks decided to seek the help of the relics of St Remacle, patron of the abbey of Stavelot. They took the bones from Remacle's shrine and carried them as far as Aachen. Alarmed, the king conceded that the monks had been wronged; but still he refused to do anything about it. The monks next sought the help of the Pope. Alexander II refused to intervene.

By 1071 the monks of Stavelot concluded that they had exhausted every possibility of secular or spiritual justice. In that year King Henry, Archbishop Anno and the leaders of the Empire came to a great assembly at Aachen. Once again the monks of Stavelot took the remains of St Remacle from their shrine. In solemn procession they carried them to the imperial city and while the royal company was eating entered the palace dining-room. In the presence of the archbishop, the King and Queen and the leading men with their ladies, the monks placed on the great table an urn bearing Remacle's bones. Anno and Henry retired, as did the Queen in tears. For a day and a night the monks of Stavelot occupied the dining-room, singing psalms and genuflecting before the bones of St Remacle. Then they transported him to the church of Notre Dame amongst a huge crowd of supporters. Anno and the King gave up the struggle against this all-conquering corpse. Prostrate before Remacle's urn, they begged forgiveness for their sins and returned to Stavelot jurisdiction over the convent of Malmédy.

Humiliation of relics in order to obtain justice, when all other remedies failed, continued for over two more centuries. But some church leaders began to find a number of the practices involved offensive. In particular many considered it bizarre that owners of relics were prepared even to bury them in order to bring an opponent to heel, digging up the corpse again once victory had been won. Equally offensive to many was a similar practice of burying a crucifix or a statue of the Virgin Mary to get the better of some opponent. In 1274 Pope Gregory X called an ecumenical council at Lyons. His chief aim was to accept the submission to Rome of the Greek Church (which badly needed a temporary ally since it feared the ambition of Charles of Anjou who was about to proclaim himself Emperor of Constantinople). The Pope also wished to set in motion the liberation of the Holy Land from the heathen. Yet these weighty matters did not prevent the council promulgating a canon (no. 17, known as *Si canonicis*) forbidding the burying of crucifixes, statues of the Virgin or relics.

Union of the Greek Church with Rome lasted fifteen years; the Holy Land was not liberated; but canon 17 of the Council of Lyons greatly slowed down the practice of humiliating relics. Soon this quaint practice which had succeeded in bringing justice to many for six centuries disappeared from Christendom.

This did not mean that relics ceased to be interested in the course of justice. From the time of St Augustine until just before the Reformation a relic remained a powerful sanction when any person was required to take an oath. Fear of the consequences of offending the saint in Heaven after swearing on his earthly remains could keep the most powerful from breaking their vows.

Jesus seems to have disapproved of oath-taking. 'I say to you, Swear not at all,' he said, 'neither by Heaven, for it is the throne of God, nor by the earth, for it is the footstool of his feet, nor by Jerusalem, for it is the city of the great king. Neither shall you swear by your head, for you cannot make one hair black or white. But let your speech be, Yea, yea; Nay, nay: whatsoever is more than these is of the evil one.'

Slowly the churches forgot or ignored this judgment – though some Christian groups, such as Mennonites, Quakers and Baptists still take their Lord's injunction *au pied de la lettre*, and many early church fathers explicitly forbade oath-taking. After the Council of Chalcedon in 451, the eastern churches allowed men and women to swear oaths on the Gospels. And perhaps earlier many appealed to the name of God or to the saints as tokens of their sincerity. But the first reference to taking an oath in the presence of a relic is to be found in the writings of St Augustine. Augustine recounts that the people of Milan brought home to a thief the evil fruits of his larceny by making him swear before a saint not to steal again. Presumably the Bishop of Milan (later St Ambrose) supported this, but we cannot be certain. The first theologian actually to declare in writing his approval of the practice was Augustine himself. A couple more centuries elapsed before the Popes began to approve.

Once the Popes did approve they naturally felt the need to regulate the practice. Since this was a matter of justice and legal disputes, such regulation was no doubt beneficial in the law courts. In the eighth century western lawyers came to assume that every layman's oath should be made in the presence of a relic. From the ninth century onwards it was decreed necessary actually to lay one's hand on (or at least point it towards) the reliquary. Proper words were prescribed, the swearer declaring, 'Before God and this relic, I . . .' And – since most relics were found in churches – the ceremony almost invariably took place there.

Initially reluctant to sanction oath-taking on a relic, the Popes soon enthusiastically made use of the powers of a relic to keep their vassals faithful. The papacy could of course make effective use of the bones of Peter himself in this way. So in 722 Pope Gregory II heard of the untiring efforts of the Devon-born missionary St Boniface to convert the extremely hostile Frisians to Christianity. Summoning Boniface to Rome the Pope made him swear on the body of St Peter to keep the faith of the holy catholic church in all its purity. Thus fortified by contact with these sacred bones, Boniface courageously returned to Germany, where he took the immense liberty of felling the famous Oak of the pagan god Thor, at Geismar near Fritzlar, using the timber to build a missionary chapel.

This was the kind of action later recommended by Charlemagne's *Admonitio Generalis* – and as might be expected the same treatise ordered oaths to be taken either on the Gospels or on a sacred relic by town magistrates; by those swearing fidelity to another; whenever a person entered a profession or a monastery; in court cases; before ecclesiastical visitations; when a grievous public sinner wished to submit and be forgiven; in any private matter; and when enemies declared peace. In codifying the use of relics in this way, their great promoter was for the most part only giving imperial sanction to what had become common custom. For instance at a synod held in Llandaff in 560 King Mauricius swore to live in peace with his nephew Bishop Oudocco, sealing the oath in the presence of a holy relic. In Rome newly-consecrated bishops would take the oath of allegiance to the papacy on the body of St Peter – a practice that did not cease until the year 1078. Such a powerful relic was, it seems, well able to take reprisals against such as broke their oath.

In truth, all relics, great and small, could do the same. Tales abound of perjurers who had taken oaths on relics and, later, dropped down dead. As if that threat were not enough, Charlemagne's *Admonitio Generalis* also prescribed chopping off the hand that had touched a relic, if its owner failed to keep his oath. Only one group of people, so far as I have been able to discover, escaped such punishments: the poets of the Languedoc, who invented the notion of courtly love. Again and again Languedoc poetry speaks of lovers plighting their troth by (say) the head of St Catherine or the bones of St Mary Magdalen (whom Jesus forgave because she loved much). As the Jacobean dramatist Webster noted, lovers' promises are like mariners' prayers: offered in extremity and not, perhaps, to be taken seriously. No doubt the relics allowed the love-sick troubadours of Languedoc poetic licence in the matter of their troth. But these were exceptions.

Since, as we have seen, relics conferred considerable status on those who owned them, to have subordinates swear fealty on such a relic gave those in power an added superiority. The bones of St Peter would not only rightly inhibit a prelate from questioning the authority or decree of the Pope to whom he had sworn loyalty; these bones also contributed a deeper sense of awe to the very act of swearing fealty. That relics could confer superiority provided an additional motive for digging them up and cherishing them. The discovery by Bishop Ambrose of Milan of the bodies of St Gervais and St Protais in 386 greatly enhanced the stature of the bishop and his bishopric. Ambrose lost no time in transferring the relics of these two martyrs to his cathedral. As this ability of relics to offer prestige and status to their protectors became widely recognised, more and more churchmen happily discovered them. Bishop Theodore of Octodurum overtrumped his many rivals by conveniently finding the bodies of a whole Theban legion which had converted to Christianity and been slaughtered by the Emperor Maximian; but his subsequent status as a result of this fortunate windfall was nothing compared with that of Clematius of Cologne, when a vision informed him exactly where he could find not only the bones of the martyred St Ursula but also the 11,000 virgins killed with her. Sceptical historians have suggested that in the twelfth century the existing relics at Cologne were supplemented by a great number of fakes from a newly-discovered old cemetery. If it is odd to speak of a fake relic honouring a human being, one should consider what Sir Francis Oppenheimer described as 'perhaps the most glorious man-made miracle legend of Christendom': the Sainte Ampoule. The legend of the Sainte Ampoule I believe to be certainly false. Yet for nearly one thousand years it conferred a unique status on certain privileged Frenchmen; and in the late eighteenth century the enemies of those men, though most of them certainly regarded the Sainte Ampoule as a fake, took especial care to have it ceremoniously destroyed.

The origins of the Sainte Ampoule are closely connected with the legendary life of St Remi, son of a Count of Laon who was persuaded, much against his will, to become Bishop of Reims at the age of twenty-two. Apparently he was persuaded to accept the unwelcome office when a great light, signifying divine approval, shone over his head and a torrent of holy oil poured down from Heaven over him. St Remi's greatest achievement was the baptism of Clovis I, pagan king of the Franks, on Christmas Day 496. And the Sainte Ampoule enters into history at that moment.

King Clovis, it is said, had been facing defeat by the hostile Alemanni tribe. He vowed that if defeat were turned into victory, he would listen to the entreaties of his Christian wife Clotilda and convert. After the victorious battle of Tolbiac he kept his word and came to Remi for baptism.

During the ceremony a hitch occurred: Remi was waiting for the holy oil with which to anoint the king. A priest carrying the oil simply could not reach the bishop, so great was the press of the crowd. Undismayed, St Remi knelt down and prayed. Suddenly a white dove appeared in the sky, an ampoule bearing holy oil in its beak. Clovis, the first king of the Franks, was baptised with this miraculous chrism.

Now Gregory of Tours's history of the Franks, written in 575, gives a detailed description of Clovis's baptism. Gregory, as we know, loved miracles and miraculous relics. But he nowhere mentions the descent of the dove with the Sainte Ampoule. The tale is found three hundred years later in a life of St Remi written by his successor Hincmar, Bishop of Reims from 845 to 882. By this time the body of St Remi had been translated at least three times. At first his relics lay buried under the church of St Christopher outside the walls of Reims. In the sixth century the church was enlarged, as St Remi's popularity grew, and his remains were placed in a stone coffin behind the altar. (His chasuble, tunic and some of his hair were kept on top of the coffin for use in healing the sick; the body was put back, rolled in a purple cloth.) Thirdly Hincmar built a completely new church for the relics of his illustrious predecessor and put them in a silver reliquary. He kept back Remi's face cloth and some of the purple in which the body had been rolled. These he carefully placed in Reims cathedral in a reliquary made of ivory. And although King Louis of France wanted a small piece of the saint, the possessive Hincmar refused to give him one.

Here then is another classic example of a saint's relics bestowing lustre and prestige to a less distinguished successor. Hincmar so cherished the bones of St Remi that when the Normans invaded in 882 he carried the silver reliquary and the saint's remains with him in flight to Epernay. There Hincmar died. But before that time he had produced the Sainte Ampoule, and with it anointed King Charles the Bald, at Metz in 869.

Did Hincmar himself fake the Sainte Ampoule? Sir Francis Oppenheimer charitably suggests not. His supposition is that the Ampoule of oil had been placed sometime before in St Remi's tomb, and that Hincmar took it out. Instead of being either a miraculous gift from Heaven or something invented by Hincmar, the Sainte Ampoule was a secondary relic of St Remi himself.

Whatever it was, the Ampoule took on enormous significance. With the remains of its sacred oil, every French king until the Reformation was solemnly anointed at his coronation.

Naturally great care was taken of it. The abbot of Saint-Remi and the grand prior were alone allowed to carry it. Even so, a great fire in 1774 reduced the abbey to ashes, and only the quick wits of a Benedictine monk saved the Ampoule. A description of it remains from the age of Louis XV: 'The Sainte Ampoule is a small phial of somewhat ordinary glass; its whitish and opaque colour is to be attributed rather to the calcination of time than to any quality of the material, which, like crystal glass of a certain age, has lost some of its transparency.' The oil too was described: 'The body of the phial appears less transparent than the neck, because it is filled with a reddish balm, the colour of which approaches that of dried roses.'

Whatever this reddish balm did for a French king, it obviously had accumulated enormous symbolic power. Philosophers sometimes analyse what they call 'performative utterances'. The late J. L. Austin gave the following examples: 'When I say "I name this ship the *Queen Elizabeth*" I do not describe the christening ceremony, I actually perform the christening; and when I say "I do" (sc. take this woman to be my lawful wedded wife), I am not reporting on a marriage, I am indulging in it.' To my mind anointing a French king with oil from the Sainte Ampoule was an analogous action: it actually made the man king – even though, as I believe, the relic was not what it purported to be.

Small wonder, then, that the French revolutionaries abhorred it. In 1793 the Convention issued an order for the destruction of the Sainte Ampoule. A 'Citizen Rühl' was given the task. He ordered it to be brought to him on 7 October 1793 at 2 o'clock in the afternoon, to be destroyed publicly in the Place Nationale. While the crowd cried 'Vive la République', Citizen Rühl smashed the relic with a hammer on the pedestal of the statue of Louis XV.

Some brave citizens collected bits of the glass. In 1819 the Archbishop of Reims put them in a silver casket and then made a new ampoule, incorporating the rescued fragments of the old glass. In 1825 the ultra-reactionary King Charles X was anointed with oil from this new ampoule. But times had changed. As J. L. Austin observed of 'performative utterances', the circumstances must be right for the utterance to be effective: otherwise, for instance, we might have to say that 'we "went through a form" of marriage, but we did not actually succeed in marrying.' The ampoule of 1825 was not the old Sainte Ampoule. And of course in 1793 the reddish balm had disappeared, and with it some of the old glory. More: after the disastrous reign of Charles X, people no longer wanted a revival of the old days. In 1830 the citizen-king Louis Philippe came to the throne of France without a religious ceremony and without the aid of the much reduced ampoule.

St Remi, however, though long dead, was still active. His peregrinations had not ceased on arriving at Epernay with Hincmar in 882. Archbishop Fulcro of Reims brought the bones back and placed them temporarily in his cathedral. On Christmas day 901 Fulcro's successor, in the presence of Charles the Simple, put them back in the abbey of Saint-Remi. To bless a council held at Reims under Pope Leo IX, the sacred relics were again displayed in the cathedral. In 1533 Cardinal

Lenoncourt of Reims decided the bones deserved a new tomb; they were translated to the finished shrine four years later. Four times during these travels the opportunity was taken to examine the saint's physical condition. Though withered, he was each time found to be whole. Later, in the seventeenth century, the silver reliquary was opened again. St Remi's corpse was still all connected together. Such a remarkable corpse clearly still retained great power.

Happily too the relic survived the great abbey fire of 1774. Quick-witted citizens dragged out the reliquary and carried it with its precious burden to the church of Saint-Nicaise. Even more remarkably, St Remi's remains survived the French Revolution. His relics were lain in a grave alongside the body of a dead soldier. Fortunately their great age and the fact that they were embalmed made them easily recognisable; the pious saved St Remi's bones, thus enabling them to continue to help the pious.

Yet it must be conceded that even so notable a relic as St Remi is no longer as active today as were relics in the past. If a medieval man were asked what relics do, his list of their activities would be a long one. Relics, he could answer, visibly join earth and Heaven, the natural and the supernatural, this life and eternity; they repel enemies and defend cities; they heal the sick; they soothe sore throats and cure cattle of all sorts of diseases; they ensure a good harvest; they undergird the law and promote justice, bringing evil ones to repent; they force men to keep their oaths and rightly punish perjurers; they confer prestige and great renown on those who protect sacred bones; they concern themselves particularly with the rights of the poor and of the church; they remind us that all power comes from the just Saviour, in whose name they act; they anoint kings; they promote morality; they perform godly miracles.

Today relics are rarely called on for such a range of activity. Usually the faithful nowadays look to them merely for miracles – though miracles are of course no small matter. St Remi is one who, in life and after death, has never ceased to serve those who need him in this way. Saint-Rémy-de-Provence, now a fashionable tourist centre, is so-called because the saint performed a miracle there in 500 as he was accompanying Clovis to besiege Avignon. After his death even the pall from his tomb, carried in procession in 543, warded off the plague. When Archbishop Fulcro in the late ninth century brought back the corpse in triumph from Epernay by way of Orleans to Reims, the miracles performed *en route* could scarcely be counted.

Nor would it be possible today to tally the miracles performed by the relics of St Remi since his body was dragged out of the grave in 1793. One reason for this is that his corpse is no longer in one piece – though as we have seen, this rarely hampers a dead saint. You are not disappointed, visiting what remains of the abbey of Saint-Remi at Reims, by the large particle of its patron's corpse still there. Undoubtedly too, the martial yet charitable St Remi would himself have approved both that till recently the abbey buildings served as a hospital and that now they house a museum of warfare (though this does not intrude on the great abbey church).

Yet the dispersal of St Remi's bones surely makes them available to far more supplicants than before. The great historian and novelist of the Périgord, Eugène Le Roy, writing in 1899, remembered a cult of St Remi at Auriac and another at Saint-Raphaël, between Cherveix and Excideuil. St Remi had apparently chosen to allow part of his body to rest at Saint-Raphaël, for earlier it had lain under a great stone at the crossroads leading to the four parishes of Cherveix, Anlhiac, Saint-Médard and Saint-Raphaël. Le Roy tells how the people of Anlhiac brought their best oxen but were unable to move the great stone over St Remi's tomb. The powerful oxen of Saint-Médard were equally useless. Even the huge oxen from the plains of Cherveix failed to budge the stone. But the poor people of Saint-Raphaël managed to move it with their one and only donkey, after their parish priest had invoked the help of the saint himself.

The villagers were fortunate. St Remi had never ceased to perform miracles of healing. Now even his very effigies could heal. In one Saintonge village, if a child was seriously ill, two candles were lit, one to St Remi, the second to the non-existent St Finit. If St Remi's candle lasted longer than St Finit's, the child would recover.

As described by Eugène Le Roy, the crowds who on the 23 August gathered at Auriac to celebrate the feast of St Remi relied neither on candles nor simply on prayers before the saint's bones to cure their ailments. In the local church was a little stone model of St Remi. Each in turn approached the parish priest who placed his stole on their heads while reciting those verses from St Matthew's Gospel which recount how Jesus cured many diverse illnesses. Then in turn each grabbed the little statue and rubbed away fiercely at whatever part of the body was giving trouble. If the pain was in the back or kidneys, a friend was enlisted to do the rubbing. 'They rubbed the saint on their stomachs, arms, legs, thighs and skin,' recalled Le Roy. 'This good saint possessed such a reputation for healing,' he added, 'that people called him in the local patois *saint Rémédy*, that is St Remedy; and during the rest of the year when the church was closed, people passing by who were suffering some affliction rubbed themselves with complete confidence on the church wall near to the statue's niche.'

So, long after his soul had departed this life, and after the famous Sainte Ampoule he once may have used had been discarded, the relics of St Remi were still succouring the faithful: as no doubt they are to this day, in the same fashion as many other relics throughout the Christian world.

4

Relics as creators of wealth

As more and more people realised what relics could do, along with the prestige that came from owning them and the blessings that flowed from their presence, some grew to covet relics belonging to others. In the second half of the fifth century, for instance, the Emperor Leo I, seeing that the city of Antioch was rich in relics, asked them to give him the body of the famous St Simeon Stylites. Simeon had only just died. Born in Cilicia around the year 309, he had set himself almost impossible goals in fasting and self-discipline. Then in 423 he conceived the idea of living on a pillar. At first he tried a fairly low one, but soon he managed to live on one that reached sixty or so feet above the ground. There he stayed for the remaining thirty-six years of his life, inspiring many imitators and much awe.

The citizens of Antioch refused Leo's request. They had no intention, they replied, of giving up 'the holy corpse, which is for our city both a rampart and a fortress'.

Antioch was clearly looking after itself. But other rulers were similarly to be disappointed, though perhaps for less selfish reasons. Until the seventh century the Roman church tried to stop people even touching relics – a legacy of the old Jewish attitudes, perhaps – let alone moving them around. When Justinian, not yet enthroned as Emperor, wrote to Pope Hormisdas in 519 asking for relics of St Peter, St Paul and St Laurence, he conceded that his request was a most unusual one. It was turned down. As late as 594 Pope Gregory the Great was politely but firmly excusing himself for refusing to send the head of St Paul to the wife of the Emperor Maurice.

This was not mere churlishness or selfishness on the part of Popes Hormisdas and Gregory. In these years many western Christians preferred to build basilicas where a great saint had been buried, rather than transfer the corpse elsewhere. Pope Symmachus in the early sixth century preferred to build the basilica of San Pancrazio obliquely over the relics of St Pancras, rather than lay sacrilegious hands on the body of the child martyr.

During the middle ages this hesitant awe disappeared. In this chapter I want to examine how relics became big business, to be bought and sold at will. Relics increasingly brought employment and generated a huge economy of their own. Middlemen traded in them, cathedrals and humble churches were enriched by them and those who coveted them were provoked to theft and chicanery. The tender reverence of the early church passed away.

It is true that western Christians never scrupled to bring home the relics of saints martyred in exile. Holy bones miles away seemed somehow unlikely to care for their home town and its needs. Ambrose brought back to his relic-starved Milan in 356 the body of a native saint, Denis, who had died in Cappadocia. Again, westerners were willing to shift around their relics in times of persecution. Bishop Urbanus of Toledo thus saved a good many sets of bones when the Vandals invaded Spain in the fifth century.

Yet western Christians considered all this unusual, even unseemly. Not so in the east. In contrast to the refusal of the Popes to spread their relics around, from a very early stage in the cult eastern Christians were liberally sharing their saintly cadavers. Bones of the forty martyrs of Sebaste were generously parcelled out by the church in that town to churches throughout the Greek orient. The first recorded deliberate translation of a complete relic to a new church occurred in the 350s when St Babylas was transferred to a church in Daphne.

Eastern Christians seem to have taken the view that to distribute parts of their holy martyrs around the world spread their influence and glory. At Sinope in Pontus on the south shore of the Black Sea lived a Christian market-gardener named Phocas. Soldiers sent to kill him actually called on him asking for directions and telling him of their task. Phocas put them up for the night and dug his own grave in his own market-garden. The standard fifth-century account of his martyrdom says that the soldiers were truly sad next morning when they killed their kind host. Proudly the church at Sinope distributed bits of their martyr to many other churches; and soon they had the satisfaction of seeing their market-gardener adopted as the patron saint of sailors on the Aegean, the Adriatic and the Black Sea.

Eastern Christians, willing to cut up and distribute their relics in these ways, naturally showed little compunction at transporting them to places they specially wished to honour. Constantine took the body of St Timothy in 356 to his new city of Constantinople. It was followed the following year by the bodies of St Andrew and St Luke. Next the head of John the Baptist arrived there. Antioch, so curmudgeonly when Leo asked for St Simeon Stylites, had a hundred years previously obtained from Caesarea the bodies of the martyr St Pamphilus and his simultaneously slaughtered companions, to go into the new church of Santa Sophia. The trade in relics was gathering pace.

All this would have horrified fellow-Christians in the west. In a letter to the Empress Constantia Pope Gregory I deplored the dividing up of relics. It was alleged that the forty martyrs of Sebaste had appeared in dreams begging not to be distributed around the Christian world. When St Savinus, Bishop of Assisi, was condemned to have both hands cut off, a widow got hold of them and embalmed them. But when the saint died, she placed them with his stumps in his coffin, thus ensuring that his corpse was kept intact.

Undoubtedly such attitudes were reinforced in the west by Roman law, which guaranteed the inviolability of corpses. Until the second half of the second century, even to transfer a corpse required the consent of the Emperor himself. This was later changed so that the consent of the governor of a province sufficed – but only in urgent cases. And for breaking this law the punishment was severe. Clearly when St Martin of Tours at the end of the fourth century brought the relics of St Gatien, his predecessor who died in 250, from the cemetery outside the town to a basilica west of the city, he was taking the considerable risk of offending both the law and popular mores. In 410 the Bishop of Toulouse needed the reassurance of a dream, telling him to transfer the bones of St Saturnin from their little oratory to a great new basilica west of the city, before he dared move the martyred relics.

Yet cracks were appearing, as the translations of St Gatien and St Saturnin reveal. Even Gregory the Great, refusing Constantia a piece of St Paul, sent her some filings from St Peter's chains. It is said that he was persuaded to give some of John the Baptist's hair to a king of the Visigoths. And the Venerable Bede, recounting how Gregory equipped St Augustine of Canterbury with everything needed to convert the English, lists among them 'relics of the holy apostles and martyrs'.

At a pinch, then, even western Christians were beginning to trade relics with each other. Moreover, as the thirst for relics overcame their scruples, they would salve their consciences by sternly declining to cut up any relics themselves while joyfully accepting any saintly bits and pieces cut up by their fellow-Christians in the east. Queen Radegund happily accepted one of St Mamme's fingers from the Patriarch of Jerusalem, as well as a piece of the true cross from the Emperor Justinian. Historians continue to turn up examples of westerners quietly breaking the rules in this matter. Towards the end of the sixth century Pope John III placed the relics of St James the Less and St Philip in the basilica of Santi Apostoli, Rome. Over the centuries that followed the church was several times damaged and restored, receiving also in the course of Christian history numerous other relics. Then in 1872 a savage fire led to a further extensive restoration. The altar containing the relics put in Santi Apostoli by Pope John was opened. Amongst them was found a single tooth which perfectly fitted a root in a jaw guarded in the cathedral of Ancona and said to be St James's. Clearly, whichever saint owned the tooth, the jaw and the rest of the relics concerned, some people around the year 565 had taken to the eastern habit of dividing up the holy dead.

Soon the evident desire of western Christians to emulate the east in transferring relics or parts of relics began to be supported by alleged dreams in which the saint in question endorsed the removal of his corpse. In France and Italy bishops began exhuming the relics of their predecessors on a grand scale and placing them in finer sarcophagi inside larger churches. Then the invasions of Saracens, Normans, Danes and Hungarians accustomed Christians to fleeing with their relics, and thus helped to break down the old taboos. Finally the consecration of Charlemagne as Holy Roman Emperor made the transfer of relics a Christian duty.

Under Charlemagne the supply of martyrs naturally dried up. In any case churches north of the Alps were built where saints had so far not been numerous. Christianity was now penetrating Germany, Denmark and Sweden. These countries too thirsted for relics. Charlemagne proved particularly adept at getting hold of them. Two of his greatest acquisitions were the body of St Cyprian of Carthage followed by another Carthaginian, St Servetus, who died around A.D. 180. But most relics travelling north into Europe came from Italy, several of them the bodies of illustrious Popes.

The Crusaders added to these saintly spoils – though for the most part they brought back not so much bones as secondary relics: stones, earth and dust from tombs; bits of the true cross; some of St Stephen's blood; Jesus's sandals, and so on. Where they could, western travellers to the Orient did bring back the human remains of the saints. So much of St Catherine of Alexandria's body left Mount Sinai for Europe that the monks who once possessed her whole body today retain only the skull and one hand.

Some of this booty was no doubt given voluntarily. The monks of Mount Sinai gave King Henry II of Brunswick one of St Catherine's ribs. Their business acumen persuaded them to send one of her fingers to Rouen cathedral, in exchange for regular donations from that city. A monk named Simeon of Syracuse had already taken three other fingers to Normandy in the eleventh century. He left them with Abbot Isambert who was constructing a monastery close by Rouen. The relics cured Isambert's toothache. Oil continued to flow from them, as it also flowed from the rest of the saint's body on Mount Sinai. Isambert dedicated his abbey to St Catherine; and her oil healed many sick people.

More and more accustomed to deploying bits of saints, Christians sometimes took to improving the value of their relics by cutting them up for their own use. As soon as great St Hugh of Lincoln had died, his head was cut away from his trunk, to double his value as a relic. During his own lifetime St Hugh had himself been an enthusiastic divider of relics. He cut a sinew from the arm of St Oswald in Peterborough Abbey. And at Fécamp in Normandy he scandalised onlookers by biting two bits of bone from the arm of St Mary Magdalen. When they remonstrated, St Hugh countered brilliantly with theological flannel: he had, he argued, without irreverence just handled the bread and wine of Holy Communion, even presuming thus to eat and drink the sacred body of Jesus; why then should he not treat the bones of the saints in the same way, acquiring them and also increasing his reverence for them?

St Hugh barely got away with this. But the practice of cutting up relics had come to stay. At the abbey of Saint-Denis in Paris, for instance, the monks, once Abbot Suger had built his superb Gothic church over the old Carolingian martyry where their patron saint's bones were kept, realised that the corpse of St Denis no longer was adequately displayed. They broke off one of the relic's hands and put it on show in a much more accessible gold reliquary.

Perhaps no-one was spiritually cheated by all this. 'When the body is divided,' the church father Theodoret had decreed, 'the grace remains undivided.' But so many bits and pieces of relics passing through the Christian world gave rise to a new species of middleman making a living by trading in the bodies and possessions of the holy dead. The most famous of these was a man named Deusdona, who made his mark in the early ninth century when the Christians north of the Alps were desperate for the bones of saints and martyrs.

Deusdona tirelessly toured the Alps, Italy, Germany and France, trading in relics. He continually buttered up the Popes on behalf of his customers. And he was successful. He even managed to supply the abbey of Fulda with the bodies of Priscilla and Aquila, whom St Paul in his letter to the Romans called 'my helpers in Christ'. Sometimes his success disconcerted not only his rival middlemen but also those religious foundations that could not match the relics Deusdona had sold to their neighbours. He persuaded Pope Eugene II to let him take the body of St Sebastian to France. There he sold the relic to Soissons. Now Soissons already had the corpse of the illustrious St Médard. But St Sebastian was altogether superior in the eyes of many of the faithful, for legend had greatly elaborated the account of the death of this early and famous martyr. First St Ambrose, ever keen to exalt his own see, claimed that St Sebastian had been born in Milan. Then the story arose that St Sebastian had been an officer of the imperial guard, sentenced to death for converting to Christianity. Archers filled his body with arrows and he was left for dead, but a saintly widow healed his wounds. Hearing of this, the Emperor Diocletian ordered Sebastian to be clubbed to death.

St Sebastian was buried on the Appian Way. Now he was in Soissons, and the monks of nearby Mulinheim were deeply disturbed. Desperately they turned to another relic-trader named Ratleicus, commissioning him to find for them a saint or martyr equal in fame to Sebastian. Ratleicus managed to bring them the bodies of St Marcellinus and St Peter, two men also martyred under Diocletian. Almost certainly these two saints had more historical substance than the Sebastian Soissons had bought. Pope Damasus as a boy had actually met and talked with their executioner, and he wrote an epitaph for their tomb. But none of this counted in the medieval mind. Soissons basked in the reflected glory of its new relic; Mulinheim went into decline.

Such rivalries very much favoured commerce in relics, as did the temper of the age. Long before, St Augustine had lamented that vagabonds were clandestinely selling relics. Now the trade was in the open and had the approval of Popes and bishops. In 1032 the relics of Augustine himself suffered the ignominy of being bought by the Archbishop of Canterbury for the sum of 100 talents of silver and one of gold. After the fall of Constantinople in 1204 Crusaders so blatantly trafficked in relics that the bishops assembled at the Lateran Council eleven years later tried to put a stop to it. They failed.

Shortly after that council Christendom witnessed one of the most astonishing sales of relics in its history. King Baldwin II, the Latin King of Jerusalem, found himself in extreme financial difficulties. In 1238 he offered Jesus's crown of thorns to King Louis IX in Paris, in exchange for financial help. Although the transaction was set out as if Baldwin's offer was a loan, in effect he was selling one of the east's holiest relics. Louis IX wasted no time. He dispatched two preaching friars to Constantinople to bring back the crown of thorns. In the meantime however Baldwin had decided on a better deal: he would sell the crown of thorns to his own family and several other imperial families for the sum of 13,134 gold *hypobères*. Unfortunately, these families failed to raise the money. King Louis's friars snapped up the crown of thorns for 10,000 *hypobères* and speedily returned to France. The crown of thorns reached Paris on 19 August 1238. There it stayed until 3 October, when the king solemnly transferred the relic to Saint-Denis, to remain in the abbey while Louis built a new chapel worthy of such a great prize.

Clearly by planning such a building Louis had abandoned all pretence that the gift of the crown of thorns would one day be returned to the east. In 1247 Baldwin conceded that the relic truly belonged to Louis, who handed over a final payment of 21,000 lbs of fine silver. Neither the papacy nor the church's hierarchy disapproved. On the contrary, the arrival of the crown of thorns in France only confirmed God's special favour on Louis IX.

Although, as we shall observe, Louis IX paid lavishly to rehouse this crown of thorns, for very many places to own a great relic was an extremely profitable investment. The historian should not be too cynical about this. Writing about the campaign by Osbert de Clare to promote the canonisation of King Edward the Confessor, Professor Frank Barlow commented that 'if his sanctity was recognised, pilgrims to his tomb would increase not only the monastery's fame but also its revenue'. To my mind this underestimates the sheer fanaticism involved in Osbert's efforts on behalf of the saintly monarch. Nonetheless it is true that a famed relic brought pilgrims, and pilgrims brought gifts. Already in the sixth century people offered to the relics of St Cuthbert a candle the height of the person for whom they were supplicating. Five centuries later in some parts of northern Europe supplicants were expected to leave at the shrine of a relic their own weight in gold, or silver, or at the least corn, if they were persons of status. In the early eleventh century Count Robert II of Namur was obliged to offer his own weight in wheat to appease St Gengulphe and gain pardon for his own wrongdoings.

Poorer persons were expected to pay less, offering wax, oil or candles, cheese or cloth, bread and wine. And many paid cash. The diversity of gifts at a shrine can be gauged from an imperial decree of 822 setting out regulations for dividing up such gifts at the tomb of St Martin of Tours. Wax, oil and candles were to be used for lighting the church. Vestments and gifts of cloth were to embellish the relic's sepulchre. The rest was to be divided, one-third going to the monks and two-thirds to the abbot.

The most profitable shrine in Europe was almost certainly that of St Thomas Becket. Legends abounded of the saint's own anger if his relics were not suitably honoured. For putting off their pilgrimage to his shrine a certain Jordan and his wife lost a son. A knight promised to walk barefoot to Canterbury in honour of St Thomas. He forgot, and a knife accidentally pierced his foot. A farmer named Elias, commanded in a vision to offer his best bullock to the saint's shrine, refused. The next day he found the bullock dead and already putrefying.

Partly under the stimulus of such tales, but also – and probably much more – out of genuine devotion to the relics, pilgrims were amazingly generous. In 1120 the various shrines of St Thomas in Canterbury cathedral drew the colossal sum of £1,071. In one year when Becket's relics drew in £954, the altar of Our Lady at Canterbury drew scarcely £4 and that of Christ himself brought in nothing.

If a great church or abbey considered itself to be falling behind in this profitable trade, it could always discover a suitably eminent relic with which to attract the rich and the faithful. As Dr Warwick Rodwell had justly observed, 'The lure of money often overcame scruples, and many false claims were made.' He adds that, 'Glastonbury Abbey was a prime culprit in this field: the monks persistently claimed to have the body of St Dunstan, one of their former abbots, who died as Archbishop of Canterbury and was buried, as Eadmer tells us, in the corridor-crypt of that cathedral. The abbot of Glastonbury was eventually rebuked by the Pope for this blatant dishonesty.' The monks of Glastonbury were hardly abashed by this papal rebuke. Needing funds to rebuild their church after a devastating fire of 1184, 'the monks duly dug in their cemetery and produced bones which they announced to the world as the remains of King Arthur and Guinevere.' In consequence pilgrims virtually deserted Wells cathedral seven miles away and flocked instead to Glastonbury. As if these deceptions were not enough, in the later middle ages the notion was put about that Joseph of Arimathea had brought to Glastonbury Abbey the chalice used by Jesus and his disciples at the Last Supper, the legendary Holy Grail.

Less dishonest than the monks of Glastonbury were the clergy of Troyes. Unable to pay for the rebuilding of their cathedral after fire destroyed most of it in 1188, they borrowed relics from Garnier de Tranel of Constantinople and thus drew new flocks of paying pilgrims. Other French clerics were as cunning as the English monks of Glastonbury. The monks of Saint-Ghislain's priory lived in poverty until they discovered the relics of their patron saint in the year 930 or so. And whereas the monks of Glastonbury were rebuked for their duplicity, many others reaped the praise and approval of their superiors for similar behaviour – to their further financial profit. In 1010 yet another head of John the Baptist was discovered, this time at Saint-Jean-d'Angély. The King of France offered those who found it the reward of a gold plate. Two years previously the canons of Tournus had managed to recover the bones of St Philibert. Delighted, the Bishop of Châlons and Macon decreed that once a year all his diocesans should visit the relic bearing gifts.

If pilgrims were slow in visiting the shrines of relics, those who needed to raise money through these holy bones often took the relics from their shrines and travelled them on fund-raising tours. The abbot of Evesham who mocked, as we have seen, the relics of saints Egwin, Odulf, Wystan and Credan, after the Norman conquest, took a different line when he needed to rebuild. The English saints were taken about the surrounding countryside soliciting building-funds. England was long famed both for its love of relics and its supposed wealth, so that foreigners were frequently drawn here on their fund-raising tours. When the Bishop of Benevento decided to raise money by selling an arm of St Bartholomew, it was to England he came. King Cnut's wife bought the relic after the bishop swore an oath that it was genuine.

It is pleasing to relate that at this time Englishmen had a keen eye for a bargain in relics for sale. When Abott Aelfsige of Peterborough was in Normandy in the first half of the eleventh century, he was able to pick up the corpse of the patron saint of Saint-Florentin-de-Bonneval cheaply. A famine was raging, the monks were starving, and they had sold everything else. Usually however, starving clerics managed to hold onto their relics – their last assets in an unkind world. In the early tenth century the monks of Saint-Ghislain, ravaged by the depredations of the Normans, put all their relics in a cart and trundled them into Belgium; but instead of selling the corpses, they displayed them for cash. Two centuries later a common sight was a procession of monks and laypeople, led by the crucifix, carrying relics from town to town, collecting money. The monks of Notre Dame of Laon were even tempted to pay such a visit to England. They received a frosty welcome. Their visit, it was feared, might harm the profits of local relics.

Trade wars of this kind made fund-raising processions increasingly unpopular, especially when (as many rightly suspected) the relics involved were frequently fakes. The austere Cistercian monks found the practice of traipsing about with a relic to raise money particularly repugnant and did their best to discourage it. Soon too the papacy lost patience especially with those who attached to fake relics fake papal bulls authorising collecting tours. But the profitability of these tours made attempts to discipline them extremely difficult. Only in the sixteenth century did a decree of the twenty-first session of the Council of Trent manage to put a stop to this abuse of the cult of the relic.

Relics in any case made money for those who owned them without recourse to fund-raising tours. Since the sick and needy were willing to pay in goods or cash at a shrine whose relic could perhaps grant a divine favour, might not also the faithful wish to take away some tangible sign of the relic's continuing interest in their well-being? The clergy became adept at manufacturing these. When the canons of Rochester made a new shrine for St Ithamar, they fixed to it an image of the saint. To cure cripples, mutes, sick animals and the blind was said to be a speciality of water poured over this image's feet; and the canons did a brisk trade in this holy liquid. The monks of Canterbury for many years sold watered down blood reputably taken from the bleeding corpse of Thomas Becket. Over the centuries, until well into the nineteenth century, dust scraped from the tomb of St Eutropius at Saintes was considered specially powerful at curing fevers (and indeed was probably a safer remedy than most others: squashed earthworm poultices, eggs blended with chimney soot, carrot seeds in pig's urine, to name a few).

Secondary relics also had the merit of being usefully portable. In the early fifteenth century the Bishop of Durham, perceiving that St Wilfrid's signet ring had the power to keep cattle free of the murrain, added to his income by going about signing them with it.

And a last profitable spin-off from possessing a popular relic was the scope it gave for organising fairs. Especially on the saint's feast-day a vast concourse of supplicants would converge on a noted relic. 'People beat on the doors of the abbey,' wrote Suger at the end of the eleventh century, describing the feast of St Denis, 'and jostled against the altar itself. Women swooned. Others heaved themselves on men's shoulders and ran over the heads of the assistant priests in order to be the first to reach the choir, where the monks were proffering the relics for kissing. These monks, to escape harm, were often obliged to jump through the windows with their precious burdens.' These supplicants brought gifts – corn, wax, oil, wool, even animals. Now the clergy in charge would suddenly have a superfluity of beasts and perishable goods which would need to be sold quickly. The logical solution was to sell them back to those who gave them. Increasingly monks obtained charters to organise fairs coinciding with the anniversaries of their relics. Soon of course these fairs began selling far more than simply the gifts of the supplicants at the relic's shrine. The English word 'tawdry' in fact derives from the Anglo-Saxon name of St Etheldreda, i.e. St Audrey, and was first used to describe the cheap knick-knacks made for and sold at her fair.

Relics then were big business. Commerce in saints' bones, bodies, handkerchiefs, vests and shoes created a group of busy middlemen, trading sometimes in shady goods. Bought and sold, the relic was an investment, bringing its owner the opportunity to raise money, to attract supplicants and their gifts, to create an apparently inexhaustible supply of secondary relics for sale to the faithful laity. Relics raised money for building abbeys, cathedrals and shrines. They generated work. They encouraged fairs. They enriched the men of God.

Few found anything unseemly in this. As Eugen Weber has

observed, 'That priests and their parishes profited from such religious undertakings does not make the undertakings any less valid or the participants any less sincere. Utility underlies most human enterprise, and in no way demeans it. The mother who trudged off carrying her child that it might be strengthened or healed was an admirable figure. The priest who sought funds to glorify the source from which such healing sprang – and perhaps its guardian too – was human and perhaps even saintly.' In the middle ages no-one involved in the commerce in relics felt cheated, for everyone was acting in good faith. When Elizabeth, wife of King Henry VII of England, bought one of the Virgin Mary's girdles from a monk for 6s. 8d., she did so because such a precious relic would ease her pains in childbirth. There is no reason to believe the monk thought the girdle was anything other than Our Lady's. And Queen Elizabeth's physicians were as little likely to save her in childbirth as the relic.

Secondly, relics generated wealth for many people other than medieval clerics. The clergy profited from annual fairs on the anniversaries of the saints whose relics they guarded. But so did merchants and tradesmen and jugglers and local farmers. St Denis's fair developed in Paris as an offshoot of the annual procession in which the saint's relics were carried around the parish; soon its connection with the relics became no more than a matter of history, as the fair took on a momentum of its own. And when Charles the Bald granted the abbey of Tournus a five-day fair after the relics of St Philibert had been translated there, the whole region rejoiced at this boost to its economy.

And above all pilgrimages to the shrines of celebrated relics opened up new sources of wealth for very many layfolk as well as for ecclesiastics – for innkeepers, guides, market-traders and thieves.

The greatest of these shrines was undoubtedly that of St James the Great at Compostela in Spain. Curiously enough, the bones of St James are mentioned by no-one in connection with Spain until the late seventh century, when the tradition arose that he had preached there. The earliest account of the transfer of his relics to Compostela was written in 912. Earlier traditions, based on the Acts of the Apostles, report that after his execution his corpse was buried in Palestine, and some historians have speculated that the whole Spanish connection derives from a scribe who misread 'Hierusalem' (Jerusalem) and copied it down as 'Hispania' (Spain). I do not find this speculation plausible. Nor, in the ninth century when Charlemagne was Holy Roman Emperor and enthusiastically populating Christian Europe with the bones of innumerable saints, did anyone anxious to discover the remains of a powerful saint look for documentary evidence that his or her corpse might be lying around. Bishop Theodomir of Padron simply happened on St James's body in a neglected cemetery.

There was much for such a powerful relic to do. The King of Spain was busily repulsing the Moors, and St James the Great could help. Both Charlemagne and the Pope were delighted at his excavation. Few cared to question the authenticity of the relics (though Richard Fletcher, in his diverting book *St James's Catapult*, has recently suggested that they were the remains of the early arch-heretic named Priscillian who prayed with naked women). Moreover, the newly-discovered bones brought enormous prosperity to a region that had been hitherto desolate. The city of Santiago de Compostela was built around the tomb of the saint. Soon it merited its own bishop. The most ambitious of these men, Bishop Diego Gelmires, was consecrated in 1100 and ruled for forty years, tirelessly promoting the cult of St James and building around his shrine a splendid cathedral. His soul must have rejoiced when Pope Sixtus IV in 1478 put a pilgrimage to Santiago de Compostela on the same spiritual footing as one to Jerusalem.

Spain was easier to reach than Jerusalem. Even so the journey could be arduous. The monks of Cluny published a guide for pilgrims, the *Liber Sancti Jacobi*, warning the pilgrim of the dangers ahead. Gascon boatmen were said to be particularly keen to let pilgrims drown and rob their drowned corpses. At Lorca horses died if they drank the foul water. Spain was rendered disagreeable by swarms of huge flies.

But the *Liber Sancti Jacobi* also hints at the great prosperity the pilgrimage to Santiago de Compostela had brought to countless innkeepers, boatmen, guides and toll-keepers throughout western Europe. In Paris a hostel catering for pilgrims to Spain looked after up to eighty a day. The facilities there were far better than those offered in Gascony where, the guide noted, people of all stations in life slept together on miserable straw mattresses.

Gradually four separate pilgrimage routes were established through France to Roncevaux high in the Pyrénées, each of them providing a living for the many fortunate suppliers of victuals, beds and also of spiritual refreshment on the way. For the relic at Santiago de Compostela stimulated the shrines of lesser relics to renewed vigour, as pilgrims made their way through them to Spain. The route to Santiago from the Auvergne passed through the town of Conques, whose abbey of Sainte-Foy preserved the relics of St Foy. Initially her bones had lain elsewhere, at Agen south of Toulouse. Then at the time of Charlemagne bits of her spread throughout western Christendom (a piece ending up in St Paul's cathedral, London). Conques managed to get hold of most of the saint, and you can still see her reliquary in the church treasury there. In the form of a complete effigy of St Foy, the reliquary depicts her sitting in a sumptuous chair, arms pointing outwards, crowned and rather frightening. (Ian Robertson's guide to France describes this reliquary as 'a curiously hideous idol, uptight in its throne, as if sitting on a carbuncle.') In 1050, to cope with the press of pilgrims, Abbot Odolric of Conques built a superb Romanesque church designed to ease the flow of visitors who queued to pray before her shrine and offer gifts. Not all the monks of Conques were as good businessmen as Abbot Odolric. Instead of persuading pilgrims to leave by St Foy's relics a reasonable diversity of gifts, they once nearly ruined themselves by collecting too many candles, flooding the market with them and depressing the price.

From Conques tourist/pilgrims *en route* to Roncevaux would pass through Sarlat, pausing to worship before the relics of St Sacerdos, and through Rocamadour, where they marvelled not at a relic but at the miracle-working 'black Virgin'. Meanwhile other pilgrims were converging on Roncevaux from Arles in Provence, where they had begun their journey by praying before the remains of St Paul's assistant Trophimus. From Arles their route passed through the town of Saint-Gilles, where they knelt by the bones of the eighth-century hermit who gave his name to the abbey church and the town itself. They passed through Montpellier and reached Saint-Guilhem-le-Désert, where the body of the saint who gave that place its name lay in a tenth-century crypt. But these were minor relics compared with their next major goal: the corpse of St Sernin in his great basilica at Toulouse.

Further north pilgrims were gathering around the relics of Lazarus, one of the few saints to have died twice (since Jesus had raised him from the dead once). Lazarus's bones had been bought by the monks of Autun in the tenth century when the cult of relics was at its peak. Next these pilgrims were privileged to worship before a saint whose bones were as exalted as those of St James himself, for their route took them to Vézelay, whose great abbey church housed the relics of St Mary Magdalen. 'How should the body of St Mary Magdalen, who was born in Judaea, have been translated to France, a country so distant?' asked a late-eleventh century life of the saint, answering glibly, 'All things are possible to God.' In fact the monks of Vézelay claimed to have obtained the relics from St Maximin in Provence, where the Magdalen is said to have died. To their chagrin, in 1280 the Provençals claimed still to have the relics, and the cult of the Magdalen at Vézelay never totally recovered from this. Pilgrims to Santiago de Compostela by the route from Autun had to rest content with kneeling before lesser – though powerful – relics, such as St Front at Périgueux and St Leonard, whose relics had freed so many prisoners that their former bonds littered his church at Saint-Léonard.

The fourth great route to the relics of St James at Santiago de Compostela began at the shrine of St Denis in Paris. The number of pilgrims travelling this route would be greatly swollen at Orleans, whose cathedral would display a chalice blessed because it had belonged to the fourth century Bishop Evurtius. At Tours further south they marvelled before the shrine of St Martin; and they passed through Saintonge where, if any pilgrim felt feverish, the dust on St Eutropius's tomb was conveniently at hand to cure their ills. At Poitiers they were privileged to bring their supplications to one of the numerous heads of John the Baptist scattered throughout the Christian world. Those pilgrims intending to get every ounce of merit out of their journey would here also visit the church of Sainte-Radegonde, where the bones of Queen Radegund had been cherished since 587, and also the church of Saint-Hilaire-le-Grand, which sheltered not only the relics of St Hilary but also those of his daughter St Acra. Finally, before joining the three other pilgrimage routes to Roncevaux, the journey from Paris and Orleans allowed pilgrims to kneel before the relics of Charlemagne's paladin Roland, who was buried at Blaye in 778, before travelling on to admire his legendary horn preserved in the church of Saint-Seurin, Bordeaux.

Even today to follow the pilgrim route from Roncevaux through Spain to Santiago de Compostela overwhelmingly confirms the wealth brought by the happy discovery of St James's grave in the early tenth century. At Estella, San Pedro's church dominates even the twelfth-century palace of the Kings of Navarre. Logroño would be a fairly backward town but for its superb cathedral and the church of San Bartolomé, whose fourteenth-century portals are an astonishing piece of medieval carving. At Najera is the huge monastery of Santa Maria la Real; and further on at Santo Domingo de la Calzada are a bridge, a hospital and a guest-house built specially for pilgrims to Santiago de Compostela, as well as the relics of St Domingo himself. Through Burgos and Astorga, both with splendid cathedrals, through Vilar de Doñas, where are buried those knights of St James who died repelling the Moors from Spain, the pace quickens until the crowd of pilgrims finally reaches the magnificent Romanesque cathedral of St James in Santiago de Compostela itself, a building now encased in a magnificent baroque shell, with immense arched towers, each framing a statue of the pilgrim saint himself with his staff, cape and pilgrim's hat adorned with St James's emblem, the cockle-shell.

Today guides to Santiago de Compostela and its pilgrimage route are supplied not by the monks of Cluny but by the Spanish Tourist Board. Yet Santiago de Compostela and its pilgrimage routes flourish in our century far more than over the past four hundred years. For the English virtually closed down the shrine. In 1588 the Spanish Armada miserably failed to conquer Elizabeth I's navy. The following year Sir Francis Drake attacked Corunna. Fearing for the safety of St James's relics, the Bishop of Santiago de Compostela hid them, along with the bones of St James's two assistants (St Theodore and St Athanasius), in a hastily constructed tomb in the centre of the cathedral apse. The crypt where they had lain since the tenth century was walled up. The bishop died without revealing the whereabouts of the precious relics. And so the pilgrims petered out; the splendid ceremonial around the saint's tomb was no more.

Not till 1879 did the then Cardinal Archbishop of Santiago de Compostela decide to break into the crypt in search of the saints' bodies. He found the tombs empty. Under his orders, every part of the cathedral was searched, until a confused heap of bones was found buried in the apse. A group of doctors and scientists untangled them carefully. The team stated that the group of bones comprised those of an older man, along with two younger males. The scholarly team was also prepared to state that these bones could easily be nineteen centuries old. Moreover a bit of the cranium of the older man was missing: and this was found in Italy, where it lay in the cathedral of Pistoia, a gift from Santiago de Compostela in the days before St James's bones were so carefully hidden. Pope Leo XIII excitedly sent to Spain his official 'Promoter of the Faith', Monsignor Agostino Caprara, to go over the whole ground again. He returned to Rome and, along with leading cardinals and members of the sacred congregation, solemnly declared that the bones unearthed in 1879 were identical with the bodies of the three saints revered in Spain since the tenth century A.D.

So the cult of Saint James began again and flourishes to this day. A pilgrimage had always been a rare treat as well as a religious undertaking; it offered men and women the chance to leave their everyday lives and homes behind; it involved feasting and drinking and (as we know from Chaucer's *Canterbury Tales*) story-telling. The holiday mood that still pervades Santiago de Compostela is not too far removed from the spirit of many a medieval pilgrimage.

Curiously enough, the pilgrimages were revived at a time when elsewhere in western Christendom modern-minded clergy were often ridding themselves of what they conceived to be an embarrassing entanglement with out-dated superstitions. Some clergymen were strong-minded enough to do this even when it meant a loss of income. At Carnac in Brittany, for instance, is the church of Saint-Cornély, which houses the shrine of St Cornelius, patron saint of horned beasts. For centuries at the September fair in Carnac oxen and calves had been driven to the church door, made to kneel before the saint's statue above the porch, and then sold in the market. The priests of course took their tithe of these beasts. Even so in 1906 they decided they would no longer bless the animals. Nonetheless pilgrims still converge on Carnac in September, and animals are still driven up to the church porch before being auctioned in the streets. As we have observed before, the clergy do not always fully control the laity in such matters. Even today a blessing from the relics of St Cornelius is too precious to be forgone.

It was primarily to seek such a blessing that medieval pilgrims were willing to shoulder the huge costs of visiting the Holy Sepulchre at Jerusalem or St James's shrine in Spain. On their return, like modern holiday-makers they brought back mementoes and trinkets. From Santiago de Compostela pilgrims would bring back a hazel-twig – a memento of St James's staff – and some cockle-shells. Bishop Richard Mayo of Hereford, who died in 1516, had these buried with him in his tomb. Effigies on tombs frequently dressed the deceased in pilgrim's clothing, with a large hat, turned up at the brim to which is pinned a cockle-shell.

Some could afford to visit more than one of the great shrines of Christendom. Chaucer's wife of Bath had been to Jerusalem three times. She had knelt before relics in Rome, in Bologna, before the Magi in Cologne cathedral and of course at the bones of St James in Santiago de Compostela. Now she was on her way to the shrine of St Thomas Becket in Canterbury. And just as the pilgrim routes to Spain sprouted lesser shrines on the way, so the ways to Canterbury developed a series of shrines, each with a revered relic. Churches were rapidly modified to display these relics with sufficient dignity, since the martyred archbishop's bones now brought many more supplicants seeking their favours. At Compton in Surrey in the late twelfth century the east wall of the Norman church was strengthened, in order to carry a new upper chapel over the high altar, where relics could be displayed. Near Guildford the chapel of St Catherine, which is today, alas, a ruin, was modified so that pilgrims could climb to an interior gallery and pray before the relics without going through the rest of the church. Stairs leading up to relic chambers and shrines were built in churches at Grantham in Lincolnshire and at Wrotham in Kent – both *en route* for Canterbury. These churches were supplying a new and genuine need. They were also cashing in on the relic business. So did the chapel of the leper hospital at Harbledown just outside Canterbury, where Henry II had paused on his way to do penance at the martyr's shrine. Since pilgrims would be understandably reluctant to come too close to the lepers, the chapel's offertory box was chained to a tree outside.

None of this matched the ingenuity of Canterbury cathedral itself in relieving pilgrims of their money. The monks managed to set up not one but four holy spots, dedicated to the martyr's memory, inside the cathedral. John Charles Wall, who in the 1930s explored the four shrines at Canterbury, observed that, 'Except in the Church of the Holy Sepulchre it is almost unparalleled that four shrines to one saint are in the same church; but visitors to Canterbury and pilgrims of St Thomas have four sites, once sacred to the memory of the martyr, at which to pause and meditate: spots [Walls adds] which are holy to the memory only, as no vestige remains of the relics or the shrines of St Thomas in the cathedral.'

Medieval pilgrims to Canterbury were conducted to all four shrines in the east end of the cathedral whose rebuilding in 1174 had been dominated by the need to glorify Becket's relics. First they paused at the spot in the west transept where he was killed. Here Richard le Breton had so powerfully sliced off the top of Becket's skull as to break the point of his sword on the pavement. Here in 'the altar of the sword's point' was kept a fragment of the saint's brains, along with the point of that fatal sword, in a wooden altar.

Next, steps led the pilgrim into the crypt to the saint's first tomb – once a spare marble tomb, surrounded by a wall with two oval holes through with visitors could touch the coffin. The penitent Henry II had poked his head through one of these holes in order to be scourged. On top of this tomb was a casket with more of the saint's brains. And nearby was a well, offering water which the monks had tinged with his blood. Sale of phials of this liquid was a source of great profit to the monks of Canterbury, and they took care not to let anyone steal it. (An Irishman did so, applied it to cure his sore neck, and, it is said, developed a tumour there instead.) To complete the picture, hanging from a beam in the crypt were Thomas Becket's hair-shirt, his drawers and his own personal scourge.

From the crypt pilgrims ascended to the Trinity chapel, which contained the shrine of the corona, that is the top of Becket's skull sliced off at his martyrdom. It was encased in a reliquary representing his face in gold, further enriched in 1314 with more gold, with silver and with precious stones at a cost of £115 (maybe £60,000 in today's terms). Finally the pilgrims reached the fourth shrine of St Thomas, situated exactly above his first tomb and flanked by the tombs of the Black Prince and King Henry IV. Here the saint's bones had been transported in 1220. Soon afterwards stained glass windows were installed close by, showing Becket issuing from this tomb to heal a monk called Benedict.

The whole complex of four holy sites was immensely profitable. It is recorded that 100,000 persons came to Canterbury a year after Becket's canonisation in 1173. In 1221 pilgrims left £33. 13s. 7d. at the site of his martyrdom; £31. 3s. 3d. at his old tomb; £71. 10s. 0d. at the shrine with the crown of his skull; and £429. 8s. 0d. at his great new shrine. So much money lying around was an obvious temptation to impious hands; but the saint's relics looked after it. A female servant who stole some was rendered temporarily insane until she gave the money back.

Just as Santiago de Compostela dominated the pilgrim shrines of Europe, so Becket's shrines at Canterbury dominated those of Britain. But many smaller shrines both catered for more local communities and enriched their custodians. Some such shrines were indeed of more than local interest. St Winifred (or Gwenfrewi as the Welsh call her) repelled the lustful attentions of a young chieftain named Caradoc in the seventh century. Incensed and rejected, he cut off her head. At this the earth opened up and Caradoc disappeared underground. St Winifred's uncle, St Beuno, put his niece's head back on her shoulders and she was restored to life.

Both uncle and niece became noted relics after death. The sick were still being healed at St Beuno's grave at Clynnog, Carnarvonshire, in the eighteenth century. Winifred's relics brought fame and fortune to the Benedictine abbey at Shrewsbury. But her chief glory was a holy well, at Holywell in Flint, which sprang up at the spot where her severed head hit the ground. The noble of the land, in particular Henry VII's mother Lady Margaret Beaufort, endowed this well; and a series of sacred stones was set up to guide pilgrims to it. Yearly an enormous number came. Less important was the shrine and relics of St Candida, still *in situ* at Whitchurch Candidorum, Dorset. St Candida's body, lies in honour inside a stone tomb, through which her guardians had pierced three holes to enable the faithful to touch the saint's lead reliquary as they prayed.

On a large and small scale relics thus generated wealth in the middle ages, and some relics were very big business indeed. Those who did not have access to these divine founts of wealth were frequently covetous of those who did. Before the martyrdom of Thomas Becket, for instance, the relics of St Augustine of Canterbury drew far more people to his abbey than visited the cathedral. The murdered archbishop's bones changed all that. Desperately the Augustinians, seeing their revenues and visitors dwindle, begged the monks of the cathedral to give them the sliced-off corona of Becket's skull. The cathedral monks, as good businessmen, wisely refused.

As the Revd Sydney Smith observed, 'Poverty is no disgrace to a man, but it is confoundedly inconvenient.' Since to possess a profitable relic was a certain method of avoiding this inconvenience, those who hadn't one frequently stole from others who did. Sometimes they offered pious reasons for doing so. It was right, some said, to get back the relics of one's native saints, even if this meant stealing them. So the citizens of Tours argued, when they took back the corpse of St Martin from the Poitevins, silently taking him out through a window at night. Others said it was legitimate to steal from pagan lands. So in 828 when two Venetian merchants stole the corpse of St Mark from Alexandria, the grateful Republic of Venice readily forgave them for trafficking with the Saracens. Others claimed that they stole relics only because their owners neglected them.

The first stolen relic I know of is the body of St Hilarion, smuggled from Cyprus where he died in 371 and taken by his disciple to Jerusalem. The angry Cypriots insisted that his spirit remained with them, still able to deliver all they desired of him as if his corpse were still there too.

And this being the age of faith, these devout thieves frequently claimed that Jesus himself approved of the theft. A noted ascetic, St Isaac, died in Constantinople in 438. As his relics were being carried for burial, a nobleman named Aurelian hired a company of men to steal them. 'This', says the chronicle, 'they did with the permission of Christ our God who directs everything.'

Later Christians began to assert that the relic itself consented or even desired to be stolen. At times this would be indicated by some miracle. Thus the body of St Stephen, buried (after its rediscovery by Lucian) in a wooden sarcophagus in

Jerusalem, soon apparently conceived the desire to be taken to Constantinople. A senator named Alexander had placed the saint's relics in the Jerusalem sarcophagus, and he expressed the desire to be put after death in the same kind of coffin. His widow was a woman of Constantinople and decided to return home taking her husband's corpse and coffin with her. Stephen seized his chance to have his relics transported to Constantinople and cunningly arranged for the widow mistakenly to take his coffin instead of her husband's. The saint's relics showed their delight at being translated from Jerusalem to Constantinople by performing many miracles *en route*.

The whole anecdote was clearly invented to justify the theft by unknown persons of Stephen's corpse from Jerusalem so that it might adorn the new capital of the empire. Sometimes an alleged dream told a thief that all was well, since the relic approved the theft. Hildebert, a monk of Conques, decided to steal for his own monastery the corpse of St Vincent which was at Saragossa. Vincent revealed where he was in a dream. He told the monk that the pagans had stripped the roof of his sanctuary which now lay in a woebegone state. The monk stole the body from the sanctuary, only to be caught and punished by the Bishop of Saragossa.

The monks of Conques were now deeply anxious, for the prestige of their monastery had greatly declined since the year 838, when Pepin I had founded a new monastery at Agen where St Foy had been martyred. Pepin had even dubbed it 'the new Conques'. Conques decided that its only hope was to steal St Foy herself from Agen. A monk named Arinisdus was given the task. Posing as a secular priest, he spent no fewer than ten years in the monastery at Agen until, at last, he was made guardian of the treasury. Arinisdus broke open the saint's shrine and sped back to Conques with her body. The fortunes of Conques were restored.

In like fashion was the body of St Mary Magdalen allegedly stolen by a monk of Vézelay named Badilus. When Badilus arrived at Saint-Maximin in Provence, he found the town smitten by plague. In return for food an old man led him to the saint's relics. Badilus recognised the Magdalen's fragrant odour, and later that night she appeared to him in a dream, urging him to take her away. He did so, and only later, as we have seen, did the monks of Saint-Maximin manage to get their own back on Vézelay.

Happily for their new owners, stolen relics continued to work miracles. In his monograph on the subject, P. J. Geary studied accounts of nearly 100 thefts between the age of Charlemagne and the Crusades. Geary came to the conclusion that, 'Far from condemning them as aberrations or sins against the fellow Christians from whom the saints were stolen, most people apparently praised them as true works of Christian virtue, and communities . . . boasted of their successful thefts.' He also suggests that the celebrated middleman Deusdona took a house close by the catacombs in Rome so that he and his two brothers Lunisius and Theodorus could quietly steal sacred bones for their customers.

Theft accounts for much of a peculiar problem that faces us today: how to account for a remarkable number of 'duplicated' relics throughout the Christian world. Our own protomartyr St Alban is a case in point. Clearly he died in Britain; but eventually three places claimed to possess his body: St Albans itself, Ely, and the Danish monastery of Odense. The chroniclers tell different tales of how this came about. St Albans Abbey argued that when the Danes invaded England, Abbot Alfric, fearing the invaders would steal the relics of the protomartyr, sealed them up under the altar of St Nicholas and sent a fake set of bones to Ely, putting out that these were St Alban's. The Danish king was drowned on his way to England, and the invasion was called off. Alfric asked for his bones back. The cunning monks of Ely sent different ones, planning to keep those they supposed were genuine. Alfric accepted them with indifference, since he knew he already possessed the real relics. These he placed in a fine shrine in the centre of his abbey, leaving the dumb monks of Ely to bask in their ignorance.

The monks of Ely, however, told a different tale. According to them St Alban's bones had been brought by an abbot of St

Albans named Egfrid, who fled to Ely when his own patron was deposed in 1070. When he returned to St Albans, the monks of Ely gave him back fake relics, and Egfrid foolishly accepted them.

Clearly both monastic houses were claiming the relics of this valuable martyr. But what of the Benedictine monastery of Odense? In the thirteenth century a monk of St Albans named Matthew Paris put out the story that the Danes had in fact taken the martyr's bones. He then added a tale suspiciously similar to that of Arinisdus of Conques and St Foy. Matthew Paris says that a monk of St Albans named Egwin went as a postulant to Odense and after many years there was made sacristan. His patience at last rewarded, Egwin crept to the saint's shrine one night, bored a hole into it, took out the saint's bones, filled in the hole again, and stored the relics under his bed. Eventually he found a merchant who took them back to St Albans, disguised as 'a parcel of books'. His long task accomplished, wily Egwin feigned homesickness, and returned to Britain.

Is any one of these tales the truth? It seems to me that each group of monks claiming ownership of one of these valuable sets of bones simply invented anecdotes to explain how they got them and why their rivals' claims were spurious.

We could similarly ask whether the famous relics of St Benedict of Nursia are in Monte Cassino, where he died, or in the monastery of Saint-Benoît-sur-Loire, whose monks, it is alleged, stole them from the Italians in 703. We have no way of knowing. Monte Cassino never admitted losing the bones. But the relics at Saint-Benoît-sur-Loire undoubtedly raised its prestige and enormously increased its wealth, enabling the monks to build the astounding abbey church that stands there to this day.

Theft of relics in the middle ages threw up tales quite as legendary as those of the James brothers in the early days of the American west. So prevalent had relic-thieving become by the thirteenth century that the dying St Francis of Assisi begged his followers for an armed guard, in case the hovering Perugini stole his corpse and buried it in their own city. Fear that someone might steal Francis's body remained so strong that it was kept in a great flint sarcophagus, unexposed in Assisi until 1818. His soul-mate St Clare's corpse was shut away in a stone sarcophagus for six centuries until it was finally exhibited in a crystal coffer in 1850.

The great sarcophagus of St Francis can still be seen at Assisi, but his body now lies in a splendid shrine, along with four of his original disciples: Brother Leo, Brother Masso, Brother Angelo and Brother Rufino. H. V. Morton observed that, 'It is almost certain that S. Francis would disapprove of his tomb, unless maybe the four beloved companions, who share it with him, could point out, and no man was ever more ready to listen, that earth-bound humanity needs such anchors for the mind.' Morton goes on to speak of 'the feeling of peace and beauty' which surrounds the tomb. In Assisi itself, traders grow rich on the traffic in trinkets and tourism brought to the hill-town by its distinguished relics. At least, St Francis may expect to enjoy the peace and beauty of his tomb without fear that grave-robbers will steal him away.

Or can he? For 1200 years the basilica of Saint-Denis in Argenteuil preserved a seamless woollen robe believed to be that worn by Jesus on his way to be crucified and for which the soldiers at the foot of the cross diced. In 1982 the church authorities allowed scientific tests to be made which indicated that this robe could well date back to the very beginning of the Christian era. Charlemagne is said to have given it to the basilica in the year 800.

The seamless robe is stained with blood and is a dark, reddish-purple in colour. Extremely fragile, it has been shown to the public only at intervals of fifty years, and was due to be shown again in 1984. In December 1983 the seamless robe was stolen by a French terrorist group. An anonymous caller telephoned the French newspaper *Libération*, demanding as 'ransom' for the robe that the French Catholic church pay 300,000 francs to the Polish 'Solidarity' movement.

Relics are still big business; and brigands still break in and steal them.

5

Relics of the Holy Family

By rising from the dead Jesus transformed man's ultimate fear into hope. In a Nazi prison the martyr Dietrich Bonhoeffer could write of death as 'the supreme festival on the road to freedom'. But the manner in which the Bible recounts Jesus's ascent into eternal life is resolutely physical: Jesus led his disciples till they were opposite Bethany, 'and he lifted up his hands and blessed them. And it came to pass, while he blessed them, he parted from them and was carried up into Heaven.' No trace of Jesus's body was left behind, either to remind his followers of his earthly presence or for them to pass on to future disciples. All they could transmit to future generations was the memory of his deeds and sayings.

In the beginning, as St John said, was the word. And after Jesus's ascension too, there were only words. Later Christians might plausibly claim to possess, say, the head of St John the Baptist or the body of St James the Great. If they took seriously their New Testament, in no way could they claim to possess any tangible relic of the body of the Saviour himself.

Hence the immeasurable importance of such secondary relics

as Jesus's seamless robe. The bones of Thomas Becket were obviously of greater significance than his hair-shirt or personal scourge. In the case of Jesus the only relics Christians could possibly discover and cherish were the secondary ones.

Cherish them they did. The mystery surrounding the discovery of the true cross was soon forgotten. Tradition established as fact that St Helena had discovered it in 326. The church dedicated 14 September as its feast-day. And within half a century St Cyril of Jerusalem could observe that 'the whole world is filled with fragments of the true cross'.

To give somebody a small piece of the true cross was an enormous favour. In 586 or so Gregory the Great sent a fragment in a reliquary (shaped like a cross) to Recaredo, the first Christian king of Spain. These chippings from the tree on which the Saviour ransomed the world soon acquired a colossal monetary value. The Venetians bought a piece for 25,000 livres and then sold it for a profit to Baldwin I of Jerusalem.

Fragments of the true cross could be incorporated in an individual's store of treasure more easily than the entire corpse of a saint or martyr. In consequence during the high middle ages many people regarded such a relic as part of their personal wealth. Fragments of Christ's cross began to make frequent appearances in the wills of richer folk. In 1356 Elizabeth, Countess of Northampton, declared 'I do will to the church of Friar Preachers, London, the Cross made of the very Cross of Our Saviour's Cross, wherein is contained one of the thorns of His Crown.' In 1371 Thomas Earl of Oxford willed all his relics to his wife Maud, including a piece of wood said to have come from the true cross. William of Wykeham, Bishop of Winchester, in 1403 bequeathed to Winchester cathedral 'one cross of gold with relics of the Cross of Our Lord'.

Soon no great house or great foundation in the Christian world counted itself rich in either spiritual or worldly terms without also possessing one of these ubiquitous bits of wood. Some places had managed to get hold of more than one piece. In 1425 the provost and fellows of Eton handed over to King Edward IV a list of all the college's assets. The list included a sizeable, diverting number of relics: a bone of St Andrew, set in the middle of diverse other holy relics; the arm of St George; a piece of St John of Beverley; St Nicholas's tooth; bits of St Stephen, and so on. It also itemised:

> a cross of silver and gilt enameled with the figures of the four Evangelists and garnished with diverse stones counterfeit and therein is contained a large piece of the holy cross; a double cross of silver and gilt standing upon a foot with diverse escutcheons enameled contained therein diverse pieces of the holy cross;
> a double cross with part of the holy cross silver and gold without a foot with diverse counterfeit stones.

The reliquaries containing these pieces of the true cross were clearly valuable works of art in themselves. The bits of wood inside them were virtually invaluable. Such precious relics of wood spread throughout the Christian world. Some of them can be seen to this day.

Initially however about half the true cross stayed in Jerusalem, its main beam annually exposed on Easter Day by the bishop and clergy. For six hundred years the cross was safe in its original home. Then in 614 Chosroes II, King of Persia, captured the Holy City and with it its patriarch and the remains of the cross. Both were taken to Chosroes's capital, Ctesiphon, and the king set up the true cross in a throne standing to the right of his own.

Thirteen years later the Emperor Heraclius defeated Chosroes in battle and saved the honour of the true cross. Triumphantly it was carried to Constantinople by four elephants in front of the Emperor's own chariot. Two years later he took it back to Jerusalem. Heraclius took off his shoes, laid aside his imperial garments and dressed as a peasant carried the sacred relic on his own shoulders to Calvary. The patriarch, now restored, is said to have recognised his own seals still intact on the casket of the true cross.

For some years the cross, though endangered, remained safe

in the Holy City. The Moslems who took the city in 637 allowed the cross to stay there unharmed. When in 1009 El Hakim, Caliph of Egypt, destroyed Jerusalem, the rock of the sepulchre where Jesus's body is said to have been laid resisted the fire. Prudently the Christians claimed (perhaps truthfully) to have hidden the true cross there and thus preserved it. At any rate it was joyfully produced again when the Crusaders regained the city in 1099.

In 1187, however, Saladin finally defeated the Christians. Part of his booty was what remained of the true cross. Christendom anguished. Richard Cœur de Lion failed to persuade Saladin to sell him the great beam of the cross. It is said that Hubert Walter, Bishop of Salisbury, was granted permission to kiss it in Jerusalem. And then it was lost for ever. In the words of J. C. Wall, 'Saladin either hid or destroyed that talisman whose invisible power he could not understand; and now it probably forms part of the soil of Palestine; or was it burnt (as reported) and the dust wafted by the winds over the face of the globe to sanctify the whole earth?'

Not all was lost. As we have seen, bits of the cross had fortunately already been chipped off the original long before the Moslem invasions, and these had spread miraculously around Christendom. King Sigurd of Norway had in 1127 offered part of his navy to help Baldwin I to reduce the port of Sidon in exchange for a piece of the true cross. Sigurd built a church for this relic in his castle at Konighelle. After Baldwin's death another piece reached Britain. One of his chaplains, an Englishman, tried to sell a fragment first to St Albans abbey. The monks there rejected his offer. So did other communities. Finally the chaplain's offer was accepted by the impoverished Cluniac priory of St Andrew, Bromelholme, Norfolk. Their foresight was rewarded. The fragment of the true cross worked many miracles at Bromelholme, and in recognition of the relic's powers, King Henry III granted the priory an annual fair on 14 September, the feast of the Exaltation of the Holy Cross.

Other pieces reached Scandinavia. Queen Dagmar of

Denmark owned a fragment set in a Byzantine reliquary and had it buried on her breast when she died in 1212. The relic was considered too precious to lie there merely to help ensure her resurrection. It was exhumed and is now in the Museum of Copenhagen.

Naturally Constantinople kept a large chunk of the true cross, frequently allowing pieces to be cut off and given to worthy recipients. Again, Richard Cœur de Lion, notwithstanding his failure to persuade Saladin to sell him the great beam of the relic, is said to have bought two other small pieces that the Moslem leader had secretly spared for the Christians. And soon it was reported that the Emperor Heraclius long ago had cut nineteen huge pieces off the cross, distributing these for safe keeping to Cyprus, Antioch, Crete, Edessa, Georgia, Alexandria, Ascalon and Damascus as well as Constantinople and Jerusalem.

Despite the irreparable loss of the great beam of the true cross, the Christian world was thus able to take comfort from the belief that many powerful fragments of this relic of the Saviour were still dispersed throughout their holy places. Many remain to this day in the Greek Orthodox monasteries of Mount Athos. In the monastery known as the Great Lavra is a piece no less than seven inches long, presented to the fortunate monks by the Emperor Nikephoros Phokas.

Seven inches of true cross, considerable though it may be, cannot compare with a fragment still to be seen in France in the valley of the Loire. This piece of wood came from the Holy Land in 1241 to the Cistercian monastery of La Boissière, eighteen kilometres or so east of Baugé, a gift of the Crusader knight Jean d'Alluye. Today this relic has been officially placed high in the second class of national monuments in France. (This sort of classification of course takes no account of the status of the fragment as a holy relic possibly endowed with otherworldly powers.) Altogether it contains 104,000 mm of oak (and is thus smaller only than two other such relics of the true cross: that placed by Louis IX in the Sainte-Chapelle, which comprised 220,500 mm; and the world champion, that of the convent of Sainte-Gudule, Brussels, comprising 514,590 mm).

In 1790 the Revolutionaries, instead of destroying this relic as they had destroyed many others, took it from La Boissière to Baugé. There it was kept in the chapel of a hospital for incurables run by the Filles du Cœur de Marie. In the chapel there you can see it to this day. And in a curious fashion this relic has continued to exert its influence over the fortunes of France. In the fifteenth century the wood was carved into the shape of a double-beamed cross. From this cross Duke René II of Anjou derived the symbol of his banner; and by his marriage to Isabelle of Lorraine, the cross of Baugé became what we now call the cross of Lorraine – that cross adopted by Charles de Gaulle in the Second World War as a symbol of the struggle against Hitler.

As with the true cross, so with the nails of the true cross: both relics miraculously seem to have had the gift of multiplying. No fewer than twenty-nine places in Europe alone claim to possess a holy nail: Aachen, Ancona, Arras, Bamberg, the convent of Andechsen in Bavaria, Carpentras, Catana, Colle in Tuscany, Cologne, Compiègne, Cracow, the Escurial, Florence, Livorno, Milan, Monza, the monastery of St Patrick in Naples, Paris, both Santa Croce and Santa Maria in Campitelli in Rome, Siena, Spoleto, Torcello, Torno on Lake Como, Toul, Trèves, Troyes, Venice (which claims to have three nails) and Vienna.

Now some explanation for this remarkable number of sacred nails is called for. Most early Christian writers assume that Jesus was nailed to the cross by four spikes, though a few (Gregory Nazianzen, the fifth-century Greek poet Nonnus, etc.) believe that he was obliged to cross his legs, so that three spikes would suffice. The earliest known crucifixes, which were drawn in cemeteries on the Via Flaminia in the seventh century A.D., show the Saviour's feet separated, as does an eighth century crucifix at Lucca – assuming therefore four nails.

Four nails obviously cannot account for even twenty-nine European relics, leaving aside the rest of the world (and assuming Britain not to be part of Europe, for naturally foundations like Eton College possessed holy nails). But need we assume that these nails are necessarily those that pinned Jesus to the cross or even that they claim to be these nails? Some of the nails may, it is suggested, have held the cross together and not be the ones that held the Lord onto it. Secondly, legend has it that St Helena had the four nails which pierced Jesus's flesh made into twelve smaller ones. The nails of the true cross now dispersed throughout the world are not necessarily *whole* nails. Thirdly, it is highly likely that Christians seeking to multiply these relics would create new nails incorporating filings from the original ones, just as for example the monks of Canterbury thinned down St Thomas Becket's blood with water without thinning down its healing powers. The holy nail in Santa Croce in Gerusalemme, Rome, discovered there in 1492 and certified as authentic by Pope Benedict XIV in the mid-eighteenth century, has certainly been much filed down. Finally, analogy with the way cloth allowed to rest on the relics of holy martyrs was often deemed to have become a secondary relic leads one to the justifiable suspicion that sometimes a new relic was created simply by touching a new nail against one truly supposed to have come from Christ's cross. With such techniques available, why not multiply nails *ad infinitum*?

These considerations may help to ease the minds of those troubled by questions about the authenticity of the many holy nails whose exploits, to my mind, form one of the more diverting aspects of the history of relics. Since the holy nails so readily multiplied themselves, one thrown into the sea by Helena to calm a storm (as Gregory of Tours relates) was not necessarily a lamentable loss. Another fixed into the head of Constantine's statue and a third stuck onto his helmet would have constituted an indulgent waste, had not more been available. Constantine's deployment of these relics was in fact odd, since he refashioned one as a bit for his horse. Some church fathers – Cyril of Alexandria, Ambrose – suggest that he was inspired to do so by a verse in the Old Testament prophet Zechariah (chapter 14, v. 20): 'In that day shall there be upon the bells of the horses HOLY UNTO THE LORD' – an explanation rejected as absurd by St Jerome. Whatever possessed Constantine to order this somewhat ridiculous treatment of a sacred relic, it is certain that travellers to Constantinople as late as the eleventh century were still being shown the holy bit. Did the Crusaders then bring it to France? Certainly at Carpentras in Provence numerous references occur to the Saint-Mors ('holy horse-bit') in the early twelfth century. Within a hundred years the Saint-Mors was on display in the cathedral of Saint Siffrein and had been incorporated into the city's coat-of-arms.

Constantine is said to have been generous with his nails, in spite of also clearly using them to glorify his own image. He sent one to Russia, and that nail can now be seen in Moscow, in the Synod of the Ascension, where it was brought from Georgia in 1686. And a yet more historic nail is said to have been brought to Europe by Pope Gregory the Great. He gave it to Theodolinda, the Frankish princess who converted the Lombards from Arianism. Theodolinda used the nail as a band around her crown, which she donated to the church at Monza in Italy on her death in 628. Eleven-and-a-half centuries later Napoleon Bonaparte used the crown of Theodolinda to crown himself King of Italy.

Jesus himself was crowned differently. 'The soldiers of the governor,' wrote St Matthew, 'took Jesus into the palace and gathered unto him the whole band. And they stripped him and put on him a scarlet robe. And they plaited a crown of thorns and put it upon his head, and a reed in his right hand; and they knelt down before him and mocked him, saying, Hail, King of the Jews!' This crown of thorns became the third great secondary relic of Jesus to pervade Christendom.

In the early years of Christianity few gloried in it as much as they did in the true cross and the nails, but by the time of Bishop Gregory of Tours, the crown of thorns was exciting the imagination of Christian historians, and by the time of Charlemagne, who obtained some thorns from the Patriarch of Jerusalem, it ranked with the true cross and the nails as a relic much coveted. Like them it was seemingly inexhaustible. Peterborough abbey boasted a huge thorn in the twelfth century. Eton College in 1465 treasured 'a little pinnacle of gold standing upon a small foot containing therein one of the thorns of our Lord', and what must have been a lovely reliquary: a marble statue of a Grey-friar, holding a table and two angels guarding a second thorn from Jesus's crown.

The crown of thorns, it seems to me, only narrowly escaped the fate of the burning bush that once was alight but unconsumed on Mount Sinai. The monks of St Catherine's monastery joyfully built a chapel in honour of this famous memento of the manner in which God had long ago manifested himself to Moses. For many years and certainly well into the Christian era travellers reported seeing this bush still alight on Mount Sinai. Regrettably, so many of these travellers snipped away pieces of the burning bush to keep as souvenirs that today it is no more. (In 1980 a monk of Mount Sinai showed me what he claimed was a bush developed from a shoot of the original; but that is not the same.) Similarly, so great was the demand for thorns from Christ's crown of thorns that the original virtually ceased to be a crown at all.

This reached Paris along with many other relics when Baldwin II, expelled as Latin Emperor of Constantinople and in desperate need of cash, sold it to Louis IX – though, as we have already noted, to avoid the sin of trafficking in holy goods he 'freely' gave the relics to Louis, who in return 'freely' offered 13,134 perperi in thanksgiving for the gift of the crown. Presumably Louis knew that the relic would be short of at least some of its thorns, since the nearby abbey of Saint-Denis already boasted one whose authenticity had been attested by many miracles. History does not record whether or not he was prepared for what finally arrived from Baldwin: a bundle of shrunken reeds in a circle, without a single thorn; a kind of interior hat-band to the crown of thorns proper. Unfussed, Louis hastened with the building of the Sainte-Chapelle to house this and his other treasured relics.

At the time of the French Revolution, Louis XVI in 1791 ordered this crown of (non-existent) thorns to be taken for safety to the basilica of Saint-Denis. From there it was taken two years later to the Hôtel des Monnaies and thence to the Bibliothèque Nationale. In 1804 the French government ordered its removal to Notre Dame de Paris. There it remains, in a ring of six pieces of crystal held together by three gilt leaves. Still thornless, even this circlet of reeds is incomplete; bits of it today can be found in other parts of France: at Arras, Autun, Chablis, Lyons, and Vaugirard.

After the soldiers guarding Jesus had mocked him as king of the Jews, spat on him and beaten him, they dressed him again and led him to be crucified. Almost certainly they crucified him naked, and St John's Gospel tells us that they divided his clothing amongst themselves. His coat, however, was seamless, and they decided not to cut it up. Instead they played dice for it. Now as we have already noted, this seamless robe was given by Charlemagne to Argenteuil in 800 and stolen by left-wing terrorists in 1983. Fortunately western Christendom possesses a duplicate seamless robe of Jesus, which is still kept in the cathedral of Trier, Germany. A number of Popes have indeed indicated their belief that the Holy Coat of Trier is the genuine seamless robe of Jesus, and not the one stolen from Argenteuil. Popular acclaim too warms to the Trier coat and not the French one. When the Holy Coat of Trier was devoutly exposed in 1933, it drew over two million pilgrims.

One more garment of Jesus was to play its part in the savage events of his death, before entering into the history and lore of relics. After Jesus's death, he was placed in a tomb belonging to Joseph of Arimathea. 'Joseph,' noted St Matthew, 'took the body and wrapped it in a clean linen cloth.' Since 1578 in the chapel of the Dukes of Savoy, close by Turin cathedral, a length of ivory-coloured linen measuring 4.5 by 1.1 metres, has been preserved as the holy shroud of Jesus. When it was exposed for six weeks in Turin cathedral in 1978, more than three million pilgrims went to see it.

A most unusual aspect of this exposition was that although it cost 20,000 dollars to put the holy relic on show, with special lighting and behind bullet-proof glass, the cathedral authorities decided to avoid all show of greed by welcoming pilgrims entirely free of charge and banning all attempts to exploit the occasion commercially. The vast crowds were by no means all members of the Roman church. Ian Wilson has recorded that 'The last Mass of the expositions, on the evening of Sunday, 8 October [1978], was one vast sea of people, Anglicans, Episcopalians and even Greek Orthodox among them, some so moved that, like the Anglican bishop John Robinson, they felt it entirely natural to receive Roman Catholic Communion.'

The ecumenical nature of this act of reverent adoration and the laudable lack of commercialism point to the truly remarkable nature of this major secondary relic of Jesus Christ. For the Turin shroud, as it has come to be called, bears the imprint of the front and back of a human being, a bearded, naked man who has apparently been crucified. We can see that he must have been about 170 centimetres tall, perhaps more. His hair was long. He wore a beard and a long rope of hair hung down his back. Blood appeared to have flowed from his body to the shroud, from his wrists, from his feet, from his side, and from what appear to be the wounds of severe beating about the head and back.

The visitors in 1978 also knew of a yet more remarkable phenomenon in connection with this relic. For centuries the imprint of the man's back and front had been visible to the naked eye: but only just. The image is pale, like a faded sepia-tint. The feet are a mere blur. The indistinct head with its wide staring eyes seems virtually separated from the rest of the corpse. The back view of the image is similarly indistinct. But in 1898 the then owner of the relic, King Umberto I, allowed an amateur photographer named Seconda Pia to photograph the shroud. Black and white cameras of that era required the photographer first to make a negative image, with the dark and light areas reversed. Seconda Pia took two exposures, one lasting fourteen minutes, the second twenty minutes.

Developed, these plates were astounding. Instead of what Seconda Pia had expected, namely a negative rather ghostly picture, he found an extraordinarily lifelike image of a man's body, bloodstains (showing white) flowing from his head, hands, side and feet. Pia was deeply moved because the image so closely corresponded to the picture of Christ built up over centuries of Christian art. Clearly, to him, the image represented what two weeks later a newspaper described as 'the long and thin face of Our Lord, the tortured body and the long thin hands.' After centuries, the Italian journalist continued, 'are revealed to us what no-one has seen since the ascension into Heaven.'

Subsequent photographs with far more advanced cameras have confirmed the power of the negative image. Pope Pius VI found it 'so true, so profound, so human and so divine, such as we have been unable to admire and venerate in any other image.' The French Catholic poet Paul Claudel described the picture on the shroud as 'something so frightening and yet so beautiful . . . that a man can escape it only by worship.'

Such pious expressions of reverence do not of course prove that the amazing relic at Turin is in fact the winding sheet of Jesus; and later we must examine the question of its authenticity. Suffice it here to note that not only are the wounds on the image of the shroud clearly consistent with those of a man who had been crucified; in addition the wound in this man's side corresponds closely with one unusual feature of the crucifixion of Jesus.

St John's Gospel tells us that as Jesus and those crucified with him had been put to death on a Friday, the Jews did not wish their bodies to hang on the crosses overnight into the Sabbath day. They persuaded the authorities to order the soldiers to break the legs of those still alive (so that the weight of their crucified bodies would speedily bring about death) and then remove the corpses. However, wrote St John, 'When they came to Jesus and saw that he was dead already, they did not break his legs. Nonetheless, one of the soldiers pierced his side with a spear, and immediately water and blood came out.'

The flow of blood that would have been caused by such a spear clearly appears in the negative photographs of the image on the Turin shroud. That, however, is only incidental to our purpose here. For Christians soon realised that in piercing the Saviour's side as he hung on the cross, the Roman soldier's lance had suddenly become a secondary relic! Soon it had turned up in the chapel of the Virgin at Pharos, Constantinople, brought there in haste, it was said, to escape the plunder of Jerusalem by King Chosroes of Persia in 614.

Like the crown of thorns, the true cross, the holy nails and Christ's seamless robe, the holy lance had the gift of duplicating itself. In the late eleventh century the Crusaders conquered Antioch. Weary and half-starved (as Sir Steven Runciman movingly recreates their plight), when they realised 'that they had now to face a siege by an enemy more formidable than that which they had beaten, they hungered for a miracle to console them'. Two days later a man of Provence who was with them, Peter Bartholomew, announced that in a vision St Andrew had revealed to him that the holy lance which pierced Jesus's side lay buried in Antioch in St Peter's cathedral. The Crusaders rushed to unearth the relic, and another Frenchman, Raymond of Aquilers, carried it into a victorious battle against the besiegers.

In spite of this victory, one person present, the papal legate Bishop Adhemar of Le Puy, refused to accept that this was truly the holy lance of Jerusalem. For one thing, Adhemar was annoyed by Peter Bartholomew's gratuitous announcement that St Andrew in the vision had incidentally criticised Adhemar's preaching. Another more cogent reason was that Adhemar had already seen the other holy lance in the chapel at Pharos. Peter Bartholomew gave the lance from Antioch to his own lord, Raymond of Toulouse, but his enemies continued to insist that the relic was a fake. Incensed that people doubted the authenticity of his vision, Peter agreed to undergo ordeal by fire in its support. The ordeal killed him.

The lance was discredited – or partly so, for Peter's friend Raymond of Aquilers claimed that Bartholomew had in fact survived the test and been forced back into the fire by his enemies. In addition Pope Paschal II congratulated the

Crusaders on finding the lance in Antioch. Emboldened by this, Raymond of Toulouse went to Constantinople and gave the relic to Emperor Alexis, notwithstanding the fact that Constantinople already possessed its own holy lance. The Emperor diplomatically accepted Raymond's gift, privately deciding that it really had been made out of some nails from the true cross, and therefore was no miserly present.

Meanwhile two more holy lances turned up. One, known as the lance of St Maurice, appeared in the imperial treasury at Vienna and became part of the insignia of the Holy Roman Emperors. This lance, too, some decided, must have been welded out of nails from the true cross. The Lombard Count Samson gave it to Rudolf II, King of Burgundy. He gave it to Henry the Fowler, King of Germany; and when the relic was not accompanying the Holy Roman Emperor in triumphal procession, it was henceforth kept in the abbey of St Maurice in Nuremberg. The fourth holy lance, that kept at Etchmiadzin, belongs to the Armenian church, to whom (according to the earliest document to mention it – a thirteenth-century chronicle) Jesus's disciple Thaddeus had donated it.

So four relics, all purporting to be the holy lance that pierced Jesus, coexisted in Christendom fairly happily until 1241, when Baldwin II's notorious 'gift' of relics to Louis IX included one of the lances from Constantinople. Louis accepted it as genuine. But Constantinople still possessed a bigger one, as many later witnesses testified, made of dark iron, two fingers wide, with a double blade and (some said) a dark stain of the Saviour's blood still disfiguring the point. This relic of the passion of Christ finally reached Rome, a gift of Sultan Beyazit II to Pope Innocent VIII, where it has remained ever since.

Naturally its authenticity was doubted. After all the holy lance at Rome had three other rivals, all supported by enthusiastic cults. The Popes entertained no such doubts. Benedict XIV in the eighteenth century roundly declared the one discovered by Peter Bartholomew to be a fake. But Benedict was no bigot. He observed that the tip of the holy lance in Rome was missing. He sent to Paris for a picture of the lance in the

Sainte-Chapelle, compared the picture with his own lance, and announced that the French one was only the tip. Rome possessed the shaft of the sacred relic, which Baldwin must have kept back from Louis IX six centuries previously.

The two lances were never brought together to test the Pope's conclusion. Now we shall never know, for the holy lance in Paris was destroyed in the Revolution. But Sir Steven Runciman has put forward another delicious hypothesis. Perhaps Baldwin II gave King Louis not the tip of the holy lance at all, but instead the lance dug up in 1098 at Antioch. 'History is full of ironies,' observed Sir Steven; 'and it would be in keeping with them if Peter Bartholomew's lance, denounced by Benedict XIV as a fraud, should have been reverenced for so many centuries under a false name at the Sainte-Chapelle and should then be destroyed by godless Jacobin mobs as a gesture against the Faith.'

One constant feature of Christian history revealed by these multiplying relics – nails, pieces of wood, holy lances, seamless robes and endless thorns – is an unslakeable thirst for tangible remembrances of Jesus. In the end secondary relics were not enough. Above all people thirsted for the holy blood of Christ. If, after all, the bread and wine of the Eucharist became the body and blood of Christ, might it not be possible for some of the sacred blood shed at his crucifixion similarly to succour the faithful?

So speculations grew as to who could have saved this most precious relic. The soldier who pierced the Saviour's side was named Longinus and is assumed to have been converted by the events of Good Friday. He would have saved the holy blood. The Virgin Mary was present at the crucifixion. Would she have allowed her son's blood to have seeped away? St John and Nicodemus would have collected some. Joseph of Arimathea would have mopped it up. St Mary Magdalen would have treasured much.

Soon drops of this most precious relic were on show in Rome in Santa Croce in Gerusalemme, Santa Maria Maggiore and St John in the Lateran. It turned up at Fécamp in Normandy.

Quantities of the holy blood reached Constantinople, and in 1244 Lambert de Noyon, chaplain of King Baldwin, brought a phial of it thence to the abbey of Saint-Jean-des-Vignes at Soissons.

Three years later the holy blood reached England, when the Grand Master of the Templars brought a phial of it from the Patriarch of Jerusalem to King Henry III. Some doubted whether or not this precious liquid really could be what it claimed to be. At a public discussion the Grand Master argued that if he had sworn wrongly that this was the holy blood, he had sworn to his own damnation. At this the Bishop of Norwich announced an indulgence of six years and 140 days to all who devoutly worshipped before this wondrous relic, and the king joyfully carried the phial from St Paul's to Westminster Abbey.

In Britain the most famous shrine of the holy blood was undoubtedly the one at Hailes Abbey in Gloucestershire. The Cistercians here had, like Henry III, obtained a phial from the Patriarch in Jerusalem. They rebuilt the east end of their abbey church to make it worthy of the precious relic, which became a huge attraction for pilgrims. Chaucer's pardoner in his *Canterbury Tales* would take an oath:

> By Goddes precious herte, and by his nailes,
> And by the Blood of Christ that is in Hailes.

The psychological effect on a supplicant who came to worship before some of the shed blood of his Saviour was often overpowering. St Jerome many years previously described the overwrought behaviour of men and women in the presence of much less moving relics: men howled like wolves, some hissed as if they were snakes, others bent their bodies backwards till they arched over to touch the earth with their heads, and women seemed to hang upside down in the air (though their skirts did not fall, said Jerome). Similar behaviour occurred at Hailes. In 1417 Margery Kempe went there to see the holy blood:

there she was shriven and had loud cries and boisterous weepings. Then the religious men had her in amongst them, and made her good cheer, save that they swore many great oaths and horrible. And she rebuked them therefor, after Gospel, and thereof had they great wonder. Nevertheless some were right well pleased, thanked be God for His goodness.

You can no longer find any of Christ's blood at Hailes. For that you must visit Bruges. In the twelfth century Thierry d'Alsace on a pilgrimage to the Holy Land was given clots of Christ's blood by King Baldwin III and the Patriarch. On his return in 1148 he build in Bruges a chapel to house it. William the Norman, Bishop of Tournai in the fourteenth century, claimed to have touched this relic, which liquefied every Friday between the early morning and the ninth hour. He commissioned a new tube of crystal to contain the blood, sealed at each end by a jewelled crown and censing angels of silver. And in 1617 the Archduke Albert of Burgundy gave an exquisite canopied reliquary, fashioned by Jean Crabbe, to shelter and glorify the crystal tube and its precious relic. Still today on feasts of the holy blood, a priest takes the tube from Crabbe's reliquary. The faithful file past, each reverently kissing the glass, while the priest with a kerchief perfunctorily wipes the crystal after each supplicant has passed.

Of course the miraculous properties of the holy blood gave scope for many tricksters to offer dubious remedies to the sick. As late as 1591 in the England of Elizabeth I John Alleyn, an Oxford recusant, was claiming to possess a quantity of Christ's blood which he sold at twenty pounds a drop, claiming that those who carried it with them would not suffer any bodily harm.

By this time in truth far more dubious relics purporting to derive from the earthly body of Jesus had brought the cult into disrepute. In the twelfth century monks of Saint-Médard-de-Soisson claimed to have obtained from Constantinople one of Jesus's teeth. This roused the anger of a Benedictine theologian named Guibert of Nogent, who pointed out that after the resurrection no physical relics of Jesus could have been left behind. To the claim of the monks that this was a milk tooth, which the infant Jesus shed and thenceforth never again needed, Guibert responded that in that case he would expect to see several others preserved throughout the Christian churches, not to speak of some of the hairs that Jesus undoubtedly shed when he walked in Palestine.

Guibert spoke too soon. Clermont-Ferrand was soon claiming not only hair cut from Christ's head by his mother but also five fingernails from his left hand, two from his right, pluckings from his beard and an eleventh part of the bloody cloth that had covered his eyes after his death. And a letter from St Alban's, Namur, dated 1249, reveals that spot too claiming to possess a relic of Jesus's sacred hair.

This was not the end of absurdity. The town of Lucques in the thirteenth century boasted a crucifix said to contain Jesus's holy navel, brought to the Auvergne by St Austremoine. Worse, a second holy navel was venerated at Rome in the church of Santa Maria del Popolo. A third one was exhibited at Châlons-sur-Marne. Some explanation was offered to account for these last two navels, both claiming to be Jesus's. The Virgin Mary is said to have picked up her son's navel after his birth and guarded the precious relic all her life. It greatly comforted her after his death. On her own death she gave the relic to St John, who in turn left it to his successors as Bishop of Ephesus. Eventually the navel fell into the hands of Charlemagne, who cut it in two and gave one half to Rome, as a gift to Pope Leo III, and the other to the church of Notre-Dame-en-Vaux, Châlons-sur-Marne. In the year 1707, after many faithful Christians had been misled, the shrine at Châlons-sur-Marne was opened up and found to contain gravel.

As absurd as the cult of the holy navel of Jesus was the devotion paid to his holy tears, a cult exclusively promulgated in France. Jesus certainly did weep, if we are to believe the Gospels: over the fate of Jerusalem, and before raising Lazarus from the dead. If we are to believe legendary explanations of the source of his surviving holy tears, he also wept when he washed the disciples' feet.

Holy tears in France made their appearance in Saint-Maximin-la-Sainte-Baume, Provence; in the church of Saint-Léonard at Chemillé in Anjou; in the cathedral at Marseilles; in the abbey of Fontcarmont; in the church of Saint-Pierre-le-Puellier, Orleans; at Thiers in the Auvergne; in the abbey of Saint-Pierre at Sélincourt, Picardy; and in the church of the Holy Trinity, Vendôme. Sometimes the displayers of these tears claimed to know precisely when Jesus had shed them. Saint-Maximin-la-Sainte-Baume protested that its tear dropped as Jesus washed the feet of his disciples. Saint-Léonard at Chemillé claimed that a seigneur of Chemillé had accompanied Godfrey de Bouillon to Palestine and there obtained a tear shed by the Saviour at the death of Lazarus.

At Vendôme the holy tear had been brought, it was claimed, by Geoffrey Martel who had been fighting the Saracen under the banner of the Emperor Michael of Constantinople. Because of his tremendous feats of arms the Emperor would have given Geoffrey the hand of a princess of the blood plus many treasures. Martel modestly refused the princess but hesitated over the treasures. Suddenly a Greek leaned towards him and, whispering in his ear, held out a crystal (set with diamonds) with the words: 'Here is a treasure without price, a tear which Jesus himself shed on the tomb of Lazarus.' Geoffrey brought it back to France, along with an arm reputed to be St George's.

The church of the Holy Trinity, Vendôme, still boasts inscriptions and carvings depicting and describing the holy tear. The tear itself has gone. Yet in the middle ages it drew immense crowds of pilgrims. It is said to have continually trembled in its vase of crystal. Louis de Bourbon, prisoner of the English after the battle of Agincourt, is reputed on his release to have burned before the holy tear a candle weighing thirty-three pounds – one pound for each of the Saviour's years on earth. But, as with many relics, the tear was finally shed as a result of the French Revolution. In 1783 along with other relics from the church of the Holy Trinity, this tear was taken to the Hôtel des Monnaies, Orleans. Pious Christians managed to rescue it in 1803, and the tear eventually found its way into the hands of Cardinal Caprara, the papal legate. No-one heard of it from that moment on.

Not surprisingly, all these holy tears occasioned much controversy as to their authenticity, even among the clergy. Fr Honoré de Saint-Marie in the early eighteenth century desperately contended with the absurdity of these tears being totally confined to France by suggesting that they fell, not from the Saviour's actual eyes but from one of his effigies in the church of Saint-Pierre-le-Puellier, Orleans – thus accounting for one virtually incredible phenomenon by something even less likely. The more radical clergy suggested that the Benedictines of Vendôme had perhaps faked their holy tear and other churches, not to be outdone, had followed suit.

This development from secondary relics to physical ones, from the plausible (or at least possible) to the absurd, can be paralleled in cults devoted to the relics of Jesus's mother, the Blessed Virgin Mary. Many medieval Christians supposed her to have been bodily assumed into Heaven, without passing through death – a miracle which had the unfortunate consequence of taking her physical remains out of the reach of human hands. But her clothing was a different matter. So in the fifth century two patricians from Constantinople came upon what they convinced themselves was the robe of the Virgin, lying in a small village in Galilee. They decided to steal it, first begging the Virgin's consent (readily given in a dream), and take it to their native city. Soon Constantinople was claiming to own not only this robe but also the Virgin's shroud – otiose, presumably, in view of her bodily assumption to Heaven – and one of her many girdles. In addition the city boasted of possessing a relic once greatly cherished by the Virgin herself: her son's swaddling clothes.

And these last three relics were further enriched, so to speak, by the coagulated drops of milk that had fallen on them as the Virgin mother fed her divine son. Soon the Virgin's milk would spread as an infinitely precious relic throughout much of Christendom. Mme Nicole Hermann-Mascard has traced sixty-nine sanctuaries of the blessed milk, forty-six of them in France. Eton College, as might be expected, possessed no less than two drops of this milk. And in Norfolk the pilgrims' route to the great abbey at Walsingham was known as the Milky Way, after the phial containing drops of Our Lady's milk which were displayed there.

Walsingham Abbey was built round a small wooden chapel which, legend insisted, had been built under the auspices of the Virgin herself as a copy of the house she once lived in at Nazareth. But to see what purports to be the actual house itself, and not a copy (albeit one supervised by the Virgin), you must go to Loreto, a town in the Italian province of Ancona, on the Adriatic Sea. The Virgin's Nazareth birth-place did, in truth, take a long time to decide to make its final home there. After the aged Helena had commissioned a basilica over the house in Nazareth, countless Christians worshipped God there before this humble dwelling, until the Saracen invasions put a stop to the cult and ruined Helena's basilica.

At this point the legend becomes scarcely credible. The Virgin's birthplace, the house where she also is said to have been told by an angel that she would bear the son of God, no longer is in Nazareth, but was transplanted by the hands of angels to the Dalmatian coast, to a spot lying between Fiume and Tersato. Three years later, in 1294, the angels came again by night and moved the holy house to a wood near Recanati. From this wood (*lauretum*) or else from the name of the widow who owned it (*Laureta*) this unlikely secondary relic took its present name: 'the house of the glorious Virgin in Loreto'. And a year later the angels moved it again to its present site.

Now our earliest account of all this dates from around 1470, long after the events are deemed to have happened. Papal bulls were issued commending the shrine of Loreto in 1491 and 1507 – though the latter was understandably cautious about the miraculous translation of the relic, ascribing the story to 'pious belief' and 'popular report'. The inhabitants of the region displayed no such reticence and have assiduously promoted the cult of the holy house – with considerable success. Their efforts were rewarded in 1598 when Pope Sixtus V afforded Loreto the status of a town. At the end of the seventeenth century Pope Innocent XII appointed a mass with a special office, to be celebrated on December 10th, the feast of the translation of the holy house. Sixtus V's statue today towers over the entrance to the church of the Casa Santa, which the people of Loreto built around the holy house. Inside this magnificent, much decorated building is the simple brick home of Our Lady, 13½ feet high, 28 feet long and 12½ feet wide.

Impressive though I find the Casa Santa, I cannot bring myself to believe that the Blessed Virgin Mary once lived in it, or that it was miraculously transported, intact and undamaged, twice in the thirteenth century. Indeed, most of the relics connected with Jesus's mother easily give rise to scepticism. In the seventh century was discovered the stool on which she allegedly was sitting when the archangel announced her divine role as the mother of Jesus. Soon the credulous were treasuring a pitcher and bucket said to have been near her at the time. Men discovered a stone on which they believed she rested on her arduous journey to Bethlehem, where Jesus was born. In the late tenth century Pope Gregory V even found her wedding-ring.

None, however, ranks in absurdity with the cult of her son's holy foreskin. Properly one ought to say foreskins, for many communities claiming to possess this relic are scattered throughout the west. Charroux in the diocese of Poitiers insists that Charlemagne gave its abbey a holy prepuce. In the early twelfth century the monks of Charroux carried their most precious relic in triumph to Rome, exhibiting the foreskin (alongside a piece of the true cross and Jesus's sandals) before Pope Innocent III. Yet at that time another foreskin, also claiming to be Jesus's, was on show in the parish of Calcata, a medieval village in the province of Viterbo north of Rome. Another was displayed in the abbey of Coulombs in the diocese of Chartres. A fourth rested at Puy, a fifth at Metz, a sixth at

Anvers, a seventh at Hildesheim and an eighth holy foreskin in the church of Notre-Dame-en-Vaux, Châlons-sur-Marne.

Naturally enough, each religious foundation possessing such a relic disputed the authenticity of the others. Pope Innocent III refused to judge the issue, declaring that only God could know the truth about something so delicate. In consequence a spate of newly-discovered foreskins added to the number of such relics already exhibited in Christian churches. Santiago de Compostela obtained one. Another turned up in the abbey of Saint-Corneille at Compiègne. In 1527 one of the soldiers pillaging Rome spotted a sacred prepuce on show in St John in the Lateran. He stole the relic; and as he lay dying confessed to having buried it. Pope Clement VII ordered a search, and eventually one Magdalena de Strozzi discovered the relic. Her own hands stiffened as she tried to prise open its container. The relic gave off a beautiful odour (further convincing the onlookers that it was genuine). Finally a young girl of great sweetness and some nascent sanctity opened the container, and the relic was returned to the church.

The relic at Charroux similarly disappeared and was rediscovered. And whereas the church in the Lateran possessed so many other relics that the loss of the Saviour's foreskin could be considered a minor matter, the monks of Charroux were devastated by the loss. Their very name, deriving from *chair rouge* (red skin) glorified the precious relic. Pope Clement VII had granted indulgences to anyone who was present at the exposition of the piece of Christ's flesh. (Some say that a mistranslation of his bull granting this led to the claims of Charroux to possess the relic, since – it is argued – the Pope's scribe wrote *praeputiam*, instead of *praesepium*, i.e. cradle, referring to the infant Jesus's little bed, but I do not find this plausible. Why else call Charroux *chair rouge*?)

Then during the French Wars of Religion the protestant Huguenots captured Charroux. The relic disappeared. In the mid-nineteenth century it was a mere memory at Charroux. But in 1856 a workman discovered some reliquaries hidden in a wall. The diocesan bishop, Monsignor Pie, after a long and minute examination, declared that the holy foreskin of Jesus had at long last come to light again. The local Ursuline convent was given the honour of caring for it, until Monsignor Pie could persuade the Ministry of the Interior to build a new church worthy of the relic. In 1862 this was complete, and amid a huge crowd the relic was solemnly translated to its new home. Monsignor Pie preached a panegyric on it, during which he told the people that he had perceived on the relic of Charroux the same coagulated blood of Jesus that Pope Clement VII had mentioned in his bull long ago.

Of course some theologians doubted the very possibility of such a piece of Jesus remaining on earth. Was it not clear that at his resurrection Jesus ascended whole and perfect into Heaven? Fortunately for those who approved of the cult of these particular relics, the Spanish Jesuit theologian Francisco de Suarez countered this argument at the time of the Counter-Reformation. Surely, he declared, Jesus's risen body was capable of growing again any lost part. So the faithful were reassured.

In any case, these relics seemed well able to look after themselves, turning up again many centuries after being lost. They also gained much fame and favour by their success in protecting women in childbirth. The holy foreskin at Coulombs, near Nogent-le-Roi, was especially renowned for rendering the sterile fertile again. It also greatly protected the pregnant. In 1422 Henry V of England, who at that time also dominated part of France, persuaded the monks of Coulombs to lend him the relic, since his wife Catherine was about to bear their first child. Doubtless partly due to the power of the holy remains, she safely gave birth to the future King Henry VI. Since the Hundred Years' War was raging in France, Henry V returned the relic for safe-keeping not to Coulombs but to the Sainte-Chapelle in Paris. Only when times were safer did the relic return to its true home. And in April 1464 King Louis XI honoured the abbey by kneeling humbly before its exposed piece of the Saviour.

The relic at Coulombs escaped destruction at the time of the

French Revolution. The abbey became a parish church and the cult continued, though with less ostentation. When in 1860 the archaeological society of the *département* of Eure-et-Loire wished to examine the famous relic, they found it shut in a cupboard. In 1872 the parish priest took the relic, in its silver-gilt reliquary (which embodied an ivory cross dating from the twelfth century), into his presbytery. He would, we are told, put on his surplice and stole and then allow women to come to kiss the reliquary, praying and kneeling as they did so.

The practice has, I believe, been discontinued. Until very recently the only way of viewing one of the relics of Jesus's circumcision was to visit Calcata in Italy. Even here one did so in the face of official Catholic disapproval. On 3 August 1900 the Holy Office in Rome had threatened anyone writing or speaking of what the locals called the *carne vera santa* (real holy flesh) with excommunication. As the Vatican put it, such devotion to dubious relics of this kind encouraged 'irreverent curiosity'.

The devout of Viterbo paid little attention to this threat. In their folk-memory, the relic had been given by Charlemagne to Pope Leo III. Subsequently, in a tale suspiciously like that of the parallel relic at St John in the Lateran, the relic was rescued from the sack of Rome in 1527, along with a tooth of St Martha. (Once again a mature lady failed to open the relic's container, and a young girl managed to do so; and again the powerful, beautiful odour was exhumed.) Since that time the relic has done many favours in the impoverished village. So in spite of Vatican disapproval, the parish priest of Calcata, Dom Dario Magnoni, was still exposing the sacred *carne vera* on 1 January (the feast of the circumcision) until 1983.

After the closure of his old church (with its frescoes of the nativity and the circumcision of Jesus), Dom Dario Magnoni took charge of a new concrete church a mile away. He decided to keep the relic in the wardrobe of the bungalow that served as his presbytery. This was an error, for in 1983 thieves broke in and stole it. Heartbroken, the priest did not notify the police and avoided telling the laity of the loss. But as the feast of the circumcision approached, he was forced to make a public announcement: 'This year,' he declared, 'the holy relic will not be exposed to the devotion of the faithful. It has vanished. Sacrilegious thieves have taken it from my home.'

In Fr Magnoni's own view, the thieves probably wanted the reliquary – fashioned three hundred years ago in the form of two angels, holding a silver jewelled vase – rather than the relic. But many of the laity of Calcata claimed that the church authorities – including their bishop – disapproving of the veneration of the *carne vera*, had stolen their relic. Possibly under the influence of these authorities, the local police seemed reluctant to devote much energy to tracking down the thieves, observing merely that the relic was 'old, in bad condition and small'.

Certainly the authorities were obviously relieved that the embarrassing piece of skin had gone away. 'We would prefer not to have too much publicity about the affair,' said the local bishop, Monsignor Rosina. 'The church would actually prefer it if it were not discussed.' In spite of my own passion for relics, my sympathies here are with Monsignor Rosina. The holy navel, the *chair rouge*, holy tears, Virgin's milk and the like, in my view, bring into disrepute worthier relics, relics in whose authenticity even the sceptic might be constrained to believe.

In 1912 a French folklorist named Pierre Saintyves wrote a distinguished monograph drawing attention to some of the absurdities connected with such relics as the holy blood and the Benedictine speciality of collecting teeth said to have fallen from the mouth of Jesus when he was a child. Saintyves was not an atheist or an enemy of the church. On the contrary, he wished to rid the church of unnecessary and stupid excrescencies. As he observed, 'A beautiful woman who covers herself with false jewels throws them away once she finds they are no more than rubbishy bits of glass.'

6

Great British relics

Many of our greatest saints have been conscious that after death the power of their relics might be even greater. No doubt this partly accounts for the anxiety of a man so humble as St Francis lest thieves deem even his lowly body worth stealing. For similar reasons saints have sometimes left detailed instructions about what to do with their relics. Bishop Henry of Uppsala, for instance, now the patron saint of Finland, suspecting that he was about to be murdered, told his servants to place his corpse in a cart drawn by a couple of unbroken oxen. Wherever these beasts stopped, a cross was to be erected. But where they lay down, there his remains were to be placed in a church built on the spot.

Henry was murdered; his servants obeyed him; and thus was built the church of Nousis, where his relics remained till the year 1300, comforting many and performing countless miracles. In 1300 they were translated to a silver shrine in the cathedral at Äbo. It is touching to relate how these relics took care of themselves, since they are today lost. Henry's murderer had incidentally cut off the saint's thumb. Some time later an old blind man and his son were crossing a marsh when the boy noticed a raven pecking at some flesh on a floating lump of ice. The blind father urged him to row to the spot and drive off the bird. They found the bishop's thumb stuck in the ice, recognisable by its gold ring. Yet, sadly, Bishop Henry's relics later seem to have lost this art of self-protection. In 1720 his remains were taken from Äbo by the Russians and today they are nowhere to be found.

Like all the major saints whose relics fill this chapter, St Henry of Uppsala was born in Great Britain. Although naturally these include relics of which an Englishman is especially proud, my purpose in limiting myself to British bones is principally to show how nationality mattered little during the golden age of the relic. One relic alone, that of Henry of Uppsala, has already taken us to Sweden, Finland and Russia. Others will reach France, Ireland, Germany, Italy, even the New World. For where a saint was born was often of far less significance than where his relics would be enshrined. Relics belong to the universal church, not to any one country.

So St Boniface, the great eighth century missionary and martyr who was born at Crediton, lived as an English monk till the age of forty or so. Then in 718 he left Britain, never to return. Long after his death, his relics were venerated by countless pilgrims to the monastery he founded at Fulda in Germany. In his own lifetime he shrewdly understood the power – for good or ill – of a relic, so that when he found an opponent named Aldebert of Gaul handing out his own fingernails and hair to the faithful, Boniface persuaded Pope Zacherias to condemn the man as a magician. Then Boniface himself became a famous relic, enshrined in his own monastic foundation at Fulda. Yet, as the distinguished hagiographer Donald Attwater noted, although a contemporary Archbishop of Canterbury had hailed the saint as England's special patron, his own countrymen soon virtually forgot him.

To look closely in this chapter solely at British relics is not therefore chauvinism. Indeed, some British relics hardly redound to their country's credit. The cult of Little St Hugh of

Lincoln, for instance, reveals a disturbingly anti-Semitic medieval England. As Matthew Paris, monk of St Albans, tells the story, on 31 July 1255 a Jew named Joppin inveigled into his home the nine-year-old son of a widow, a boy named Hugh. There the child was imprisoned until Friday 27 August, when he was tortured, scourged, crowned with thorns and crucified. After the earth had, it is said, miraculously refused to cover St Hugh's corpse, the body was thrown down a well. Joppin was arrested, along with many other Jews, and confessed that it was a Jewish custom to crucify a Christian boy once a year. Henry III ordered Joppin to be killed by being dragged along after a young horse. Eighteen other Jews were hanged. The rest were ordered to pay large fines. And the corpse of Little St Hugh, having brought back the sight of a blind woman, was instantly transferred to a shrine in Lincoln cathedral: a symbol of race hatred for many years, the subject of an absurd and malicious legend, and a fomenter of future anti-Semitism.

Of course hatred of the Jews flourished elsewhere in medieval Europe. Between 1336 and 1339, for instance, hundreds of south-German Jewish communities were massacred by Christians. And as if the Jews were responsible for the Black Death itself, in 1349 the Christians of Nuremberg wiped out the Jewish community, building churches on the desecrated sites of synagogues. Soon these churches became centres of pilgrimage. Yet the relic of Little Hugh of Lincoln reminds us that for three hundred years in one of Britain's loveliest cathedrals was enshrined a corpse charged with an emotionally black current of racial hatred, capable of provoking Christians to immense cruelty.

But the relics of Britain are of particular interest also because of her peculiar Reformation. In the sixteenth century Britain swung sometimes violently between Catholicism and Protestantism, sometimes tolerant, sometimes not. In consequence, there was no lack of new martyrs and therefore a good number of new relics to be cherished by their co-religionists or abominated by their enemies. The bones of St Frideswide, patron saint of Oxford, entertainingly illustrate the passions of sixteenth-century England. Frideswide, probable foundress of a monastery at Oxford in the eighth century, which Augustinian canons refounded in the twelfth century, was translated to a fine shrine in the priory in 1180. At the Reformation the priory church became Oxford cathedral. The relics of the saintly foundress, unacceptable to the Protestants, were dug up, preparatory to burial in some unknown spot. This, however, was not sufficiently discourteous to her bones to satisfy an extreme Protestant named Calfhill, who in 1561 went so far as to mix together St Frideswide's relics and the bones of a nun who had renounced her orders and married a friar. He reburied in the cathedral the mixed bones, with the legend *Hic jacet religione cum superstitione* (Here lies religion with superstition); and there they lie today, the relics paradoxically saved for posterity by Protestant fanaticism.

But many other venerable British relics disappeared for ever at the Reformation. St Swithun, Bishop of Winchester in the mid-ninth century, entered popular mythology a century later when, apparently against his will, he was translated to the cathedral and in anger caused rain to fall for forty days. The notion that if it rains on St Swithun's day rain will continue to fall for forty more days is still strong. In 1093, in spite of his apparent irascibility, Swithun's relics were translated again and placed in an even costlier shrine. Swithun proved a great draw, raising money for rebuilding the cathedral, for restoring his own shrine after an accident in 1241, and healing many supplicants at his altar.

All this was anathema to the Protestant Reformers. Moreover King Henry VIII cast greedy eyes on the rich trappings of the saint's shrines and reliquaries. In 1538 the cult of St Swithun at Winchester was suppressed. The saint's relics were secretly buried. And though to the Reformers' chagrin the precious stones and the gold on his shrine were discovered to be fake, the silver on it was estimated at 2,000 marks.

Either, then, from deliberate dispersal or simply out of indifference, neglect and forgetfulness, some of the greatest British relics were lost for ever. Others, fascinatingly, were lost – sometimes for centuries – and then rediscovered as the British began to reappraise their own religious heritage and the passions of the Reformation waned. Not only did the British Catholics, once the days of persecution were over, reassert the cult of the British relic. Anglicans and sometimes even Calvinists discovered old bones and began to read afresh the legends of their owners. Though not always without controversy, the great British relics returned from their graves.

None did so more dramatically than St Magnus of Kirkwall. In 1114, the cousins Magnus and Haakon, both Earls of Orkney, met on the Island of Egilsey to make peace with each other. Instead there ensued what St Magnus's biographer John Mooney described as 'a tragedy that should send throughout the earldom, and far beyond, a thrill of horror which has not yet ceased to vibrate.'

As joint rulers of the Orkneys, the cousins had been at odds for many years. Now Magnus had arrived on Egilsey virtually alone, in order to come to terms with Haakon. By contrast Haakon brought heavily armed retainers. His cousin seemed to have some inkling that all was not well. After hearing Mass, the Earl, according to the *Shorter Saga of St Magnus*, went 'down to the shore to a certain hiding-place and there prayed to God'. Eventually Earl Haakon found his cousin on the beach and apprehended him. Magnus offered to give up his rights over the islcs. Hc would, he promised, make a pilgrimage either to Rome or Jerusalem 'and so make amends for both our souls. This I will swear also: never to come back to the Orkneys.' But Haakon refused to believe him. Magnus next begged, 'Let me be maimed in my limbs or let my eyes be plucked out, and set me thus in a dark dungeon from which I may never emerge.' Haakon weakened and seemed ready to agree to this savage punishment; but many of the chiefs with him demurred: someone, they argued, must die – either Haakon or Magnus – to bring peace to the islands. Haakon then sentenced Magnus to be slain.

Magnus fell to prayer, while Haakon tried – and failed – to persuade one of his henchmen to slay his cousin. Eventually the

Earl ordered his cook Lifolf to do the work. Magnus stood and faced the reluctant executioner, saying then, 'Stand before me and hew a great wound on my head; because it does not become a chief to have his head severed from his body as if he were a thief. Be strong, wretched man, for I have prayed God to forgive you.' Then Magnus signed himself with the sign of the cross, and Lifolf clove his skull asunder.

Magnus, as Herbert Thurston and Donald Attwater observed in their edition of *Butler's Lives of the Saints*, 'was regarded as a martyr, in spite of the fact that he was murdered on political rather than religious grounds'. In case anyone should doubt his sanctity at the time, his relics almost immediately performed numerous miracles, straightening the hump-backed, making cripples walk, illuminating their own grave with a heavenly light. The bones were buried first in the church of Christ at Binsey. Soon, records the *Shorter Saga*, 'people were travelling from Shetland and the Orkneys who were past cure; they watched at the tomb and were healed of their hurts.' Twenty-one years later the local bishop acceded to popular request and declared Magnus to be a saint. Early in 1136 the bishop, a great crowd of churchmen, and many rejoicing laity carried the relics to Kirkwall. Magnus was placed over the high altar of the old church, waiting for Earl Rognvald to build a new cathedral in his honour. As soon as the choir of this cathedral was ready, the saint's relics were carried there.

The bones were prized throughout Europe. The *Sagas* tell that portions of this renowned British relic reached Kirkjubø, Farø; and a cache of bones claiming to be from Magnus can still be seen in the unfinished church there. Other bits of the Scottish saint reached Aachen, and on St Magnus's day, 16 April 1372, Aachen sent part of his shoulder-blade to the King of Bohemia, who placed it in St Vitus's church, Prague. In 1298 part of the saint had reached Iceland, to be reverently enshrined in Skalholt cathedral.

Meanwhile the saint's relics did not rest at peace in Kirkwall. Rognvald had joined his to Magnus's after his own canonisation in 1192, and both corpses were in considerable danger from grave-robbers anxious to own a piece of such valuable relics. In the thirteenth century the cathedral authorities took the opportunity of continued building works to hide both bodies, somewhere in the apse, high up and out of reach.

Soon the hiding-places were forgotten. For nearly seven centuries no-one again saw the relics of St Magnus, though in 1314 on the eve of Bannockburn he appeared in a vision to Robert Bruce, promising him victory over the English.

In 1919 craftsmen and stonemasons were engaged in preserving and renovating the fabric of Kirkwall cathedral. They noticed that some of the ashlar on the large south pier of the choir was loose. Pushing his footrule through a crack in the ashlar facing, the clerk of works struck wood. Stones were removed, revealing a wooden case containing a skull, the bones of legs and arms, and some other smaller bones.

Under the direction of the provost and magistrates of Kirkwall cathedral Dr Robert Heddle officially examined the relics. By this time many discounted the record of the *Sagas of St Magnus*, with their apparently legendary account of his death by cleaving. Dr Heddle was therefore amazed to discover that these, clearly the relics of a man dead for many centuries, showed evidence of precisely such a blow. As Dr Robert Heddle reported:

> The skull showed a clean cut hole in the parietal bones which had evidently been done by a sharp instrument such as an axe; the hole showed a sharp perpendicular cut through both layers of the bone; the instrument had then turned and glanced backwards off the skull removing a piece of the outer layer of the bone.

Dr Heddle continued:

> The hole in the skull and the cut through the jaw still showed distinctly, even after the long time that has elapsed, showing that they have been done while the bones were in their living state.

Magnus is still in Kirkwall. Centuries after his horrific death a cool autopsy had confirmed the truth related in the supposedly legendary *Sagas* of a famed Scottish relic.

Grotesque dismemberment, subsequent loss and accidental rediscovery of a martyr's alleged bones have been the fate of many British relics. Magnus's bizarre death, gruesome though it was, was surpassed in horror by that of the English martyr Thomas Becket. The chronicler William Fitzstephen wrote that 'The holy archbishop received in all four strokes, all of them on the head; and the whole crown of the head was cut off. It could then be seen how his members were at the service of the Holy Spirit. Neither in mind, nor by raising or flinching his limbs, was he seen to struggle against death.' Then Becket's body was desecrated by one Hugh of Horse, surnamed Mauclerk, who, 'planting his foot on the neck of the holy martyr, as he lay dead, cut with his sword's point the blood and brain from the cavity of the severed crown.'

Horrific though this was, the manner of the saint's death did enable his body instantly to be divided into several relics, usefully displayed in various parts of the cathedral, and eventually elsewhere too. Immediately after the martyrdom, the terrified monks watched over the corpse all night, mopping up the blood that flowed from it. Later, mixed with water, this blood was conveniently multiplied, and a monk was given the special task of caring for this profitable legacy of the murdered archbishop.

Becket's clothing also provided secondary relics. Before his consecration as Archbishop of Canterbury the saint, as chancellor to King Henry II, had been noted for his sumptuous way of life. On the day before his consecration he had renounced gracious living and henceforth preached austerity. But the monks were unprepared for what they saw when they undressed his body for burial. Not only did they find him wearing drawers and a shirt both made of haircloth; Edward Grim, who had witnessed the martyrdom, records that the hairshirt was 'swarming with vermin'. The monks were filled with admiration for the dead prelate. 'So infected with worms' was the hairshirt, according to Grim, 'that anyone would judge the martyrdom of the previous day light in comparison to wearing it'. The monks, he added, 'burst forth in these words: "See, see how true a monk he was, and we knew it not".' Now that filthy hairshirt and those saintly drawers were deemed relics almost as precious as the saint's corpse itself. Soon other garments worn by Becket were treasured similarly; and from the point of view of the relic-hunter today, this is extremely fortunate, since as we shall see the whereabouts of the saint's corpse, so long treasured at Canterbury, is not readily ascertainable. You can, happily, see his pallium and pectoral cross in the public library of Douai in France. His chasuble, dalmatic, tunicle and green cope went to Aachen. The Eton College chapel inventory of 1465 listed 'a tablet of gold garnished, standing upon a foot with the escutcheon of arms of Warwick, containing therein of the brain of saint Thomas of Canterbury'; but that, alas, has disappeared.

Becket's body was (apart from such bits as were parcelled out elsewhere) cherished at Canterbury for four-and-a-half centuries, during which time his various shrines drew fully a quarter of the cathedral's total revenues. But Henry VIII, like his forebear Henry II deeply at odds with the papacy, would not tolerate the reverence afforded to the relics of a saint murdered for protecting ecclesiastical privileges from an over-weening monarch. On the king's orders, all the shrines at Canterbury were destroyed after the jewels and precious metals had been removed. The spoiled shrines were carried away in two great chests, each borne by six or seven strong men. The saint's relics, kept in separate places for so long, were brought together in an iron chest.

What then happened to them remains a fascinating, unsolved mystery. The bull of Pope Paul III, excommunicating Henry VIII on 17 December 1538, alleges that, 'the King had caused the said St Thomas, for the greater scorn of religion, to be summoned to trial and condemned for contumacy and declared a traitor.' The notion of a posthumous trial and condemnation of Thomas Becket is entrancing; but apart from the Pope's bull, there is little evidence that any such event took place. What

Nicholas Harpsfield (Catholic Archdeacon of Canterbury in the reign of Mary Tudor) says in his *Life of Sir Thomas More* is: 'Albeit we have of late (God illuminate our beetle blind hearts to see and repent our folly and impiety!) unshrined him and burned the holy martyr, and not only unshrined and unsainted him, but have made him also (after so many hundred years) a traitor to the king that honoured him.' There is no reference to any crazily vindictive show-trial of the centuries-old bones.

Holinshead's *Chronicles* corroborate Nicholas Harpsfield's statement that the relics were burned: 'the shrine of Thomas Becket in the priorie of Christ's Church was . . . taken to the king's use and his bones, scull and all, which was there found, with a peece broken out by the wound of his death, were all burnt in the same church by the lord Cromwell.'

But other equally respectable witnesses disagree, suggesting that the relics were not burned but simply buried. The Royal Injunctions of 1541 'cause the images and bones of such as they resorted and offered unto, with the ornaments of the same, and all such wrytings and monuments of feyned miracles, wherewith they were illuded, to be taken away.' The bones were by royal command given ordinary graves. Thus St Cuthbert was buried in the same place his shrine had occupied. St Swithun of Winchester was buried in a secret spot to put an end to superstitious rites connected with his bones, but buried he was. Why then should Becket's relics have been treated differently?

In 1888 the question was raised again by the exciting discovery of a coffin with a man's skeleton inside it, during excavation work on the Trinity Chapel of Canterbury Cathedral. At the head of the coffin was a boulder-like stone, hollowed as if to form a pillow and broken across the middle. The bones themselves were lying higgledy-piggledy, in an untidy heap, as if buried hastily. A piece from the left side of the skull was missing, and the skull itself was in two or three pieces, lying by itself on the stone pillow.

Now all the witnesses to Becket's martyrdom say that virtually the top of Becket's skull – not just a piece from the left side – was hacked off at his martyrdom. Yet speculation immediately began that the saint's long-lost relics had been found. The cathedral authorities had no record of that coffin, as if the man inside it had been buried not only hastily but secretly. The cathedral surveyor sent for the Bishop of Dover and the dean. The relics were carried off to the surveyor's house, where a doctor came and rearranged them into their proper shape.

The whole cathedral chapter was filled with excitement. Canon Holland's daughter Agnes made a pall of thin white sarsnet silk with a broad edge of lace at either end, to dress the new find decently. 'The bones look most curious and strange,' she commented, 'lying there all arranged, with the skull set up straight over a clay mould at the neck.' Agnes Holland clearly longed for the corpse to be Becket's. Not only had it been found in a broken coffin, shallowly buried 'in the crypt under the Trinity Chapel . . . exactly in the middle behind the Chapel of our Lady'. She also argued that although the corona of the skull was more or less intact, the notion that Becket's attacker sliced away the whole of it could well be no more than tradition, rather than fact. In any case, she reported, 'The fracture begins on the top and extends all down the left side, and it was on the left side and shoulder that the blow was struck.'

Others too were willing to believe that they had uncovered a long-lost, great English relic. One such was the cathedral's surveyor, Mr H. G. Austin. Another was an old man from Margate, who on 23 January 1888 brought his son to Canterbury cathedral. The boy's eyesight was failing and doctors had proved helpless. Miss Holland described how 'the gentleman made the boy kneel down and put his eyes close into the sockets of the skull, saying to him, "Now no doctors can heal you; you must pray for yourself".'

But others were sceptical. The seneschal of Canterbury Cathedral, Dr W. Brigstocke Shepherd (who was at daggers drawn with H. G. Austin) said, 'Piff paff; All rubbish,' and scouted the bare notion that these might be Becket's bones. His views prevailed, and on the orders of the Dean of Canterbury the bones were reburied in the eastern part of the cathedral crypt, the skull (as Agnes Holland observed) looking 'more frowning and terrible than ever'.

For the time being no more parents, anxious for the health and welfare of their children, can bring them to seek solace from the bones of Thomas Becket. Yet his relics continue to do us service, most recently by indirectly helping to find another long-lost and distinguished British relic. For in 1928 a sarcophagus made of stone was discovered in the courtyard of Douai College, France. During the reign of Elizabeth I of England Cardinal Allen had set up the college to train English priests, many of whom returned to Britain hoping to convert their native land away from Protestantism. Douai already possessed the pallium and cross of Becket. When the sarcophagus was found to contain a leaden shell, which in turn was found to be the coffin of a bandaged corpse; and when a hairshirt and some sacramental vessels were found next to the corpse, intense speculation arose that some seminary priest or priests might have brought back from England the relics of the murdered archbishop. Was *this* Becket?

But the Douai corpse turned out not to be Becket's but that of St John Southworth, martyred at Tyburn on 28 June 1654.

The relics of John Southworth have left France and are now in London. What is astonishing is that they are also virtually intact. John Southworth was born in Lancashire in the reign of Elizabeth I in one of the most dangerous eras for Roman Catholics in the history of Britain. The Pope had excommunicated Elizabeth. Catholicism had been officially dubbed as treason. Yet remote Lancashire remained a largely Catholic part of the country. John was sent to the English seminary in Douai around the age of twenty to study for the priesthood. He was ordained at Cambrai in 1619 and was sent to try to bring back his fellow-countrymen to the Catholic faith.

In the mid-1620s he spent some time in the safety of Belgium, but he was back in England in 1626. Soon he was arrested, interred in Lancaster gaol and condemned to death. But seventeenth-century England was a country half-tolerant, vacillating between persecuting Catholics and Nonconformists and turning a blind eye to their activities. For twenty years Southworth lived and worked on parole, so to speak. Moved to the London gaol known as the Clink, he was allowed to minister to fellow-Catholics during the plague years of the 1630s. His heroic labours in the noisome streets around Holborn and Westminster persuaded many who had renounced Catholicism once more to embrace the old faith. Southworth even made an appeal for money to relieve the wants of the poorest Catholics to whom he ministered. He raised 800 gold crowns. But every time he offered the last rites to one who had converted on his death-bed, John Southworth technically committed treason against the Protestant régime of Britain. He lived therefore on borrowed time. And when King Charles I, who had married a Catholic queen, provoked half his kingdom to rebel, Southworth's time ran out.

'Priest-catchers' found Southworth in his bed, in a small room in the midst of London's poor. Although the judge at his trial begged him to plead not guilty, Southworth refused to deny that he was a priest. So the sentence that dismembered his relics was ritually carried out. On the day of his execution he was dragged from Newgate prison to the gallows at Tyburn, where Marble Arch stands today. He was allowed to speak to the crowd for a moment, declaring, 'I plead not for myself, who am come to die, but for the poor distressed Catholics whom I leave behind me.' Then he was hanged. But before he was dead the rope was cut. His body was cut into quarters. And then, quite unusually for the time, it was saved and thus survives as a relic to our own day.

The Spanish ambassador bought the four quarters of John Southworth's body for the sum of forty shillings. He gave the relics to a surgeon named James Clarke, instructing him to sew the pieces together again and embalm the whole. Almost certainly Clarke cut off the martyr's hands and gave them (or sold them) to others, for they are missing today. Then the relics were taken to Douai.

Legend has it that John Southworth foresaw his fate. The president of the seminary, Fr George Leyburn, had forbidden the saint to return there during his lifetime, because he was such a fine missionary. 'Well Sir,' said the resigned martyr, 'if you will not let me go with you, at least I shall follow you.' So he did. He left behind a legend. The Italian ambassador to Britain (admittedly a man prone to exaggerate) found it 'incredible that the blood of a priest recently martyred' could have so 'fertilised the soil of the church and brought back very many heretics to the Catholic faith.' The Vatican allowed the fathers at Douai to expose the precious corpse as a holy relic. They reverently placed it under the altar of St Augustine in their seminary chapel.

A relic so venerable was obviously enormously at risk when the French Revolution broke out. The fathers at Douai in 1793 decided to try to preserve it. Taking up the refectory floor, they placed St John Southworth six feet underneath it and then filled in the hole. The community did not survive the Revolution. Their seminary was converted into a barracks and the old buildings replaced. The relics were effectively lost.

In 1863 an attempt to recover them failed, though it was later discovered that a metal rod probing the ground had actually penetrated both the sarcophagus and the lead coffin. Sixty-three years later the barracks were demolished and navvies began to build a road across the site. On 15 July 1928 the unlooked-for discovery was made. Apart from some decay caused by water seeping into the tomb, the martyr's relics (save for his hands) were beautifully preserved.

Once the body had been correctly identified, the French allowed it to return home – though not to Lancashire but to the Catholic convent at Ware. In 1930 the relics were triumphantly brought thence to London. For a time they rested in a convent set up by the Catholic church at Tyburn, before being transferred to the magnificent neo-Byzantine cathedral in Victoria Street, Westminster.

Leading those who dressed the relics in priestly vestments, before enclosing them in a glass feretory and carrying the saint to the chapel of St George on the north side of the cathedral, was Fr Derek Worlock, later Catholic Archbishop of Liverpool. He

St Edmund's head

A Suffolk bench-end shows the hound rescuing the head of St Edmund

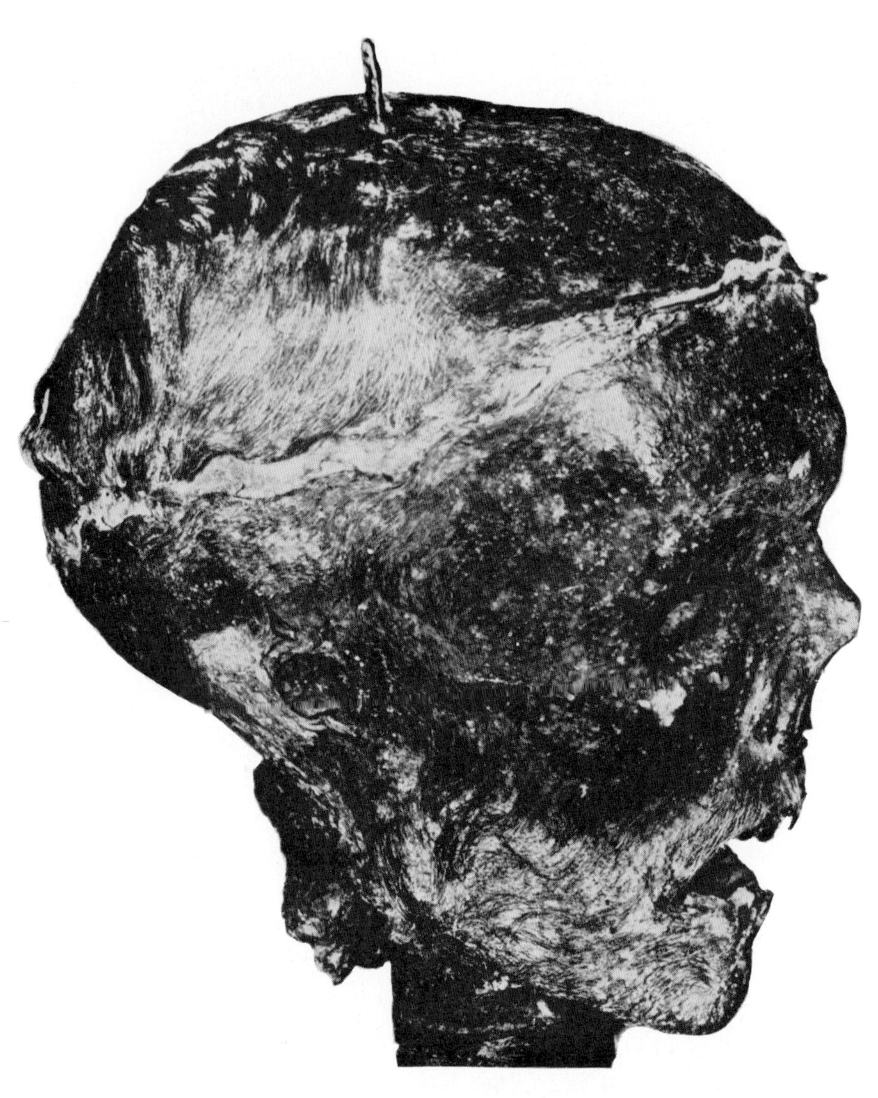

Cromwell's head
The head of Oliver Cromwell, still fixed to its pole

Jeremy Bentham
The corpse of Jeremy Bentham in University College, London

A ninth-century Irish reliquary
This reliquary, made in Ireland in the ninth century, was stolen by Vikings and is now in Copenhagen

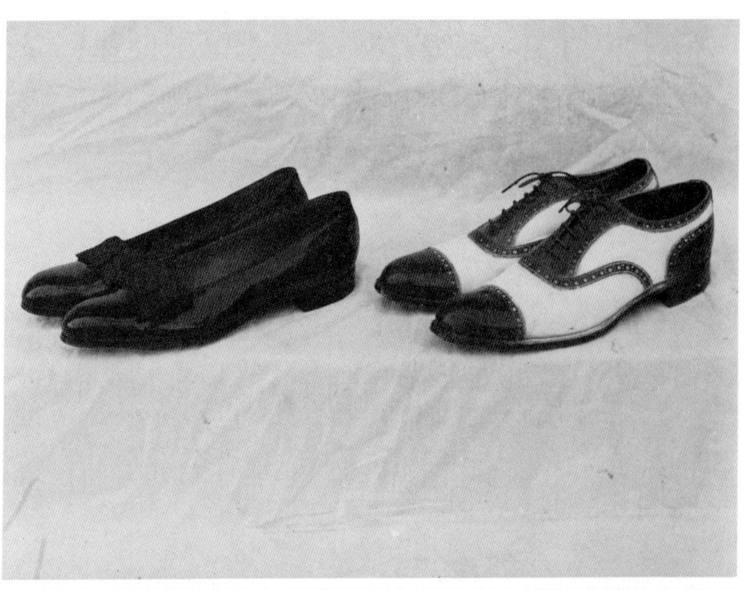

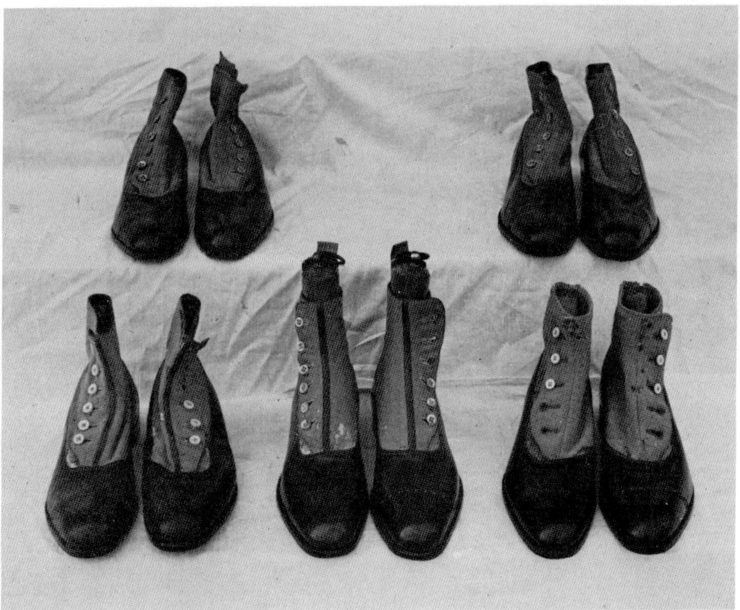

Mr Jinnah's shoes

Mr Jinnah's shoes: 'the best dressed gentleman in India'

The Sainte-Chapelle

The Sainte-Chapelle, built specially to house relics by Louis IX of France in the early thirteenth century

Three saints, depicted on a reliquary carrying their severed heads

St Maxim, St Lucian and St Julian, carrying their severed heads on a reliquary in the Cluny Museum

Riemenschneider's Holy Blood Altar
The limewood altar at Rothenburg ob der Tauber, carved by Tilman Riemenschneider to house the Holy Blood of Jesus

never forgot the experience. There was, he recalled over half a century later, 'nothing particularly hoodoo about it. Indeed,' remarked the archbishop, 'I hope John Southworth thinks kindly of the man who put him into priestly vestments, in a place of honour.'

This bringing together of Southworth's remains in one place strikingly contrasts with what has happened to the relics of his co-religionist St Oliver Plunket, who was also hanged, drawn and quartered at Tyburn. It is difficult to decide whether Plunket would have approved of being classed as a great British relic, since he was born in County Meath, Ireland, in 1625. But the present Republic of Ireland was governed by the British at that time. And the British certainly put Plunket to death.

It is hard not to find their action ridiculous, for Plunket was the gentlest of men and an ecumenist before his time, a great friend of the Protestant Archbishop of Armagh and a meditative Christian of singular piety. Pope Clement IX chose him to be Catholic Archbishop of Armagh and Primate of All Ireland in 1669. In 1681 he was sentenced to death for alleged complicity in the Popish plot. A contemporary pamphlet observed that he was killed because he sought 'to carry on his Hellish designs of Murther and Subversion, for having the *Pope's* Commission; he was owned as head of the Conspirators, and endeavoured to bring and establish Popery and arbitrary power; in order to which having levied vast Summs of moneys, treated with the French about landing an Army of 70,000 thousand men to joiyn with such papists as should be in readiness.'

The condemned Plunket was amazed at his own steadfastness. To a former secretary in Rome he wrote: 'Sentence of death was passed against me on the 15th without causing me any fear or depriving me of sleep for a quarter of an hour.' He added, 'I die most willingly.' And then in a passage of deep perplexity Plunket revealed his profound spirituality, by asking himself, 'How am I, a poor creature, so stout seeing that my Redeemer began to fear, to be weary and sad, and that drops of his blood ran down to the ground? I have considered that

Christ, by his fears and passion, merited for me to be without fear.'

Thus fortified, Plunket, accompanied by Edward Fitzharris, a Wexford spy and forger, was dragged for two miles from Newgate to Tyburn. There he was hanged, cut down before dead, disembowelled (his entrails cast into the fire while he watched) and beheaded, before being cut into four parts. And in Plunket's case the tradition of dismembering British relics continued after his death. His head had been cast on the fire, but was raked out only scorched and collected along with the rest of the corpse by one Elizabeth Sheldon. She had the king's permission to inter the remains of the martyr, and she put him into a large chest.

Before burying the various bits of Plunket, however, Elizabeth Sheldon engaged a Catholic surgeon named John Ridley to cut off his arms below the elbow. She put these in a long tin box, transferred the martyr's head to a round tin one, and kept them, burying only the rest of the corpse in the churchyard of St Giles.

The relics of Oliver Plunket were thus almost immediately after his death parted from each other. Eventually his scorched head reached Rome as a present to Cardinal Howard, and after his death it passed to the Dominican convent of Santa Sabina. It did not stay there long. In 1722 the niece of Archbishop Hugh MacMahon of Armagh, Catherine Plunket, founded a Dominican convent at Drogheda in Ireland. The Archbishop obtained Plunket's head as a present for the convent, and in Drogheda it lies to this day, mummified in a glass case, on display in the church of St Peter.

The rest of the martyr's bones lie elsewhere. His torso and legs rested in St Giles's churchyard no more than two years. Fr Corker, head of the English Benedictines, had them exhumed and sent abroad to the German abbey of St Adrian and St Denis at Lampspringe, near Hildesheim. But in the early nineteenth century the Prussian government expelled the monks and secularised the abbey. The holy torso and legs were placed in the churchyard outside. This deeply disturbed the British historian Cardinal Gasquet, and in 1883 he managed to get the relics translated to St Gregory's monastery, Downside, near Bath. However, a piece taken from the torso before it left Lampspringe eventually reached the Siena Convent in Drogheda, to be put on show there in 1921.

Plunket's relics were still not entirely exhausted. One of the lower arms was given in part to Sarnsfield Court, Herefordshire, and travelled thence to the Franciscan convent at Taunton. The upper part went to the English Benedictines in Paris, who lost it. The right arm was similarly divided. Archbishop John Brenan of Cushel took most of it, though part reached the Convent of the Dominicans at Cabra. They preserve it still. And not content with blessing the old world, this protean relic graces the new in the form of a piece of skull which reached Chicago, to be transferred to Boston in the 1950s.

Secondary relics following such a one might seem to be otiose; but so great has proved the desire of the devout for Plunket's remains that the Mayor of Wrexham even managed to buy the old oak door of his Newgate cell and give it to St Peter's, Drogheda, in 1951. The bishopric of Meath preserves Plunket's mass vestments. Lord Dunsany took his episcopal ring. And the relics still work wonders of healing. In April 1958 supplication before the relics of Plunket cured a Neapolitan lady, Signora Giovanna, Marchese of Martirigiano, of a rupture of the womb and what her doctor described as 'incurable necrotic inflammation of the bladder'. Pope Paul VI canonised the martyr in 1975.

The location of these relics is symbolically as well as historically significant. Oliver Plunket, a saint of the universal church as expressed through western Catholicism, is dispersed throughout much of the western Catholic world. St John Southworth by contrast, sewn together and enshrined in the senior Catholic cathedral of England, symbolises the determination of English Catholics to cherish and proclaim their own history (for many years one of persecution by Protestant England) as a source of identity and pride.

Relics never lie accidentally enshrined. Their tombs are

found in their several places because that is the way our history has run. So the patron saint of Sweden, St Anskar, lies in Bremen and not in the land he is supposed to protect; for Anskar symbolises the *failure* of Charlemagne's Christianity to overcome the paganism of the north. Anskar was tireless in promoting the Christian faith. He mitigated the evils of the Viking slave-trade, without succeeding in entirely abolishing it. His bodily mortifications matched those of Thomas Becket. Like St Alcuin, he embodied the educational zeal of the Carolingian empire. But his base was northern Germany, not Sweden; and to savour his relics you must visit St Peter's cathedral in the city whose first bishop he was and descend into the crypt where (as Nagel's guide quaintly puts it) 'are a number of centuries-old mummies'.

In Sweden relic-hunters find not the bones of her patron saint Anskar but those of the great British Christians who actually succeeded in establishing Christianity there. St Sigfrid died in extreme old age and is enshrined under the altar of the cathedral at Vaxjö. So successful was he that the German chronicler Adam of Bremen tried to claim him as a native of that city; but his name was one adopted by many Englishmen in the eleventh century when he flourished; and Adam's extreme nationalism is well-known to historians of the middle ages for leading him astray.

And this successful English missionary and Swedish relic astutely deployed relics himself during his life's work (though an English Bishop, John Wordsworth, in 1911, went so far as to deem this story 'a puerile extravagance'). Sigfrid, it is said, instructed his three nephews to carry on missionary work at Värend in his absence. The Swedes murdered them, cut off their heads and flung them in a lake, hiding the rest of their bodies in a wood under a huge heap of stones. A heavenly light shining down on these headless trunks forced the murderers to transfer them to a yet more secret spot. The heavenly light thenceforth transferred itself – hovering over the lake where the heads lay concealed. When St Sigfrid waded in and lifted out his nephews' heads, he was delighted to find them still incorrupt.

Clasping them to his breast, he asked whether the crime would be avenged. 'Yes,' replied the first head; 'When?' asked the second; 'In the third generation,' replied the third. And so it was.

However much that story has been embroidered in the telling and retelling, St Sigfrid obviously knew how to use the relics of his murdered allies to terrorise their murderers and terrify his enemies in general. A dead missionary, properly deployed, could be more useful than a living one.

In Finland too this proved to be the case. In the mid-twelfth century Nicholas Breakspear, the one Englishman to become Pope, consecrated his fellow-countryman Henry as Bishop of Uppsala. Henry worked with St Erik, King of Sweden, to conquer and convert the neighbouring Finns. Both were martyred, and Erik became co-patron of Sweden alongside St Anskar.

At Turku in Finland, Henry imposed a penance on a murderer who, rather than submit, murdered Henry as well. This was the making of him. Such a cult grew up around Henry's bones that soon the martyr was being hailed as the patron of Finland. The obscure English missionary became Finland's greatest relic.

To find the relics of Anskar (a monk of Corbie in Picardy and co-patron of Sweden) enshrined in Bremen; to find St Sigfrid's bones resting at Vaxjö; to contemplate St John Southworth, sewn up again and brought back to London, illuminates the continuing significance of a dead saint's remains. The relic's final home is a culmination of the saint's earthly mission. Thus some saintly relics may yet make the last leg of their journey to their ultimate shrines. In particular the divided relics of the English St Edmund appear ill-at-ease in their present homes, more than 1,000 years later.

Edmund was chosen King of the East Angles while still a boy. He grew to be a mighty opponent of the marauding Danes, but in 869 his army was defeated, and he was slain at Thetford in Norfolk. A continental scholar, Abbo of Fleury, who lived for some time at Ramsey Abbey and assiduously checked his sources, alleges that the Danes, infuriated because the captured king constantly called on Jesus for help, scourged Edmund, tied him to a tree and shot so many arrows into his body that he resembled 'a thistle covered with prickles'. Then they beheaded him. The Danes left his body where he was executed, but hid the head in brambles in Hellesdon wood. Their aim was to stop the king's friends decently burying his corpse, since it was incomplete. However, the dead king's followers heard a dog howling (unless it was the severed head crying for help) and found Edmund's head between the paws of a huge hound.

From that moment on we possess an almost continuous account of what happened to the martyred relics until our own century. (At only two points do the narratives seriously disturb the historian.) The dead king's relics were translated to a place known as Bedricesworth, after having lain for several years near Hellesdon in a make-shift chapel. Bedricesworth was soon to be known as Bury St Edmunds. There a devout woman is said to have pared the nails and cut the hair of the saint (which continued to grow long after his death), and these hung over his shrine until the Dissolution of the monasteries under King Henry VIII.

Again and again the relics protected their own protectors. When King Cnut's father, Sweyn Forkbeard, threatened to destroy the town unless the citizens paid a heavy ransom, he was struck down dead. In 1294 King Edward I, who had proposed to tax Bury St Edmunds, woke up screaming that 'Edmund was making another Sweyn of him'. The relics of the slaughtered king were making amends for his inability while alive to overcome his people's enemies. Even the Danes who slew him came off worst in the end. In what he called an 'Essay in Necrobiography' on the body of St Edmund, Norman Scarfe described him after death as 'one of the most effective symbols of English resistance to the invader ever recorded . . . King Alfred and the West Countrymen were able to hold the Danes and bring them to terms, and to Christianity.' Edmund's prodigious medieval fame, Sharpe conjectured, both inspired and also derived its own strength from the revival of English

Christianity and English patriotism, against the renewed incursions of raiding Northmen.

Naturally few could resist having a closer look at such powerful relics from time to time. But the unworthy could suffer for doing so. A young magnate insisted on having the coffin opened and the moment he saw King Edmund went out of his mind.

Others took care to placate this potentially dangerous relic. Edward the Confessor gave much land to enrich the saint's shrine. When the Vikings savagely attacked England between 1010 and 1013, the guardians of Edmund's corpse anxiously moved him to St Paul's churchyard, London. King Cnut, however, mindful of his father's untimely demise, decided the best way to cope with the relic was to endow for it a great monastic church at Bury St Edmunds, to be staffed by a community of Benedictine monks.

At this point the chroniclers record one of the two curious features of the long history of this relic which disturb the historian. Edmund by all accounts met his death by beheading. But when in the mid-eleventh century Abbot Leofstan of Bury St Edmunds, stung by a woman's complaint that the shrine of Edmund was covered with cobwebs, decided to inspect the whole body, he found the trunk and head miraculously joined together again. Leofstan was amazed. He told a young monk named Turstan to take hold of the relic's feet. Leofstan seized the head. Both pulled and pulled. Instead of the martyr's head and body coming apart, Abbot Leofstan had a stroke.

Whatever one makes of this miraculous joining up of a severed head and a dead trunk, it is something of a relief to learn that the relic as we know it today is once again beheaded.

In spite of Abbot Leofstan's stroke, the monks of Bury St Edmunds remained willing to uncover Edmund's relics from time to time – though always circumspectly. In 1198 an examination became a necessity. The guardian of the shrine fell asleep at his vigil, his candle tumbled over and the whole area around the shrine was set alight. Many supposed that the head of St Edmund might at the very least have been singed. Abbot

Samson decided he must inspect the sacred corpse. Along with his sacrist, physician and twelve strong monks, he opened the coffin. Silk and linen wrappings were removed, till Samson saw the outline of the body and dared proceed no further with undressing it. He touched the saint's eyes, nose, breast, arms, fingers and toes.

Eighteen years later occurred the second difficult episode in the history of this relic. In 1216 the French prince Louis le Lion was at the head of English rebellious barons. His principal ally, the Earl of Winchester, along with other opponents of King John, offered Louis the English crown. Unfortunately for this plan, the Earl was defeated at the battle of Lincoln the following year. Retreating to London, he passed through the village of Sempringham, from whose monastery he stole the body of the recently canonised Gilbert of Sempringham. Then, as a contemporary French chronicle records, Louis sent soldiers to contest the country around Bury St Edmuds.

The body of St Gilbert of Sempringham was never seen in England again – even though he was the only Englishman to found a religious order throughout the entire middle ages. What is more curious, neither was the relic of St Edmund ever seen again in his native land. Two years later Louis le Lion was besieging the city of Toulouse. Soon the surviving lists of relics belonging to St Sernin's basilica in that city were claiming possession not only of the relics of St Gilbert of Sempringham but also ('in the top container' of the cupboards of the deambulatory) of 'St Edmund, once King of England'.

Historians pause for two reasons: one, there is no evidence that the marauders sent by Louis le Lion did necessarily steal or buy the corpse of St Edmund from Bury St Edmunds. And secondly, the monks of that foundation never admitted that they had lost their most famous relic. They carried on the cult of the saint as if he were still there, till his shrine (and body?) were destroyed at the dissolution of the monasteries in 1539.

Yet no-one ever recounts seeing the body at Bury St Edmunds again. Between 1217 and 1539 a corpse once so frequently examined disappears from view. The strong presumption remains that with the connivance of a handful of monks, it had left the monastery in 1217, never to return. And because of this, the great relic survived the Reformation.

By the mid-fourteenth century or so, Edmund had been designated one of the eight protectors of the city of Toulouse. In the late sixteenth century his image was painted on one of the great hexagonal columns of the basilica, with the legend 'S. EADMUNDUS REX ANGLAE'. The canons of St Sernin celebrated his Mass each year on 20 November. And in 1631 they successfully begged his holy bones to drive away the plague that was ravaging their city. So great was the city's gratitude that the Archbishop and other dignitaries solemnly opened Edmund's sarcophagus to verify the relics, count the teeth and generally see that all was in order. They found the skeleton lacking only one small bone; the lower jaw with its seven teeth detached from the skull; the rest of the skull in good order, save for three loose teeth in the upper jaw. To honour the English saint who had done such a signal service to the city, his trunk was now placed in a silver monumental reliquary over a new St Edmund's altar in the lower crypt. The skull was placed in another silver reliquary in one of the cupboards in the deambulatory.

As St Edmund survived the English Reformation (by not being there), he also survived the French Revolution. For a time his relics lay in the private home of the Comtesse de Comminges. They returned to the basilica in 1802.

In 1901, for the first time since men had found the saint's skull between the paws of a dog, the two parts of this sacred relic left each other's company. Herbert Vaughan, Roman Catholic Archbishop of Westminster, had begun building a magnificent neo-Byzantine cathedral in London, the same magnificent building that now houses the body of St John Southworth. Vaughan wrote to the Archbishop of Toulouse asking if he would send back the body of St Edmund, to be placed in the high altar of his new cathedral. But St Edmund was now a protector of Toulouse. Archbishop Germain refused.

Vaughan went over his head. He appealed to Pope Leo XIII, who forced Archbishop Germain to hand over Edmund's skeleton. Germain sent it to the Pope, who sent it on to Vaughan. St Edmund's skull remained in Toulouse. But the English prelate was not after all to get his own way. Learning of the news, a number of English historians set to work casting doubt on the authenticity of the relic. Vaughan took fright. Instead of transferring St Edmund's skeleton to his new cathedral, he left the relic in the care of the Duke of Norfolk, in the private chapel of Arundel Castle, where it remains to this day.

'Relics are unfashionable,' wrote Fr Bryan Houghton, Catholic priest of St Edmund's parish, Bury St Edmunds, in 1970. 'Nevertheless,' he added, 'it somehow seems improper that the mortal remains of a saintly king and patron of England should lie discredited in a private chapel.' Fr Houghton's view was that the bones should rest properly in the (Anglican) cathedral at Bury St Edmunds, a former parish church which, ambitiously extended by Mr Stephen Dykes Bower, has been described as 'an unsurpassed example of modern Gothic, superbly executed and showing, as no other building today can, how an ornate church in this part of the country must have appeared in about 1400.'

I agree with Fr Houghton. The Catholic Archbishop of Westminster has waived his right to St Edmund's remains. If Toulouse still needs protection, the skull alone of such a martyr will more than suffice. The rest of St Edmund's relics should come home.

But these are perilous waters. Throughout Christian centuries the ownership of relics has been vehemently disputed. In 701, for instance, St Bonet, Bishop of Clermont, died away from home in Lyons. There the nuns of St Peter's convent were encouraged to hold onto his corpse by numerous miracles. Only after a long struggle did these ladies accede to the demands of Bonet's see and return his relics to Clermont. Even then they kept part of his head. Again, eight-and-a-half centuries later, the marquise of Miolans gave three thorns from Jesus's crown of thorns to the Augustinian church of St Peter in Albi. Her heirs and the monks fought angrily over the ownership of these godly relics of the Passion. The dispute was resolved only in

1625, when Pope Urban VII ordered the Bishop of Grenoble to take possession of one of the three thorns and gave it to the marquise's heirs.

Similar quarrels have occurred over the disposal of the remains of British saints. For example, after the death of St Patrick, the Englishman who converted Ireland to Christianity, a contest arose between Saul and Armagh over the ownership of his body. The relics were placed on a cart, to which were yoked two untrained bullocks. They wandered where they wished, until they stopped: where they stopped, the saint was buried; and the church of Downpatrick now stands at the spot.

The twentieth century has not escaped such disputes. In 1931 Mr John Wilson Claridge, excavating the ruins of Shaftesbury Abbey, discovered the bones of Edward the martyr, Saxon king of England. Edward had been made king in 976 at the age of seventeen. His step-mother, from the start of his reign, determined to kill the young king. In 979 he was hunting near her Castle of Corfe. The queen invited him to take a cup of wine, and then ordered a servant to stab Edward in the back. He tried to mount his horse, but slipped, and was dragged to his death with one foot jammed in the stirrup. He was buried, notes the *Anglo-Saxon Chronicle* 'without any kind of royal honours'. Soon Edward's relics were translated to Shaftesbury Abbey and by the year 1001 were highly honoured in a shrine in the sanctuary. At the Reformation his remains were reburied and lost until Wilson Claridge's recent excavations. When Claridge moved to Malta, he stowed the relics in a bank vault in Woking. In 1984, having failed to persuade either the Church of England or the English Roman Catholics to take over the bones, he offered them to members of the Russian Orthodox Church who worshipped in a converted Anglican church at Brookwood, Surrey. The Orthodox built a shrine for the relics at a cost of £50,000. Only at this point did John Wilson Claridge's eighty-one-year-old brother, Colonel Geoffrey Claridge, intervene, as Shaftesbury Abbey had belonged to their mother, and Colonel Geoffrey claimed joint ownership of the relics, under the terms of their mother's will. The case reached the high court. The

Orthodox Christians held a four-hour service on 16 September 1984 in honour of the relics, but because of the dispute they were obliged to return them to the bank vault immediately afterwards. Naturally enough, the matter found space in the correspondence columns of *The Times*. 'Whatever the case, one hopes that the bones will be returned to Shaftesbury, and not end up in a Russian Orthodox Church in Exile,' wrote Dr S. D. Keynes from Trinity College, Cambridge. 'No Saxon can have deserved that fate.' The Revd Howard Weston-Smart of Sussex disagreed. Edward was martyred, buried, translated, venerated and canonised well before the Great Schism sadly occurred in 1054, he pointed out, and is consequently a saint of the Universal Church, 'as much Orthodox (even if Russian and in exile) as Catholic and Anglican'. Mr Weston-Smart added that the Russian Orthodox community in Woking had provided 'a lovely reliquary, shrine and church to house the relics'. He concluded that 'No Saxon king deserves better than this, surrounded by undoubting love, honour and veneration.'

Even so, the relics remain in the bank, and the dispute runs on. Edward is one of only three canonised English kings. One thousand years after he was murdered, his relics are still the cause of strife.

7

Relics survive the Reformation

The coolest, wittiest and indeed most courteous opponent of relics at the Reformation was undoubtedly John Calvin. In his native France Calvin had come across so many abuses, so many absurdities, so many palpably false claims connected with the cult that he concluded in his treatise on relics that there was more perversity and idolatry among Christians of his own age than ever was known even amongst unbelievers or the ancient Jews. In fact, Calvin argued, God had revealed precisely to those Jews the evil of doing any sort of obeisance before dead men's bones, for 'was not the body of Moses concealed by God's will in such a manner that it never has been or can be discovered?' He went on to ask why this revered body should have been removed from human sight and why (as the New Testament letter of Jude appeared to argue) the devil wanted it given back to us, answering, 'It is generally admitted that God wished to put away from his people of Israel all temptation to commit idolatry, and that Satan desired to bring back the body to introduce temptation amongst them.'

Calvin then turned his considerable powers of irony on some

choice contemporary manifestations of the cult. He had heard that some treasured what they deemed 'a piece of broiled fish which Peter gave to Jesus on the sea shore'. That fish, observed Calvin, 'must have been thoroughly spiced to have been preserved for so long.' He then went on to ask whether anyone could seriously suppose that an apostle would have made a relic of part of Jesus's intended supper. Calvin had come across shirts of the Virgin Mary at Chartres and at Aachen. He also knew of her amazing ability to produce milk, commenting that 'had the Virgin been a wet-nurse for all of her life, she could not have produced more milk than you can see in various parts of the land'.

Next Calvin considered the great number of pieces of John the Baptist allegedly dispersed throughout western Christendom: his face at Amiens, the top of his head at Rhodes, the back of his head at Nemours, his brains at Nogent-le-Retrou, part of his jaw at Besançon, the other part at St John in the Lateran, and a bit of his ear at Saint-Flour-en-Auvergne. Noting that the relics of St Sebastian were reputed to be a remedy against the plague, he conceded that it was useful that the corpse appeared to have quadrupled itself. 'St Giles,' he wrote, 'has a body at Toulouse and a second one in the town bearing his name in the Languedoc.' St Denis's corpse seemed to be not only in France but also in Regensburg. Mary Magdalen's had turned up both at Auxerre and at Saint-Maximin in Provence. He knew of three complete relics of St Lazarus: at Autun, Marseilles and Avalon. How could these things be?

Calvin claimed to know intimately only Germany, Spain, Italy and France when it came to relics. He warned his readers to remember 'that all the relics of Christ and the apostles displayed in the west are also to be seen in Greece, Asia and all the other countries where Christian churches are in existence.'

Calvin's translator, Count Kosinski, notes that the great Reformer had forgotten about the four bodies and several more heads attributed to St James the Great. *A propos* of the multiplication of St John Baptist's head, Kosinski added a pleasing story of an English lady visiting the château of Prince Grassalkovich in Hungary, where the parish priest showed her and other strangers round the museum. Amongst other curiosities, the priest revealed two skulls, one large, one small, saying of the first, 'This is the skull of the celebrated rebel Rayotzi,' and of the second, 'This is the skull of the same Rayotzi when he was a boy.'

John Calvin's wit was subtler than Kosinski's. When he came to enumerate the many relics of St Peter spread around the churches of the west, Calvin noted he had two sets of slippers, one pair made of satin embroidered with gold. The Reformer caustically suggested that St Peter had been smartened up after death 'as compensation for the poverty he had suffered during his lifetime'. Calvin also disposed of the soldier supposedly converted after piercing the side of the crucified Jesus: 'he has been canonised under the name of St Longinus, and after having thus been baptised, has been bestowed with two bodies, one now at Mantua, the other at Notre-Dame-de-l'Isle at Lyons.'

As to the many phials of holy blood, Calvin simply appealed to reason: how could any of it have been found after a lapse of seven or eight hundred years? Jesus's manger and swaddling clothes, the altar on which he was placed when presented in the Temple of Jerusalem, these to Calvin were equally totally unlikely to have survived, for after fifty or so years from the death of Jesus, Jerusalem itself and presumably everything in that city was destroyed. The water-pots in which Jesus created wine likewise could never have survived up to a thousand years before being rediscovered, along with some of that very wine, now to be seen at Orleans.

Calvin also set about demolishing the status of some relics by superior scholarship. Those who claimed to have the table on which Jesus and his disciples took their last supper together failed to realise that tables at the time of Jesus were of a totally different shape from the ones they now boasted of, and that in any case the last supper was eaten lying on cushions.

So Calvin continued, methodically considering the four lances that claimed to have pierced Jesus's side, the multiplication of the true cross, the countless nails, the pieces of silver with which Judas betrayed his Lord, and so on. John Calvin's treatise classically presents what many a later polemicist borrowed. What makes Calvin by far the best of them is the continual crackling of his wit, transforming tedious lists into such comments as his suggestion that the crown of thorns must have been replanted after use, so as to produce the increase visible by his own time.

Calvin perceived that a curious kind of bad faith operated when men and women of his time came to look at relics. Instead of using their brains or even their eyes, people preferred to bow down reverently and blindly. Should they look clearly, they would spot a good many fakes. The head of Mary Magdalen at Marseilles had been furnished with waxen eyes. At Geneva an arm, said to be St Anthony's, was worshipped uncritically until it fell out of its shrine and was found to be the bone of a stag. In the same city St Peter's brain was displayed on the high altar of one church, until the profane discovered it to be in truth a lump of pumice-stone. All these supposed relics, Calvin asserted, 'were inventions for deceiving silly folk – or (as some monks and priests confessed) *pious frauds* or *honest deceits* to stimulate the devotion of the people'. But such piety was worthless.

Historical veracity gave the lie to many supposed relics. If the cup said to have been used by Jesus at the Last Supper and captured by Baldwin II of Jerusalem in 1101 was genuine, then Christians must revise their accepted notions of the worldly splendour of that meal. As for the dish on which the paschal lamb was brought to his table, since three were to be found in the west – at Rome, at Genoa and at Arles – were we to conclude that instead of using clean plates for different courses the disciples actually changed the dishes for the *same* food? How many towels did Jesus really need to wash his disciples' feet: the one at Rome, that at Aachen, and the one displayed at Saint-Corneille-de-Compiègne (and bearing still the imprint of Judas's dirty foot)?

Calvin naturally enough made great play with the supposed fragments of the true cross scattered about the Christian world in the sixteenth century. 'If, as the Gospel testifies, this cross could be carried by one man, how glaring is the audacity which now pretends to display more relics than three hundred men could bear!' He added: 'if we were to collect together all the pieces of the true cross exhibited throughout Christendom, they would form a whole ship's cargo.' The multiplicity of nails from the cross; the four spears that finally proved Jesus dead, instead of the single one mentioned in the Gospels; these excited Calvin's scorn almost as much as the tail of the donkey that carried Jesus into Jerusalem (exhibited at Genoa) and the donkey's whole skeleton (preserved at Vicenza). 'One cannot really tell which is the more wonderful,' commented the Protestant Reformer, 'the folly and credulity of those who devoutly receive such mockeries, or the boldness of those who put them forth.'

Evidently enough, John Calvin's reason in opposing the cult of relics was informed by a special passion. It derived from the powerful memory of what he had perceived as a young boy in his own parish church. There, as he remembered, the faithful Christians whom he loved and later wished to save from error, had been grievously led astray. 'On the festival day of St Stephen,' he recalled, 'the images of the tyrants who stoned him (for they are thus called by the common people) were adorned as much as that of the saint himself. Many women, seeing these tyrants thus decked out, mistook them for the saint's companions and offered candles in homage to each of them.' Calvin reasonably enough thought that this kind of error was inevitably encouraged by the cult of relics, 'for there is such confusion amongst them that it is quite impossible to worship the bones of a martyr without danger of rendering such reverence by mistake to the bones of some brigand or thief, or even those of a horse, a dog or a donkey.'

Calvin did not, however, conclude from this that the chief problem was one of authenticity: identify your relic correctly and then all will be well. On the contrary, he still opposed the reverence shown to what might well be a genuine relic of a saint. 'It is equally impossible to adore the ring, the coat or the girdle of the Virgin Mary without the risk of adoring instead objects that have belonged, perhaps, to some scandalous person.' The very possibility of error outweighed in Calvin's view the merit of kneeling before a true relic.

Here the driving force in Calvin's opposition to relics was the theology of the Reformation itself. Nothing, he held, should detract from the twin pillars of the Christian faith: the *Bible* and the *Sacraments* of Holy Communion and Holy Baptism. Relics did precisely that. 'Instead of discerning Jesus in his Word, his Sacraments and his spiritual graces,' declared Calvin, 'the world, in its usual fashion, has amused itself with his clothes, shirts or sheets.' The 'spiritual graces' which Calvin spoke of were those impulses to holiness and the good life essential to Christianity. The cult of relics, he believed, tended to make men and women forget about them – in the hope that one might attain Heaven without any change for the better in one's daily behaviour. The cult, 'instead of persuading us to observe the lives of the apostles, martyrs and other saints in order to imitate their examples, directs all its attention to the preservation and admiration of their bones, shifts, sashes, caps and other similar trash.' Honour that ought to be reserved for Jesus alone was given to such material survivals. Calvin conceded with some generosity that St Helena having discovered what she supposed to be the true cross, 'did not worship the wood but the Lord who was suspended on it'. Her virtue here, however, was in his view 'a very rare phenomenon'. Most people, he said, 'not only turn from God, in order to play with vain and corruptible things; they even go so far as to commit the sacrilege of worshipping such dead and insensible creatures, instead of the one living God.' Often they seem to display genuine devotion and zeal. In fact, 'the desire for relics is never without superstition, and what is more, usually is the parent of idolatry.' And thus, worshipping idols, they neglect the true holiness, which comes from God alone.

John Calvin was not the first to have attacked the cult of relics in these ways. As early as 1120 a French Benedictine abbot, Guibert of Nogent, wrote a celebrated treatise attacking the claim by the monks of Saint-Médard at Soissons that they possessed Jesus's tooth. Yet his scepticism was far more qualified than that of the Protestant Reformer, for he held that so long as we can be certain that the relic is genuine and that the person from whom it came had led a saintly life, then 'we ought to honour and reverence it, imitating the saint's own example and obtaining his or her protection'.

Guibert was scandalised that the people of Constantinople and the monks of Saint-Jean-d'Angély both could claim to possess the Baptist's head. 'What could be more stupid,' he asked, 'than to say this great saint had two heads?' Yet Guibert still supposed that, once one had decided which was authentic, to revere the relic was entirely praiseworthy. Indeed, he devised a sophisticated defence of those who mistakenly worshipped before the bones of one saint, supposing that the relics really belonged to another. 'Some people maintain it is pernicious to honour one relic thinking it is another or one saint under the wrong name, but I believe it is not,' Guibert wrote. The reason was that the Bible maintained that all the saints, collectively, constitute Christ's body, i.e. his church. 'Did not Jesus say of the saints that they shall be one even as I and my Father are one, and that all the saints together, with Christ as the head, are one body?'* Clearly, a case of mistaken identity was a trivial matter.

So Guibert of Nogent pulled his punches. He even at one point admitted holding back when he ought to have attacked the cult. Once a noted church sent round a group of collectors, carrying relics to raise cash. One of them, in Guibert's presence, claimed to have a piece of bread which Jesus had actually chewed; he even dared to ask Guibert to agree that the relic was genuine. And the embarrassed abbot records that he shrank from declaring the relic to be a fraud.

Guibert's objections to relics often seem to be more aesthetic than rational or theological. He detested the notion of digging up a corpse and carrying it elsewhere. But he found that the devotions of the faithful were too well-established for him to

* The second point is St Paul's, not Jesus's.

make any major assault on the whole cult. In Britain too Archbishop Lanfranc found himself similarly defeated by the strength of the relic cult. In 1077 he decided not to translate the bones of the old relics of Canterbury at the dedication of his rebuilt cathedral. Instead he ordered a procession of the consecrated bread and wine of the Eucharist. As Dr Michael Clanchy puts it, 'Christ himself was to be the cult and treasure of the church and not some local bones.' But Anglo-Saxon attitudes proved too strong for Lanfranc's idealism to prevail, as he himself tacitly acknowledged when he founded St Gregory's at Canterbury ten years later. This was, writes Dr Clanchy, a good example 'of a house of canons being contaminated almost as soon as it started'. Lanfranc simply could not afford to pay for the running costs of his new foundation without transferring to the canons the miracle-working corpse of St Mildred, whose cult brought in much ready cash. 'The dedication of the church to Pope Gregory the Great, "patron of us and of all England" (as Lanfranc called him in the foundation charter), was too idealistic for the average churchgoer and so Lanfranc . . . also provided the more immediate attractions of the relics of St Mildred and two other Anglo-Saxon ladies, Sts Eadburga and Ethelburga.'

Slowly however, the attack on relics grew in intensity. Wycliff in the fourteenth and Jan Huss in the early fifteenth century both attacked the cult as superstitious. Both were condemned as heretics. So was Martin Luther; but he and his view survived condemnation.

Luther's attack on relics was even braver, initially, than that of his fellow-Reformer, Calvin, for Luther's patron, the Elector Frederick, was extremely proud of his own stupendous collection of holy remains. Built up around a thorn from Christ's crown (which, it was maintained, had certainly pierced Jesus's head), the collection had been illustrated in a catalogue drawn by Lucas Cranach in 1509. At that time Frederick possessed altogether 5,005 bits of saints or articles of their clothing and other secondary relics. The Popes by now had come to assign indulgences to the reverence for certain bones, indulgences which reduced the number of days the worshipper would have to spend in purgatory. Frederick's 5,005 relics carried indulgences reducing purgatory by no fewer than 1,443 years. He continued to collect. By 1520 his castle at Wittenberg housed the astonishing number of 19,013 saintly remains, calculated by now to reduce purgatory by 1,902,202 years, 270 days. Yet Luther presumed to attack the cult, provoking (as he himself noted) much displeasure from his protector.

The Elector Frederick became partly reconciled to Luther's preaching because the Pope himself was sending collectors into Germany carrying rival relics. But in addition the mood of the people seemed to be turning against the whole cult. When some of the Elector's relics were paraded in the streets on All Saints' day, 1522, many people booed. There was no such procession in 1523. In some parts of western Christendom, relics were at last out of favour. Luther's invective was powerful. 'What lies there are about relics!' he said. 'One man claims to possess a feather from the wings of the angel Gabriel, and the Bishop of Mainz has a flame from Moses's burning bush. And how does it come to pass that eighteen apostles are buried in Germany when Christ chose only twelve?' Yet men had preached equally powerfully against such absurdities in the past. Now, as western Christendom divided itself into rival camps, relics were seen as buttressing the secular power of the papacy. Those who opposed that power, also opposed relics. Luther, Calvin and their lesser followers found ready supporters.

One such, after his own peculiar fashion, was King Henry VIII of England. If Henry's marital problems bulked large in his eventual detestation of the papacy, his greed (and the greed of his supporters) helped him to set about destroying the shrines of holy remains. Henry's inordinate need for treasure shines through his instructions for the destruction of English relics and their shrines. At Chichester, for instance, commissioners were in 1538 appointed to take down the shrine of St Richard, whose relics had lain there since 1253. The king began by noting that these long-dead bones promoted superstition and 'a certain kind of idolatry'. He pointed out that 'men of simplicity, by the instigation of certain of the clergy, who take advantage of the same, do seek at the said shrine and bones of the same, that [which] God only hath authority and power to grant.' So Henry VIII commissioned Sir William Goring and William Ernely, Esquire, to do away with St Richard's bones. And in addition they were to make sure that 'all the silver, gold, jewels, and ornaments to the same shrine belonging; and also all other the reliques and reliquaries of the said cathedral church . . . with all the plate, gold, jewels, ornaments, aforesaid,' were 'safely and surely conveyed and brought unto our Tower of London, there to be bestowed as we shall further determine at your arrival.'

As a result, in the words of the royal commission, St Richard's noble shrine and his holy bones were 'rased and defaced even to the very ground'. Similarly at Henry VIII's command the 'shrine and superstitious relicks' of St Hugh of Lincoln were dismantled, and everything valuable connected with them – jewels, plate, copes, etc. – put in the care of the king's master of jewels.

The finest shrine in northern England was that of St Cuthbert in Durham cathedral. Here the saint's bones were happily preserved; but not without a gruesome series of events, recorded by a near contemporary chronicler. After the king's emissaries had taken away the precious stones ornamenting Cuthbert's shrine (including one 'of value sufficient to redeem a Prince') they came nearer his sacred body. Thinking it to be no more than dust and bones after so many years, they broke open the chest in which it was sealed, and there found the saint, 'lying whole, uncorrupt, with his face bare, and his beard as it had been a fortnight's growth, and all his vestments upon him'. Unfortunately the smith who had broken open the tomb also had broken one of Cuthbert's legs. 'He was very sorry for it,' recorded the chronicler, 'and did cry, "Alas, I have broken one of his legs".' At this a certain Dr Henley ordered the workman to throw down the bones – a task that proved unexpectedly difficult. The smith replied that 'he could not get it in sunder, for the sinews and the skin held it [together].'

Even such great evidence of sanctity did not suffice to persuade the emissaries of Henry VIII to risk the king's displeasure by reburying St Cuthbert without royal permission. Eventually Henry agreed that the relics should neither be burned nor buried secretly. So then, 'upon notice of the King's pleasure therein, the prior and the monks buried him, in the ground, under the same place, under a fair marble stone, which remains to this day, where his Shrine was exalted.'

That took place in 1542. Instead of lying in the richly gilt alabaster and marble shrine which Lord Neville of Raby had built in 1372 at a cost of £200, St Cuthbert's bones for the next two hundred and eigthy-five years lay under a decent but plain blue marble slab. During those years they decayed. On 17 May 1827 the Durham cathedral authorities decided to look at St Cuthbert again. The blue marble slab was removed. About eighteen inches of soil lay under it, beneath which was a large pit, dry, with stone walls. At the bottom was a greatly decayed oak coffin. Inside this unprepossessing tomb was another coffin, with a good number of bones thrown at one end: doubtless the many relics that had over centuries been gathered around the revered bones of Cuthbert himself. The workmen of 1827 removed these remains in order to discover a third coffin, partly decorated with carved symbols and saints. Inside was Cuthbert's corpse, along with an ivory comb, a wooden portable altar (covered in silver) and a linen bag which once would have held consecrated bread. The saint was by now a skeleton. On the skeleton's breast was the great pectoral cross – gold, cloisonné work, with a garnet at the centre, buried with Cuthbert in 687. Today it can be seen in the library of the dean and chapter at Durham, along with the saint's vestments and the remaining fragments of his coffin. Cuthbert's bones were again laid to rest.

But the curiosity of the deans and chapters of English cathedrals can be insatiable. In 1899, to the great distress of the gentle Bishop Brooke Foss Westcott of Durham, Cuthbert was again exhumed. A noted anatomist declared that the skeleton must have belonged to a muscular man of the saint's build and general physical condition. He also observed that the left shin-bone was missing – no doubt after being broken by the smith in 1542. Finally, the skeleton was once more entombed underneath its blue marble slab.

Cuthbert's relics were among the few that survived the assaults of the Reformation in Britain. Bishop John Latimer attacked the holy blood at Hailes because, he alleged, many superstitiously flocked there hoping 'that the sight of it with their bodily eye' would certify that they lived a clean life and were 'in a state of salvation without spot of sin'. Protestant reformers felt more was needed for the attainment of a state of grace. On 24 November 1538 Bishop John Hilsey of Rochester took the phial of blood to St Paul's Cross in London and there displayed it to the crowd, declaring that it was in fact 'honey clarified and coloured with saffron, as has evidently been proved before the King and his Council.' The centuries-old relic, which Richard Earl of Cromwell had presented to Hailes Abbey in 1270, was destroyed.

Great collections of relics, such as that of Eton College, were broken up and seen no more. Even where the success of the Reformation was limited, the attacks of men of the calibre of John Calvin helped to sort out false from genuine relics, getting rid of the absurder examples of the cult. So in 1707 the Bishop of Châlons put a stop to the veneration of the holy navel of Jesus in Notre-Dame-en-Vaux.

In the *Decameron* Boccaccio had mocked a friar who claimed to have seen a finger of the Holy Spirit ('as whole and sound as ever'), 'a few rays of the star which had appeared to the Magi' and 'also a phial of the sweat of St Michael when he fought with the devil'. Chaucer too had made fun of his pardoner who carried a fragment of the sail of the ship that carried St Paul. The sources of such harmless merriment were passing away. The French *philosophes* of the eighteenth century were judiciously circumspect in their mockery of relics, but both Voltaire in his *Dictionnaire philosophique* and the Chevalier de Jeumont in the *Encyclopédie* cited the earlier attacks of theologians with obvious relish.

In Britain the scepticism of Gibbon was less kindly expressed. He ridiculed the 'salted and pickled' heads of infamous malefactors who had been transformed as relics into gods. 'Without much regard for truth or probability,' according to Gibbon, the clergy had 'invented names for skeletons, and actions for names'. In this way 'myriads of imaginary heroes, who had never existed, except in the fancy of crafty or credulous legendaries,' were added to the invincible band of genuine and primitive martyrs. Gibbon deplored what he took to be the consequence of all this: that 'the sublime and simple theology of the primitive Christians was gradually corrupted; and the MONARCHY of heaven . . . was degraded by the introduction of a popular mythology, which tended to restore the reign of polytheism.'

Edward Gibbon wrote as a lapsed Catholic; but the derision he reserved for the relics venerated by his former fellow-Christians was as nothing compared with the virulent attack mounted by the French revolutionaries. And yet relics fought back, and by the 1850s many French cults had been revived. Jean-Baptiste Marie Vianney, the famous curé of Ars, even fostered in the mid-century the cult of a newly discovered *non-existent* saint, that of Philomena. Fifty years earlier three tiles had been excavated in the catacomb of St Priscilla near Rome, bearing the inscription:

LUMENA
PAX TE
CUM FI.

Rearranged these letters could be made to read 'Peace to you Philomena' (PAX TECUM FILUMENA). Nearby was discovered an ampulla containing what was looked on as Philomena's blood. When this supposed blood was translated to Mugnano in 1805, so many miracles occurred that Philomena was popularly deemed a saint. Fifty years later Pope Pius IX even granted the non-existent holy woman her own proper office and mass. Her fame spread enormously. Nuns at their profession took her name. Only in the mid-twentieth century did the Vatican decide that she had never lived.

Rationalistic or bored priests have never been popular with the faithful, and many such were forced to continue the cult of relics against their will. At Maizey in the Meuse, central France, the people were accustomed to an entertaining May festival when the supposed relics of St Nicholas were carried through the streets, followed by a mass in the saint's special country chapel. In 1889 the parish priest sought to cut down on the ceremony. The men of his congregation forced him to change his mind.

Many countries of course remained virtually unmoved by the turmoils of the Reformation, the scepticism of the eighteenth century Enlightenment or the occasional fanaticisms of the French Revolution. In Bavaria, for instance, the people of Oberammergau, home of the famous passion play, began to build in 1736 a beautiful new rococo parish church. Visiting the church today one is startled to see on the right-hand side, behind what I believe to be a transparent plastic screen, a full skeleton, grey, but glamorously attired, holding a golden palm in one skeletal claw, his skull visible through a white veil. The relic is St Amandus (one of several saints with this name), a gift to Oberammergau from a villager named Amadeus Eyrl who had settled in Rome as a Dominican brother. On 3 November 1760 he discovered that a fellow-Oberammergauer, Jakob Nodel, was setting off home. Nodel carried the corpse of St Amandus on his back over the Bavarian Alps. *En route* he collapsed and died. Another Oberammergauer, Melchior Faistenmantel, agreed next to transport the perilous relic; and two years later it reached Oberammergau, a symbol of Bavarian piety untouched by the Reformation.

Even where the Reformation had been successful, Catholicism remained a spiritual force that continued to foster relics. In Wales the Jesuits in the nineteenth century built a theological college, and dedicated it to St Beuno. The poet Gerard Manley Hopkins spent three years studying there before his ordination in 1877. Six miles from the college springs the holy well of St

Beuno's niece Winifred. In 1874 Hopkins and a friend walked over the hills and bathed at the holy well, returning, as he put it, very joyously. 'The sight of the water in the well as clear as glass, greenish like beryl or aquamarine, trembling at the surface with the force of the springs, and shaping out the five foils of the well quite drew and held my eyes to it,' he noted. And Hopkins was as ready as any medieval Christian to give credence to reports of the miraculous properties of St Winifred's well. 'Within a month or six weeks from this (I think Fr di Pietro said) a young man from Liverpool, Arthur Kent, was cured of rupture in the water. The strong unfailing flow of the water and the chain of cures from year to year all these centuries took hold of my mind with wonder at the bounty of God in one of His saints,' he continued, 'the sensible thing so naturally and gracefully uttering the spiritual reason of its being (which is all in true keeping with the story of St Winifred's death and recovery) and the spring in place leading back the thoughts by its spring in time to its spring in eternity: even now the stress and buoyancy and abundance of the water is before my eyes.'

Hopkins's prose, like his poetry, was usually convoluted: yet here he finely expresses the essential nature of a relic – 'the sensible thing . . . naturally and gracefully uttering the spiritual reason of its being'. So great was the impression on him made by this secondary relic that he determined to write a play, in poetry, about the saint and her holy well. He failed to complete the difficult project; but the song of the maidens in Hopkins's fragmentary *St Winefrid's Well*, which he called 'The Leaden Echo and the Golden Echo', is a superb expression of the way mortal transient beauty can express and even become immortal beauty; just as a mortal, even hideous, relic expresses immortal life.

A hundred years later Pope John Paul II visited Scotland, once fanatically ruled by John Knox, the disciple of Calvin. To St Mary's Catholic Cathedral, Edinburgh, the Pope gave one of the shoulder-blades of St Andrew, Scotland's patron saint. (You can see the relic displayed in a side chapel in a huge marble altar – though little guards the bone: only an upturned glass on a gold stand, decorated with the cross X of St Andrew.)

Catholic relics made their dignified return to every land of the Reformation. What is more remarkable is that the notion of relics themselves never forsook those lands, even during their most secular eras. In England relics continued to haunt the imaginations of her newly- (perhaps barely-) reformed clergymen, especially the poets among them. Since these clergymen had been granted the right to marry and thus take sexual cognizance of women, some boldly went so far as to connect the cult of relics with their newly-legitimised love-lives. John Donne, the Jacobean Dean of St Paul's cathedral, wrote a love-song specifically called 'The Relique':

> . . . Then, he that digges us up, will bring
> Us, to the Bishop, and the King,
> To make us Reliques; then
> Thou shalt be a Mary Magdalen, and I
> A something else thereby;
> All women shall adore us, and some men; . . .

Robert Herrick, vicar of Dean Prior, Devonshire from 1630 to 1647, was similarly circumspect. Herrick never married, though he wrote fine love-lyrics, one of which again takes hold of the imagery of the relic to suggest immortality for a mortal lover's bones:

> For my embalming, *Julia*, do but this,
> Give thou my lips but their supremest kiss:
> Or else trans-fuse thy breath into the chest,
> Where my small reliques must for ever rest:
> That breath the *Balm*, the *myrrh*, the *Nard* shal be,
> To give an *incorruption* unto me.

Without losing its power, the relic, loosed from its Catholic and Orthodox roots, was slowly becoming secularised. Mid-seventeenth-century Britain was convulsed by a Revolution in which Oliver Cromwell emerged victorious and King Charles I was defeated. Charles was beheaded; Cromwell died and was buried in state. Yet their corpses continued to exercise a bizarre fascination. Both relics still possessed a dangerous power.

After Charles's execution in 1649 his friends desired to bury him in Westminster Abbey. The request was refused because (as Anthony Wood observed in his *Athenae Oxoniensis*) '*his burying there would attract infinite numbers of all sorts thither, to see where the king was buried; which, as the times then were, was judged unsafe and inconvenient.*' So the corpse was instead placed in St George's chapel, Windsor. Anthony Wood gives the merest hint that some sign or natural wonder accompanied the transportation of such a noble relic to its grave: 'It was observed that at such time as the King's Body was brought out from S. *George's* Hall, the Sky was serene and clear, but presently it began to snow, and the Snow fell so fast, that by the time the Corps came to the west end of the Royal Chappel, the black Velvet Pall was all white (the colour of Innocency) being thick covered over with Snow.'

In former times saintly innocence was frequently attested by a holy person's relics remaining incorrupt in the grave. Innocent or not, this to some extent happened to the corpse of Charles I. In 1813 his coffin was opened up. The royal head lay separated from the rest of the body by a clear cut through the fourth cervical vertebra. Charles's hair had retained its noted beautiful dark-brown hue, his beard redder than the rest. But it was a mistake to expose the relic to the air. The king's one remaining eye lasted only a few moments before dissolving away before the eyes of the witnesses.

If the relics of Charles I were treated with reverence by his devoted followers, the bones of Cromewll were soon to be grievously dishonoured. Cromwell died, still Lord Protector of England, Scotland, Ireland and Wales, on 3 September 1658. At his autopsy, the embalmed brain was found to weigh 2,126 grammes – though men noted that it was 'overcharged' with fluid. Death masks were taken, some of which show a bandage binding the severed skull cap to the rest of the skull, after the brain had been removed. Filled with sweet herbs, placed in a lead coffin enclosed by a wooden one, the corpse was carried in state for burial in Westminster Abbey, while wax effigies of the dead ruler were put on show to impress the people.

In 1660 the monarchy was restored. Some of Cromwell's effigies were burnt with contumely. One was hanged. But the worst treatment was reserved for his corpse, along with those of the men who had voted for the execution of Charles I. The House of Commons ordered that their corpses should be exhumed, dragged on sledges to Tyburn, hanged and there buried under the gallows. Cromwell's body was taken there in a green cere-cloth. The other three regicides were buried after the symbolic hanging, but Cromwell's relics suffered the further indignity of having the head cut off. The task took six blows. Then the Lord Protector's head was placed on a pole and attached to the roof of Westminster Hall.

Cromwell's chaplain, Peter Sterry, had once unwisely confessed to having dreamed that his Lord was going to Heaven. Since the ale-house opposite Westminster Hall was blasphemously called 'Heaven', Samuel Butler was able to make a rude rhyme observing that Sterry:

> . . . in a false erroneous dream
> Mistook the new Jerusalem
> Profanely for the apocryphal
> False heaven at the end o' th' Hall,
> Whither, it was decreed by Fate,
> His precious reliques to translate.

For over twenty years Cromwell's grisly head remained on Westminster Hall, before workmen (or, some say, the wind) cast it down. The Russell family retrieved the relic, which in 1773 passed to Samuel Russell, a seedy, disreputable actor, Samuel ran a museum near Long Acre, London, and Cromwell's head became its prized exhibit, guarded by its owner when he was not performing (usually more drunk than sober) at nearby Covent Garden.

Yet more indignities were in store for the relic. Around 1814 Josiah Henry Wilkinson bought it from the Russells for £230. Wilkinson would take the head to parties. In 1822 Maria Edgeworth was present at one held in the London home of Mr Ricardo. A letter she wrote on 9 March records Wilkinson's preposterous behaviour with the relic. 'Mr Wilkinson its present possessor doats on it,' she wrote, '– a frightful skull it is – covered with its parched yellow skin like any other mummy and with its chestnut hair, eyebrows and beard in glorious preservation – The head is still fastened to a pole. Mr and Mrs Ricardo and the family by turns held the head opposite the window while we stood in the window, while the happy possessor lectured on it compasses in hand.'

Maria Edgeworth's letter describing the grotesque scene remains important evidence for the authenticity of this famous secular relic. 'The nose is flattened as it should be when the body was laid on its face to have the head chopped off,' she noted. 'There is a cut of the axe (as it should be) in the wrong place where the bungling executioner gave it before he could get it off – One ear has been torn off as it should be.' Finally she referred to the wart over Cromwell's left eye, which appears in the famous portrait by Sir Peter Lely of 1653: 'To complete Mr Wilkinson's felicity there is the mark of a famous wart of Oliver's.'

Fortunately perhaps, the bones of Oliver Cromwell no longer suffer such indignities. Eventually the head passed into the possession of Cromwell's old college, Sidney Sussex. Now Cambridge had little to thank Cromwell for, and Sidney Sussex perhaps less, since Cromwell had imprisoned its royalist master and melted down the college silver to pay for his fight against Charles I. The college named nothing after its most famous alumnus until it built 'Cromwell Court' in King Street in the 1980s. Nonetheless the authorities decided to give the skull a decent burial in the ante-chapel.

Even now the awesome symbolism of Cromwell's skull was to give the college pause for thought. The dead Englishman's most heinous crime had undoubtedly been the massacre of Irish

Catholics at Drogheda on 11 September 1649. A week later Cromwell's army butchered up to 2,000 Irish Catholics at Wexford. Memories still festered. Would Irishmen and women, even now, attempt to dishonour Cromwell's battered relic in revenge for the crimes of three centuries ago? It was decided to bury the skull secretly, in the ante-chapel as had been decided, though without identifying the precise spot. Today a plaque there reads: 'Near to this place was buried on 25 March 1960 the head of Oliver Cromwell, Lord Protector of the Commonwealth of England, Scotland and Ireland, Fellow Commoner of this College 1616–7.'

The passions roused by Cromwell's relics and to a lesser extent by those of King Charles I speak to us of an age of religious upheaval still smarting from the conflicts of the Reformation. In spite of the fears expressed by the fellows of Sidney Sussex College in 1960, such passions have happily abated. But men and women still fall in love. They continue to win and then lose the objects of their desire. And losing them, they covet relics of their *grands amours*.

When one of Agatha Christie's biographers was searching the detective-novelist's papers, she came across mementoes from the marriage of Agatha's parents, Frederick and Clara, including a pathetic envelope put together by Clara, containing strands of his hair, beech leaves from the cemetery in which he lies, and 'A Piece of the Soap He had Last Used'.

One who collected such relics with more than usual profligacy was the poet Byron. Byron had in his short life more lovers than most men aspire to. But as Henry Crabbe Robinson heard Wordsworth say, insanity was in Byron's family and Byron himself was 'somewhat cracked'. Francis Jeffrey went so far as to assert in the *Edinburgh Review* that Byron's writings tended to destroy all belief in the reality of virtue 'by the constant exhibitions of the most profligate heartlessness'. Today in the offices of Byron's publisher in London are a number of envelopes in which the poet placed quantities of differently coloured very curly hair, beside the names of his girl friends. Such behaviour, no doubt, helped to provoke Lady Caroline

Lamb's celebrated observation that the poet was 'Mad – bad – and dangerous to know.'

To collect such relics (rarely in quite so bizarre a fashion as did Byron) is to fulfil an age-old longing for security and an everlasting quality in love: in effect, to use the solid and the physical to give a permanent quality to the evanescent and insubstantial. Such functions in a lover's relics are akin to the role of a saint's earthly remains in pointing to the permanence of Heaven. Intimations of immortality are longed for even when men and women have ceased to believe in God.

Not surprisingly, then, we find secular relics still asserting a powerful sway over human imaginations both in the age of the Enlightenment and in Revolutionary France. Two remarkable devotees of relics were Jeremy Bentham and the chaplain of the exiled Napoleon Bonaparte.

Bentham, philosopher of the Enlightenment who was born in 1748, defined the ultimate good not in terms of some eternal moral principle but simply as the greatest happiness of the greatest number. Earlier philosophers, such as the atheist David Hume, had hinted at this, but Bentham sketched out the theory in its entirety. For his system, morality needed no Godhead as its source. Yet in 1832, at the very end of his life, Bentham was seriously considering the uses of relics. Ten years after his death was published his *Auto-Icon*, subtitled *Further Uses of the Dead to the Living*.

The body, Bentham noted, was already valuable to others in allowing medical, surgical and anatomical experiment after death. The dead thus gave life to the living. Bentham, musing in his last months on earth, proposed that further 'enjoyment' and 'instruction' for the living would be drived from *preserving* instead of disposing of corpses. In addition, this habit would save money. Corpses, said Bentham, 'levy on us needless contributions: undertaker, lawyer, priest – all join in the depredation'. He added that 'in the case of the poor, often are the savings of a family thrown into the grave'. Already many people had seen the value of the principles 'every man his own broker' and 'every man his own lawyer'. So now, Bentham argued 'may *every man* be *his own statue*'. Instead of being buried, we should become our own 'Auto-Icons' after death.

'Ridiculed it will be, of course,' conceded Bentham. So he pointed to some instances where the bodies of the dead already proved useful to the living. In 1831 the relics of the murderer Corder were placed inside a recess of the museum attached to Suffolk Infirmary, Bury St Edmunds, in a glass case below which was a box for donations on behalf of patients in need. By an ingenious spring the arm of the skeleton pointed towards the box as soon as a visitor approached. Receipts were said to average £50 a year. The relic obviously was far more valuable to society than the living man. Bentham also noted a report in the *Morning Chronicle* of 16 July 1831, which told of a man who kept his wife's corpse in a little room under a stable, since a near relation had left her an annuity of £30 a year '*as long as she remained upon earth*'.

These were mere foretastes of the true Auto-Icon as Bentham conceived it. Upon coming of age, he had left his own body for dissection after death. Now he suggested that the softer, corruptible bits of a man or woman's relics might so be used while the hard parts became Auto-Icons. No longer would one need stone or marble monuments in churches or graveyards. 'If at the common expense poor and rich were Iconised,' declared the great Utilitarian, 'the beautiful commandment of Jesus would be obeyed: they would indeed "meet together", – they would be placed on the same level.' Bentham's fancy played on whole-length Auto-Icons and Auto-Icons of the head alone. 'In one case many generations might be deposited on a few shelves, in a moderate-sized cupboard: in the other case an apartment of considerable size would be necessary.' The philosopher envisaged exhibitions of Auto-Icons in churches and cathedrals, with accompanying oratories and other items of sacred music (even though he was careful to insist that religion really had nothing to do with this sort of relic: 'Free as air does religion leave the disposal of the dead.').

'For many years the subject has been a favourite one at my own table,' Bentham wrote. No-one, presumably, pointed out that the sculptors he intended to put out of business gained many of their sublimest effects from distorting the lineaments of those they portrayed. Bentham enthused over the continued joy given by such relics if they could remain members of clubs they once belonged to. He particularly enthused over his own such survival. 'When Bentham has ceased to live (in memory he will never cease to live!) whom shall the Bentham Club have for its chairman? Whom but Bentham himself? On him will all eyes be turned – to him will all speeches be addressed.' Indeed he suggested that the early nineteenth-century equivalents of today's Society of Authors might make their own collections of writers' Auto-Icons. And a country gentleman could alternate the Auto-Icons of his family with the trees leading to his dwelling: 'Copal varnish would protect the face from the effects of rain – caoutchouc the habiliments.'

In death Jeremy Bentham proved his own point. His relics were dissected. Today his skeleton, clothed in his usual attire, is kept in University College, London.

Napoleon intended no such secular relics after his own untimely death. He left in his will 100,000 francs to his chaplain and confessor, Père Vignali. For Vignali this was apparently not enough. He snipped away some of Napoleon's beard and body hair, as well as bits of skin, generously dividing some of these with his friends. At Napoleon's autopsy what is generally described as a 'mummified tendon' was removed from the Emperor's body. Vignali took this too, as well as one of the death masks made by Napoleon's doctor Antommarchi.

Eventually the American firm Maggs Brothers bought these relics from Vignali's descendants by relation. They sold them to Dr Rosenbach, the New York bookseller, along with letters and documents confirming the authenticity of the 'mummified tendon'. On 30 October 1969, two hundred years after the birth of Napoleon, the relics were put on offer at Christie's in London. Alas, there they failed to reach their reserve price. Christie's hoped for up to £30,000. Bidding started at £10. After £14,000 the only bidder left was another American bookseller, Mr Brian Gimelson of Forth Washington, Pennsylvania, who was particularly interested in relics of Napoleon because his own wife was called Josephine. (*The Times* of 30 October 1969 carried a photograph of Josephine Gimelson holding a pair of the Emperor's breeches.) Earlier that year Christie's had successfully disposed of the dead Emperor's hat. And at the Hôtel Rameau in Versailles on 15 June had been sold by auction some more of Napoleon's hair, his spectacles, straw from his coffin and a willow tree that had been planted near his tomb.

Relics in the west obviously no longer needed an element of the other-worldly to enhance their potency. Oddly enough, this had always been the case in the east with the relics of Buddhism. Nichiren Buddhism in particular has been (and is today) an essentially this-worldly religion. Yet this fact has not hindered the cult of relics in Buddhist history.

Undoubtedly, part of the reason is the numinous awe that surrounds the dead. Daisaku Ikeda, the Japanese leader of the largest lay Buddhist organisation in the world, expresses this with great clarity. 'Anthropologists and archaeologists consider various markings and signs of ceremonial burial on human bones to be an indication of some kind of religious feeling,' he has observed, agreeing that 'Certainly, such markings suggest awe in the face of death, awareness of the possibility of an invisible post-mortem world, and perhaps an image of what that world might be like.' For Ikeda, however, 'in spite of vague images, the world beyond death remains impenetrable; and perhaps respect for the unknown – a higher psychological function than raw, animal fear – is the true source of religious feelings.' So, Ikeda points out, one can seek 'the fountainhead of religious sentiment in the oldest primitive human relics, specifically in bones marked in one way or another for funeral purposes.'

In Buddhism the cult of relics even precedes the age of Gautama Buddha himself, for a great tower is said to have housed the entire body of Kasyapa Buddha, Gautama's predecessor. West of the Indus the image of Gautama's footprint has been venerated. And when he died, eight fragments of his burnt body were distributed among the eight great leaders of society;

another leader, the Brahman named Drona, saved the sacred vessel in which these had been collected; and a tenth Brahman took the rest of the embers from the funeral pile.

Soon the collar-bones of the Buddha, his four canine teeth and his frontal bone were being venerated as the 'seven great relics' of Buddhism. Then other pieces of the great Gautama – his hair, the tooth-relic of Sri Lanka, his nail-parings – spread throughout the Buddhist world. Some of these, such as the bones in the great tower at Piprawa, are almost certainly authentic relics. And till this day, reverence has been afforded them. In 1902 when thieves had raided one of the reliquary pagodas of Shwebo in Burma, the royal consorts of the monarch removed the Buddha's remains for safety. A silver scroll records that by so protecting these sacred bones, they hoped for happiness and undisturbed prosperity until they attained *Nirvana*.

Amongst the followers of Mohammad, few such practices have occurred. Yet in the sixteenth century Sultan Ibrahim II brought hairs from the prophet's beard to a sanctuary in Bijapur, India. Medieval travellers saw the imprint of his foot on Mount Sinai; and in the mid-eighteenth century another of his hairs was placed in a jewelled gold casket at Rurhi, Sind.

Most fascinatingly too, the thirst for secular relics has affected *modern* Islam. A few years after the death of Quaid-i-Azam Mohammad Ali Jinnah, the founding father of Pakistan, a commission was set up to gather together all his relics and put them on display in the Department of Archaeology, the National Museum of Pakistan, Karachi. The official catalogue, published in 1980, observes tellingly:

> Even his personal effects acquired a special reverence. His relics as a matter of fact breathe with one or the other historic event which played its part in the creating of the nation. The catalogue of relics is thus not only an inventory of his personal effects but also serves as a window providing a peep into the Independence Movement.

The collection comprises addresses of welcome, poems, paintings, three-piece suits, gentlemen's braces, shirts, separate collars, bows, photographs, monocles, cigarette lighters, office furniture and Mr Jinnah's favourite sofa. ('Some of the most important decisions were taken by him while sitting on the sofa,' notes the 1980 catalogue.)

Mr Jinnah had a noted predilection for fine clothing, and the collectors of his relics remain proud of the fact. 'Many Viceroys, including Lord Harding, Lord Chelmsford and Lord Reading,' they boast, 'are known to have said that Quaid-i-Azam was the best dressed gentleman they had ever met in India. It was therefore natural to expect wardrobes filled with elegant and best tailored dresses.' Sadly, not all these secondary relics had remained in mint condition. 'As some thirty-two years have elapsed since Quaid-i-Azam passed away and his material largely remained uncared for during the period,' notes the catalogue, 'moth and white ants have played havoc with his personal garments. It was with great effort that a portion of it has now been salvaged.'

As we have by now been accustomed to discovering, a person's secondary relics often possess no small significance; and this remains true of Mr Jinnah's wardrobe. Until the collection was brought together, it was generally believed that he started wearing Pakistani dress only after being elected President of the All India Muslim League in 1934. A china silk Sherwani among the relics, tailored by Hoar and Co. of Bombay in 1925, gives the lie to this damaging suspicion.

Yet in the end Mr Jinnah's personal relics, like the other secular remains of recent centuries, can scarcely vie with the great relics of the ages of faith. When the catalogue of the Jinnah collection observes that 'The presence of three different sets of golf clubs . . . shows for the first time that Quaid-i-Azam played this game as well,' it is hardly possible not to conclude that along with the sacred, some of the old glory of relics has departed.

8

Homes fit for relics

If you wish to venerate a relic you must first of all reject the evidence of your senses and reverse your normal perception of reality. Here, for one thing, is a piece of a former human being, now quite evidently lifeless, inanimate and dead. Yet you are required to believe that this object not only represents eternal life but also in some mysterious fashion can grant it. And as we have seen, men and women have in their millions in the past managed to accept this bizarre attitude to human remains, and in many parts of the world still do so.

Equally abundant is the historical evidence that believers in relics have been able to set aside the obvious truth that the saint whose remains they revere did die, did succumb to illness, or was unable to escape martyrdom, in favour of the more glorious notion that now the dead bones have healing properties, can guard against sickness and avert the evils of our fallen world.

The phenomenon is yet more remarkable than this. We know from St John's Gospel that when Jesus was about to raise Lazarus from the dead the bystanders were appalled, partly because the body would, after three days in the tomb, stink. The relics of St Lazarus, now (as many believe) in Provence, provoke no such disgusted reaction. Often relics of the more spotless saints – Cuthbert, Charles I (perhaps), St Charles Borromeo (a saint of the Counter-Reformation), St Etheldreda, et al. – remain uncorrupted in the grave, thus giving off no repellent smell. But this is a comparatively rare achievement. Most relics, being dead bodies, decay and putrefy. I myself have experienced some discomfort because of this, when privileged to revere those bits of St Catherine of Alexandria still preserved on Mount Sinai.

Curiously enough, the Archbishop of Sinai on that occasion failed to share my discomfort, crying with evident pleasure, 'What a superb aroma!' Among the faithful the odour of death attaching to a saintly relic becomes transformed into the odour of sanctity. Whereas a corpse might normally be regarded as a possibly dangerous transmitter of disease against which danger our sense of smell above all warns, now the odour of a relic promises health. The early church father St John Damascene said as much: 'Our Lord Jesus Christ has given us the relics of saints as sources of health, from which flow numerous benefits and an unguent of agreeable odour. Let none be incredulous. If from a hard and crabby stone water gushed forth by the will of God*, and from the jawbone of an ass to slake the thirst of Samson, why should it be incredible that an unguent of agreeable odour gush from the relics of martyrs?'

My own suggestion as an historian is that this 'odour of sanctity' entered into the Christian tradition not from dead bones but through the insanitary habits of the desert saints. These men and women, living lives of intense austerity after the example of St Antony, laid the foundations of Christian spirituality as we have inherited it by way of the medieval monastics. But the conditions in which they lived were not always clean. Remarkably, these men and women usually had the stamina to survive these unsavoury surroundings. St Antony himself, for

* a reference to one of Moses's miracles.

instance, spent the last twenty years of his life in graveyards; but he died in 356 A.D. at the ripe age of 105.

The tale of another unwashed desert father illustrates how the fact that a holy man failing to wash rendered him not reprehensible but contrariwise praiseworthy. This man, a monk named Abraham, suffered anguish because his niece, whom he had brought up after the death of her parents, became a prostitute. The holy Abraham determined to leave his beloved, filthy hermit life to save the erring girl. Shedding his usual garments, he dressed as a soldier and sought out his niece as if he were a potential client. To preserve his disguise he not only forsook his customary abstinence and drank wine but also kept a hat over his face: all to no avail. 'The girl came to put her arms around his neck, beguiling him with her kisses,' says the old account of Abraham's exploits. 'And as she was kissing him, she smelt the fragrance of his austerity breathed out by his lean body, and she remembered the days when she too had lived austerely; and as if a spear had pierced her soul she gave a great moan and began to weep.' The 'fragrance of austerity', or 'the odour of sanctity', or (perhaps) the pungent smell of the desert father had saved her from a life of sin.

To wash, far from being virtuous, was often considered sinful. In his extreme old age St Sigfrid of Sweden got into his bath forgetting that it was a day of fasting. The scandalised onlookers reminded him; the saint sprang out of the water without delay, begging God's forgiveness. A few days later he died and his unwashed relics were joyfully and proudly buried in Vaxjö cathedral, their odour of sanctity unimpaired by clean water.

Such a powerful reversal of sense perception, whereby the hideous takes on an aura of beauty and the revolting is made supremely attractive, sometimes demanded more than human beings could stand. Two American scholars, Donald Weinstein and Rudolf M. Bell, have discovered a fascinating example of this: the case of St Giovanni Columbini's chamber-pot. Giovanni Columbini was a successful Sienese merchant, converted to passionate Christianity in the mid-fourteenth century, who spent the last twenty-six years of his life working as a servant in a Franciscan monastery. He died aged 98, having founded the mendicant order of the Gesuati. The American scholars note that 'Giovanni Columbini's chamber-pot emitted a fragrant odour after he died. Attracted by its fragrance and believing it would work wonders, a young woman took some of the pot's contents to apply to her facial disfigurement, whereupon the fragrance disappeared and was replaced by a normal odour.'

Robert Browning observed that whereas men and women in the nineteenth century lived 'a life of doubt diversified by faith,' in the past the opposite held true: life consisted of 'faith diversified by doubt'. Even in fourteenth-century Siena a young woman might well experience a sudden revulsion having plastered her face with the contents of a dead saint's chamber-pot, her charming faith momentarily diversified by doubt, so to speak. Giovanni Columbini's biographer did his best to explain away the unfortunate event: such a sacred relic ought not to be perverted to the service of vanity. Professors Weinstein and Bell rightly observe that this attitude to the relic perfectly illustrates the Christian notion that 'Just as every vice had its corresponding virtue and every sin its expiation, so every disgusting odour might have its fragrance.'

In consequence 'the best of all we know' and 'the unsearchable and secret aims of nature', summed up (as Robert Bridges had it) above all by *beauty*, might equally be summed up by what one would normally regard as gruesome and distasteful, namely the dead bones of a saint. So today the shrivelled body of St Clare (rediscovered in 1850), her face brown and mummified, bears little immediate relation to the gentle woman who made herself the ally of St Francis. But displayed as she is in a glass case at Assisi, dressed in her nun's habit, she still represents to the countless faithful – and even the myriad tourists – who flock to that hill town all the virtues of her order and of St Francis's inspiration.

Clearly we can still make the necessary reversal of perception and invest a saint's corpse with what ought to be an implausible beauty. In Lucca at the other side of Italy this happens each 27

April, at the festival of Santa Zita, patron saint of servant girls. A servant herself, Zita was once caught smuggling from her mistress's house a basket of eggs. The angry mistress snatched away the napkin covering the basket, to find that the eggs had all turned into flowers. This apparent divine sanction to pilfering still inspires many young Luccans, who on the appointed day fill the square in front of the church of Santa Zita with flowers, and then with other flowers rapturously stroke the glass that displays the long-dead Zita in the nave, heedless of her current physical state.

Yet there is no gainsaying the fact that a corpse, whether saintly or not, has usually a repellent aspect about it, especially long after the saint's death. Dismemberment of relics has added an extra grisly element. Martyrdom can render a relic still more gruesome. To examine the skull of St Magnus of the Orkneys has distinct historical fascination. And as we have seen, the skull of Oliver Cromwell even provided entertainment in nineteenth-century parlours. But for the most part – notwithstanding the odour of sanctity, the intimations of immortality and the miraculous gifts of many relics – even the devout feel understandably uncomfortable face to face with the most holy corpse. The natural, human reaction was to find something to put the corpse in, thus – reverently, lovingly – shielding it from the public gaze.

The very first such reliquary known to history was indeed used only as a temporary home, before the relic was returned to the grave. St Savin, Bishop of Spoleto, during the persecution of the early church, had his hands chopped off. A devout widow rescued them and put them in a glass jar. But as soon as St Savin died, she buried the hands with him. Her pious action entirely accords with the extreme reluctance of western Christians in the first four centuries or so after Jesus's birth to dig up the bodies of their saints and martyrs. The homes of the earliest Christian relics were quite simply their graves, over which were built churches to shelter those who annually came to pay homage.

A bizarre consequence is that today where the relics of

illustrious early Christian saints are sumptuously displayed often turns out to be the site of a former cemetery.

The largest Romanesque nave in the whole of northern France belongs to the basilica of Saint-Remi in Reims and shelters the shrine of St Remi himself. As we have seen, Remi's relics were translated at least five times after his death in A.D. 533 and before returning in triumph to Reims. Their splendid home is today a church consecrated by Pope Leo IX in 1049. The choir, where Remi actually lies, was started on the orders of Pierre de Celle in 1170.

Remi's relics now rest in a double shrine. The smaller one is gilded, almost baroque, with 'barley-sugar' pillars and the legend '*Ici repose le corps de St Remi*' ('Here lies the body of St Remi'). On 1 October 1896 this shrine was placed inside a stone mausoleum behind the high altar, this mausoleum ornamented with bishops and saints sculpted in the sixteenth century. Peering through a grille you can see the gilded shrine and attached to it an enamel showing Remi about to baptise a naked Clovis, half-submerged in water, his crown and sword laid to one side. To their left the Holy Spirit in the form of a dove descends from the top of the enamel picture, bearing in his beak the Sainte Ampoule. The Ampoule is no more. St Remi miraculously survives, even though much of the basilica, including the entire roof of the nave, was destroyed in a massive bomb attack on 1 August 1918. A photograph taken the following day shows the ruins, with Remi's mausoleum intact. When last I saw the shrine Remi was still working miracles – or at least being asked to do so, for five candles lit by the faithful were burning there, fourteen-and-a-half centuries after his death.

The advantages both of concealing unsightly bones and also of displaying pictorially the earthly exploits of a saint whose relics lie thus concealed are obvious. Especially welcome is the possibility of concealing under a fine shrine the relics of a saint whose end was messy. In the Unterlinden Museum at Colmar, Alsace, is a reliquary from the church of Bergheim in the Upper Rhine which once contained part of the corpse of St Hippolytus. Hippolytus, who lived from about A.D. 170 till the year 236 or so, was the most imporant theologian in Rome in the early third century. In the cemetery of St Hippolytus on the road to Tivoli was discovered in 1551 a statue of the saint, sitting in a marble chair and almost certainly made in his lifetime. On the sides of the chair are a list of his works and tables for working out the date of Easter. Already by 255, he was revered as a martyr and remembered as a good priest, though some disliked him for his opposition to the views of the Popes. In fact along with Pope Pontianus he was first exiled and then martyred during the persecutions of the Emperor Maximinus.

Around his relics was to grow a remarkable cult. In remote England a village in Hertfordshire, Ippollits, was named after him and sick horses were brought to his shrine for healing. Prudentius revered him and wrote of his death, adding that he often prayed at Hippolytus's tomb and was always healed there of any infirmity, be it of body or of soul. Prudentius tells us that on his feast day (13 August) men and women would come even from abroad to his tomb, 'pressing kisses on the bright metal of the inscription, covering it with spices, wetting his grave with tears'.

The connection with horses is no accident, for it was generally believed that Hippolytus had been before ordination a pagan prison officer, converted by St Laurence; Hippolytus assisted at Laurence's funeral, for which charitable act the Emperor ordered him to be scourged and put to death by being torn apart by wild stallions. (The Emperor also had Hippolytus's nurse, St Concordia, and nineteen others beaten to death, for good measure.) The horses dragged the saint over ditches, rocks and hedges while the weeping faithful mopped up his blood with their handkerchiefs and collected his mutilated remains.

Now if the manner of Hippolytus's death gave him a martyr's golden crown it also undoubtedly altered his physical condition for the worse. Happily the reliquary now in Colmar would conceal the rather revolting state of the holy relic. It also illustrates the manner of his death in a decently tidy fashion, causing little problem for the squeamish. On either side of the reliquary, which was made in 1477 and is of gold-painted wood, the saint lies meekly down, still whole, hands tied together, bound by his feet to a prancing horse. A horrific death has been transformed into a work of art.

A reliquary reinforced the beliefs of Christians by illustrating the miraculous acts of the saint in question to people who were often illiterate. On Mount Athos the monastery known as the Great Lavra possesses a superb silver-gilt reliquary of St Demetrios. Demetrios had been put to death by the Emperor Galerian in the fourth century after one of the saint's pupils had managed to kill Galerian's favourite gladiator. Demetrios soon became a famous worker of miracles, above all when the Slavs invaded Thessaloniki in 586. As Robin Cormack describes the scene, 'In spite of their strength, the enemy retreated. The only possible explanation that the citizens could provide was the intervention of supernatural help. Later the enemy explained that they saw a large force in the city and above all they saw its commander, "a man who dazzled them, mounted on a white horse, and wearing a white cloak".' Soon the people were convinced that their supernatural help came from Demetrios. The reliquary from Mount Athos shows him on one side with hands raised in blessing, and on the other – in a superbly animated scene – he leans over the city ramparts, his spear stretching down to the terrified Slavs below.

In the treasury of St Mark's, Venice, three of the reliquaries achieve an extraordinary beauty in the way they illustrate the meaning of the relic itself. The first is a late eleventh-century Byzantine reliquary containing an arm of St George. Doge Enrico Dandalo bought it from Constantinople in 1204, attracted no doubt by the thought of possessing the arm itself but surely quite as much by the silver saint who kills a silver dragon on top of it. The other two are both reliquaries of the true cross. One was made for Henry of Flanders, the second western Emperor of Constantinople (who reigned from 1206 to 1216) by a goldsmith named Gerard. In it no fewer than six rectangular pieces of the true cross have been reassembled into a cross (with two lateral pieces). In 1618, by orders of the Senate of Venice, this particular reliquary was made into a monstrance to display the consecrated bread of the Eucharist, and placed on the high altar of the Sacrament. The third great 'talking reliquary' (as they have been called) is the heaviest of all those in the treasury of St Mark's: a scene of Christ against a pillar, suffering flagellation. Jesus is worked in gold; those beating him in black. Such 'talking reliquaries' of the Passion are extremely rare – and worth seeking out. One – from Prague – is in the form of a crown of thorns and contains an actual Holy Thorn. Today it is treasured in the Walters Art Gallery, Baltimore.

Such reliquaries were clearly designed for public display. Others, however, were made for more personal use, even for carrying a relic around as a personal possession. In Reims cathedral treasury is a small golden ampulla with two little handles known as 'Charlemagne's Amulet'. Once it contained a lock of the Virgin's hair, and two golden chains attached to the handles show that it was designed to be worn round a Christian's neck. The amulet remained at Aachen until 1804, when the church authorities deemed it prudent to give the reliquary to Napoleon's wife Josephine. By now, oddly enough, the Virgin's hair had been replaced by a fragment of the true cross (which can still be seen through the transparent jewels on either side of the Amulet). The Bonapartes kept the relic and reliquary until the Empress Eugénie gave it to Reims cathedral.

Other such reliquaries were given as presents more voluntarily than Charlemagne's Amulet. In the late twelfth century Bishop Reginald of Bath gave to Queen Margaret of Sicily a reliquary displaying relics of Thomas Becket. (Today it can be seen in the Joseph Pulitzer bequest, in the Metropolitan Museum of Art, New York). Another Becket reliquary of the same date (given by J. Pierpoint Morgan to the same museum) was made by Rhenish goldsmiths for John of Salisbury, to contain two phials of the martyr's blood. The trade in Becket relics flourished from his death until well into the next century, and with this trade a demand for fine reliquaries to keep them in. The British Museum possesses a copper box, made in Limoges about 1190, gilded and engraved with the scene of Becket's death: three knights menace the archbishop, one cutting off the saint's head, while two monks hold up their hands in horror.

These works of art arose out of a simple need to carry relics around – sometimes from one country to another. We still possess a major work of art from the late seventh century simply because English monks needed to transport the body of St Cuthbert. They put his remains in a coffin of oak. On the lid they carved a full-length figure of Jesus. Above his head are the symbols of the Evangelists Matthew and Mark. At his feet are inscribed the bull of St Luke and the eagle of St John. At one end are carved the archangels Michael and Gabriel; at the other end a stern Virgin Mary, holding the infant Jesus. On the sides are carved the twelve apostles and five other archangels. When Durham cathedral authorities rediscovered the body of St Cuthbert in 1827 and placed the fragments of this coffin in the cathedral treasury, they also took the trouble to reconstruct it as it must have looked in 698, putting the pieces back on a new coffin 1.69 metres long. As David M. Wilson, Director of the British Museum, has observed, the style of this reliquary-coffin at first sight seems crude; 'after the sophistication of contemporary manuscripts no amount of special pleading can persuade one that this is great art'. Yet it is an almost unique survival of Anglo-Saxon wood-carving, a tiny glimpse of a genre that has almost entirely perished.

Cuthbert was translated in his coffin out of fear that pagans might steal his remains. Not every relic and reliquary escaped as Cuthbert's did. In the National Museum of Denmark is a little casket shaped like a house which was made in Scotland either in the eighth or the ninth century A.D. to house relics. Viking raiders carried it off to Norway. It still contains relics – but these date from a period *later* than that of the Vikings. The original bones must have been at some point removed. More: on the base of the casket a Viking has carved in runic letters 'RANVAIK A KISTU THASA' ('Ranvaig owns this casket'). Scholars speculate that a pagan raider looted the reliquary, took out the relics and let his lady use it for her jewels. Later, when the Vikings became Christians, the reliquary was used for its proper purpose again.

When the church christianised the Vikings, naturally a good number of homes for the relics of the saints were commissioned; and decorated in the Viking's particular ornamental style. The Scandinavians habitually decorated their buildings with fantastic beasts – especially dragons – to protect the household from malign forces outside. These appear on Scandinavian reliquaries. Two copper-gilt ones (one from Jäla, now to be seen in the Skara Museum, the other from Eriksberg, now displayed in the Museum of National Antiquities of Stockholm) are like miniature houses with double-tiered roofs, crowned with dragons' heads. In Norway a copper-gilt reliquary from Fortun (now in the Bergen Museum) portrays a seated Jesus, his twelve apostles, all the letters of the alphabet from A to Z, and the legend 'AMOR VINCIT OMNIA' ('Love conquers all'). But just in case love alone was not enough, the coppersmith wrought two fearsome dragons for the gables. In Hedal church another reliquary shows not only the Christ in Majesty, flanked by his mother and St John, but also the murder of Thomas Becket; this too is protected by dragons, rendered more terrifying by having serpents as tongues.

Reliquary-makers in Scandinavia flourished creatively till the Reformation when, alas, much of their work perished. Twleve surviving caskets from the twelfth century show the particular brilliance of these craftsmen, for they constitute the first essays in western Europe at *champlevé* work – that is enamel with colours set in hollowed out patterns. Blues, turquoises, white, reds and yellows richly adorn figures of Jesus, the apostles, the saints, outlined in copper-gilt.

Each part of Christendom, creating these homes fit for relics, enriched Christian art according to its own special genius. Eastern Christendom excelled itself to house above all relics deriving from the holy family. In the monastery of St Paul on Mount Athos twelve triangular cases hold the gifts of gold, frankincense and myrrh said to have been presented by the Magi to the infant Jesus. Philip Sherard thus describes the reliquary housing a seven-inch fragment of the true cross presented to the Great Lavra by the Emperor Nikephoros Phokas (A.D. 963–969): the case 'is of silver-gilt, opening on top with folded doors like a triptych. These doors are set with huge *cabochon* jewels – diamonds, emeralds and rubies, as well as pearls – which alternate with medallions of saints in enamel. There are twelve rows consisting of eight of each; and the two largest pearls measure over an inch and a half across.'

Philip Sherard adds that, 'With the exception of the loot taken from Constantinople during the Fourth Crusade and now in the treasury of St Mark's at Venice, such objects – and there are several on Athos – are unknown further west.' From the point of view of those who lived in the west, this looting was of course fortunate. The Church of San Francesco, Cortona, today boasts a splendid ivory reliquary of the true cross, made for the church of Agia Sofia, Constantinople, during the rule of Nikephoros Phokas. Also from Constantinople and from exactly the same period dates an enamelled silver-gilt reliquary with delicately coloured figures, again for a piece of the true cross. This is now in the cathedral treasury of Limburg an der Lahn in West Germany.

Sometimes the east benefited from western generosity. You must go to St Catherine's monastery on Mount Sinai to see a fine gold-plated sarcophagus, sent by a Russian princess in 1860 to house the aromatic fragments of Catherine still to be found there. The saint is depicted lying peacefully, hands crossed across her breast, her legs delicately showing through a blanket which reaches up to her middle. The whole is littered with jewels.

Without such treasure-stores as St Mark's, Venice, much would have been destroyed as Islam conquered Byzantium. For example, the splendid late tenth (or early eleventh) century reliquary of the true cross, ornamented by fusing together metal and coloured glass and then polishing it till it shines like a jewel, was made by Byzantine goldsmiths; but it would almost certainly be lost were it not preserved at St Mark's. A more astonishing survival, now preserved in the treasury there, is a sixth-century reliquary-throne. Made of alabaster, its style suggests that it was made somewhere along the eastern Mediterranean, perhaps in Alexandria. It stands 1470 mm high, 550 mm wide and 530 mm. deep. Stylised evangelists and a lamb of God are carved on the throne, as well as six-winged seraphim on either side. A much later inscription in Hebrew reads 'The seat of Mark the Evangelist'. And underneath where no doubt a distinguished ecclesiastic sat is an asymmetrical cavity, capable of housing a sizeable bit of a dead saint. Looting saved this amazing seat.

Before lamenting booty from the east brought to the west, we should consider the sad lack of such marvellous works of art in lands such as Britain, which came deeply under the influence of the Protestant Reformation – for the Reformers saw not works of art but the shrines of superstition in all such reliquaries. All we possess in British churches of the splendid reliquaries of the middle ages are the shrine of St Edward the Confessor in Westminster Abbey; the reliquary of St Eanswith (King Ethelbert's daughter) at Folkestone; and in St Albans the shrine of that saint, painstakingly reconstructed from fragments in the nineteenth century. To see shrines of our great British relics, we must go abroad. The relics of St Margaret of Scotland, for instance, once enshrined in Dunfermline, escaped the mob at the Reformation, were carried by Mary Stuart to Edinburgh, taken to Antwerp by a Benedictine monk in 1597 and then given to Douai. Part of her body is still there, encased in silver. The rest went to Spain, where Philip II built for her a chapel in the Escurial Palace. Into her shrine there were later placed also the bones of her husband Malcolm. The saint-queen of Scotland lies thus fittingly housed, but not in the land she loved.

To see reliquaries housing the bones of the British saint Ursula you must go to Germany, Italy and Belgium. At Bruges, in St John's hospital, part of St Ursula lies in a wooden gothic reliquary made in the 1480s and painted by Hans Memling. (He shows the saint arriving at Cologne; on the quayside at Basle;

being received by the Pope and returning with her many virgins to Basle; and finally dying at the hands of the barbarians.) Other bones of the saint are found in San Antonio, Padua, in a reliquary modelled on a perfectly-rigged ship (alluding to her emigration). A third bit of Ursula lies in her church in Cologne.

The so-called Gandersheim casket, now in the Prince Anton-Ulrich Museum, Brunswick, was once at Ely, until the Danes sacked the city in the late ninth century. Made of walrus ivory, with an interlacing design, the Gandersheim casket may well have housed a relic of the Blessed Virgin, since a twentieth-century copy of an earlier prayer, inscribed in runic letters on the casket, begs her to protect Ely.

In short, the life of a relic has never been secure. Relics in themselves rouse much passion in human breasts: men and women either covet or hate them. And their sumptuous homes similarly have excited greed or anger at various periods of Christian history. But relics belong not to one country but to Christendom, as many theologians have maintained and many faithful believed. Their reliquaries have accompanied their bones about the Christian world, or else new shrines have been made for them, far from their native lands. So in 1644, in St Sernin's basilica, Toulouse, Archbishop Charles de Montchal reverently laid the bones of St Edmund, once king of East Anglia, into a solid silver reliquary with columns that supported a classical dome, at the same time placing the saint's detached skull in another new solid silver reliquary made by a smith named Bernard Bruchon. Would the English at that time, fighting a civil war, have shown any such regard for their native martyr?

In spite of these vicissitudes, many saints remain in reliquaries today as they were first enshrined. This happily enables us to trace in some detail the brilliance and the astonishing development of the great reliquaries made in western Europe during the middle ages. Here the patronage of godly monarchs – imitated by the pious nobility – enriched the shrines of saints. The Merovingian kings covered the relics of St Germain d'Auxerre, St Denis and many others in gold and silver. The booty brought back by crusaders after 1204 boosted the ambitions of westerners who wished to honour relics. In that year the count of Châteauneuf offered the head of St Matthew to Chartres cathedral, and the countess of Evreux gave a silver vase ornamented with precious stones to house it. Louis IX gave the abbey of Vézelay vases of gold enriched with jewels to house the bones of St Mary Magdalen.

In the treasury of Conques is still preserved a reliquary shaped like a house and given to it (almost certainly) by Pepin Duke of Aquitaine, who ruled from 761 to 768. In the following four centuries this reliquary was enriched with gold and statues out of all recognition, as pious Christians sought to make it more and more worthy of the dead bones it contained.

As might be expected, Charlemagne's devotion to relics gave an enormous impetus to the building of shrines to house them. Charlemagne was himself canonised in 1166. One of his arms was placed in a reliquary now kept in the Louvre, Paris. Charlemagne, his wife Beatrix, the archangels Michael and Gabriel and the Blessed Virgin are depicted on silver plaques on one side; on the other appear Jesus, St Peter and St Paul, the Emperor Conrad III and Duke Frederick of Swabia. At either end are Charlemagne's ancestors – Louis the Pious and Otto III. And the Emperors continued to enrich the great churches of Europe with these homes for dead saints.

As mentioned in the introduction, one of the finest shrines of Christendom was created in Cologne cathedral as the result of the gift of the relics of the three Magi to the archbishop by the Emperor Frederick Barbarossa. Over the centuries many craftsmen worked on this shrine – the largest of all that have survived in the west. The greatest of these artists was undoubtedly Nicholas of Verdun. His work too can be seen on the shrine of St Anno in St Michael's abbey, Siegburg, which was completed in 1183. But his hand at Cologne – shown in the carvings of Old Testament prophets, above all – is that of a master at the height of his powers. As Peter Lasko has written, 'The work of Nicholas of Verdun formed a climax to the twelfth century. His is the case of so many artists of genius – they are not surpassed in the generation that follows them, or indeed even approached in quality. Their work is too overpowering, and at the end of their lives often too personal, to provide a fitting springboard for a new generation.' Yet, as Lasko also insists, Nicholas's achievement was part of a whole remarkable revolution in art: the great age of Gothic art had arrived. So, he observes, 'The great shrine of Our Lady at Aachen, begun in 1215 and completed in 1237, and the shrine of St Elizabeth at Marburg, probably completed in 1249, in their general design and structure continue the traditions of the twelfth century, but in their figure style, both in the large fully rounded figures under arcades, and in the reliefs of their roofs, reveal their full acceptance of Gothic forms.'

Writing about these reliquaries as if they were virtually buildings – with such architectural features as arcades and roofs – Peter Lasko could almost as easily be referring to the actual churches in which they were contained. The home of the saint was enclosed in the house of God, both often masterpieces of architectural skill. But the truth is more curious than this: for the architecture of God's house was often specifically designed with the needs of the relics in mind.

Initially churches, though often built over a saint's tomb, paid little architectural regard to the relic. But by the ninth century churches aspiring to any sort of status possessed as a major feature an impressive crypt – to serve both for burials and above all for displaying relics. Pilgrims descended steps at one side of the high altar and processed round a continuous corridor to gaze and pray before the bones visible through openings in their shrines. So bones once at rest in the soil under a church were unearthed and placed in crypts under the site of the altar. A monk of Canterbury named Eadmer described how he remembered the cathedral there before the disastrous fire of 1067. He wrote of how 'the venerable Odo had translated the corpse of St Wilfrid to Canterbury and there . . . placed it in a great altar, constructed of rough stones and mortar near the east wall of the presbytery. Afterwards another altar was placed at a reasonable distance from this one, to contain the head of St

Swithun from Winchester and the relics of many other saints.' Eadmer tells us that you had to climb steps to reach these two altars, because underneath was a crypt, 'to the east end of which was an altar containing the head of St Furseus.' From this altar, he adds, 'a single passage ran westwards to the resting place of St Dunstan.' Clearly the cathedral was devoted to the cult of such saints and one of its major functions was simply to provide them with a fitting home.

During the twelfth century the fashion for building crypts to house great relics was replaced by one of placing the holy remains either behind the high altar or else inside it. One of the last great churches in Britain to be built with a crypt was Glasgow cathedral, where Bishop Jocelyn's reconstruction of 1197 still included one containing the bones of St Kentigern. Yet often a superb building arose simply because of the arrival of new noted relics in a city. When sailors from Bari stole the body of St Nicholas from Myra, the city built the prototype of Italian romanesque basilicas to house the relic. Sometimes too Christians in possession of a precious relic would commandeer a splendid church as its home. In Pisa on the left bank of the Arno was built in the first third of the fourteenth century the astonishing Gothic chapel that still stands today near the present bridge of Solferino. It was called Santa Maria de Pontenovo. Half a century earlier rich merchants had brought from the orient a thorn from Jesus's crown of thorns, which passed into the hands of the Longo family. When Betto Longo fell seriously ill, he begged help from the Virgin Mary, promising to give the thorn to her chapel on the Arno. In fact he died, but his father (who had been abroad) returned in 1333 and handed over the precious relic. The chapel is now called Santa Maria della Spina.

Church builders grew increasingly inventive at finding suitable homes for revered relics. At Lichfield in the thirteenth century pilgrims so venerated the head of St Chad that the authorities decided to build against the south choir aisle a special chapel to contain it. A flight of steps still leads to this chapel, which is supported by an undercroft attached to a barrel-vaulted strong-room, whose walls are filled with recesses for the pilgrims' gifts. And projecting into the south choir aisle from the upper chapel is a fourteenth-century gallery constructed to display yet more relics. Chad's head, of course, also had a magnificent reliquary, ordered by Bishop Robert Stretton in the late fourteenth century to replace one made in 1296 at a cost of £2,000. Still today the chapel at Lichfield is known as St Chad's Head Chapel, even though the relic itself was removed at the Reformation. (Happily it survived, cared for by Catholics throughout four centuries until the new papal cathedral was built at Birmingham in 1841. There his head now reposes in an oaken shrine, painted, gilded and bejewelled, above the high altar beneath a gay baldacchino.)

The greatest church built especially to house relics is, however, undoubtedly the Sainte-Chapelle in Paris. King Louis IX wrote that his purpose in ordering such a house of God was for the good of his own soul, in honour of the Almighty and the sacred crown of thorns worn by Jesus Christ, and to house 'that same holy crown of thorns, a sacred piece of the cross and several other relics'. This included a fragment of Jesus's shroud, the reed that was used to give him drink on the cross, the holy lance, holy blood, part of the Baptist's skull, some of Mary's milk, and a stone from Jesus's tomb. (This stone was in a silver-gilt reliquary made in Byzantium, with plaques depicting women at the tomb and a jewelled cross between two plants.)

Almost certainly Louis IX engaged Pierre de Montreuil, the greatest contemporary architect in France, to build his Sainte-Chapelle. And as Yves Bottineau has observed, he designed a church which is itself 'like a reliquary; the skilful balance of the arches, the columns and the buttresses made it possible to reduce the outer walls to a bare framework and to increase the sense of space by bays filled with stained-glass windows.' On 26 April 1248 the papal legate, Eudes de Châteauroux, in the presence of thirteen French bishops dedicated the upper chapel of the Sainte-Chapelle to the holy cross and the holy crown of thorns. The Archbishop of Bourges dedicated the lower chapel in the name of the Virgin Mary.

Alas, the relics are no longer there. Some were given away with great generosity. A piece of the holy thorn, given to the abbey of Saint-Maurice-d'Agaune in 1262 is still there. Another relic of the thorn, sent to the Dominicans at Liège in 1267, is now in the Louvre. The rest were thrown out at the Revolution (and indeed the Sainte-Chapelle was gravely damaged, to be restored in the next century by architects of the calibre of Viollet-le-Duc and Boeswilwald). Rebuilt too was the tribune that had stood behind the high altar to display the great relics, after fragments had been found discarded in the mason's yard at Saint-Denis and at the École des Beaux Arts. But in the Sainte-Chapelle today if you want to see the relics you must be content with the great stained-glass windows that show Louis IX and Robert d'Artois carrying them to Paris and later the faithful adoring them. One fine reliquary showing St Maxian, St Lucian and St Julian, each meekly carrying his severed head, is now in the Cluny Museum. An animated statue representing the apotheosis of Germanicus, once housing another relic in the Sainte-Chapelle, is now in the medal room of the Bibliothèque Nationale. The reliquary of the crown of thorns, as reconstructed by Viollet-le-Duc, is in Notre Dame. The reliquary of the stone of the sepulchre, with the angel pointing to the empty tomb, is in the Louvre. The Sainte-Chapelle, though empty, remains (in the words of Ian Nairn) still a 'colossal stained-glass casket, scintillating rich reds and blues – all wine-coloured, were there such a thing as blue wine.'

Today in a sense every Catholic church is still a reliquary. As early as the fourth century the idea arose that a church was somehow incomplete without its relic. Gregory of Tours describes how when relics were triumphantly brought to a church, they were frequently addressed:

> Leave your old homes, saints of God, and hurry to the places we have prepared for you!
>
> Rise up, saints of God, from your old homes, to sanctify these new places, to bless the people, to cow sinners!
>
> March on, saints of God, come into the city of our Lord;

> for a new church has been built for you, where men and women may adore God's majesty!

Then the relics would be carried around the new building, with holy oil splashing everywhere.

The second Council of Nicea in 787 made obligatory the placing of relics under the altar of any church at its consecration. In the eastern churches, relics would often be pounded up with fragrant spices and placed on altars. Charlemagne in the west ordered the actual destruction of all altars that did not contain one. Such practices have continued to this day.

So a relic blesses a church and a church suitably houses a relic. Some have maintained that one may go too far in sumptuousness. Whereas, for example, at Bruges the holy blood is housed in a fine, yet simple crystal, at Rothenburg ob der Tauber in Franconia Tilman Riemenschneider carved in limewood the famous Holy Blood Altar so magnificently that one tends to overlook the golden crucifix with its rock crystal containing what is said to be a drop of Jesus's blood. Instead you are entranced by the brilliantly carved Last Supper of the Lord with his disciples, with Jesus offering Judas a piece of bread; or else you are distracted by the scenes on the wings: the procession to Jerusalem and Jesus on the Mount of Olives.

Perhaps Riemenschneider's reliquary can escape censure if only because its central scene records the moment when Jesus is about to speak of his sacred blood, offered for mankind. It is hard, by contrast, to see that the lavish surroundings of the simple house at Loreto which is said to be that once used by the holy family serves any purpose other than to *conceal* a humble brick building: Bramante's great marble screen, the stupendous bronze doors by Girolamo Lombardo, and the vast late-Gothic basilica itself, magnificent though they may be, are hardly in keeping with the relic they enshrine.

St Bernard in the middle ages argued with Peter the Venerable on this very question. We are called to revere a saint, complained Bernard, yet are in danger instead of worshipping a work of art. Against him, Peter pointed out that Jesus himself allowed Mary Magdalen to anoint his body with a most precious ointment.

Perhaps one can show a different reverence for each aspect of this rich inheritance – the relic and its beautiful home. La Fontaine, however, took Bernard's side, in his fable of 'The Ass and the Relics'*:

An Ass who bore a Martyr's bones
Thought 'twas to him the people bowed.
With head erect he paced the stones
And took the homage of the crowd.
A looker-on who twigged the joke
Explained 'twas not for him the folk
Sang canticles and genuflected
But for his burden: 'Mr Moke,'
Said he, 'you shouldn't think so big.'

A silly justice gets respected,
Not for himself, but for his wig.

* Here translated by Edward Marsh.

9

Authenticating relics

Inside Turin cathedral is a circular chapel faced with black marble, which was designed by Guarino Guarini for the private worship of the Dukes of Savoy, who once ruled Italy. It is reached by a steep flight of steps at the side of the high altar of the cathedral. The chapel is a breathtaking seventeenth-century baroque construction, lined with many white marble tombs. In the centre, beneath the cupola, is a black marble altar, surrounded by golden cherubs and hanging lamps. Six candles and a cross stand in front of a grille. Inside this locked grille is one of the most famous relics of the western world: the holy shroud of Turin.

The setting of this relic might well raise again the question of our last chapter: is this really the way to display one of the treasures of Christendom? Ian Wilson has described what lies behind the grille. First, the shroud has been

> rolled around a velvet staff and wrapped in red silk within a four-foot-long wooden casket ornamented in silver with the emblems of the Passion. The casket is kept within an iron

chest wrapped in asbestos and sealed by no fewer than three locks, for each of which a separate key is required. In turn the iron chest is within a wooden box with a painted cover. This cover is all that is visible behind the two iron grilles on the upper 'sepulchre' section of the altar in which the Shroud is stored.

Thus completely concealed is what many Christians believe to be the shroud which was wrapped around Jesus's body at his burial. More: the shroud is famous for an extraordinary double image that it bears. In a pale sepia-tint is the face of a bearded man, with staring eyes. His hands are crossed over his pelvis. And, head-to-head with this, so to speak, is a rear view of a man the same size. Those who hold this to be Jesus's own shroud maintain that it was placed under his body and then wrapped around the top of his head and down his chest to his feet. Both images, they claim, are of Jesus. Yet no-one in Guarini's chapel can see them. As the three million persons who came to view the shroud when it was on display for six weeks in 1978 demonstrate, the thirst to see it is enormous.

Yet the holy shroud of Turin raises a question of much greater consequence than how it ought to be displayed to the faithful. It raises acutely the question of authenticity. Is this a miraculous survival from Jesus's burial? Or is it yet another forgery?

John Calvin in his *Treatise on Relics* of 1543 was particularly harsh on the claims of all such shrouds because they seem to conflict with the evidence of the four Gospels themselves. In particular he cites the statement of the fourth Gospel that Jesus was buried 'according to the burial custom of the Jews'. Calvin does not mention the fact that this custom included washing a corpse, thus making the evidence of blood-stains revealed by the Turin shroud a reason for doubting its authenticity. What Calvin does point out is that the fourth Gospel speaks of two sets of grave clothes wrapped around Jesus: linen bands which had been wrapped around his body, and a sweat-cloth (or 'sudary') for his head.

Here, as always, the testimony of the Bible has become a bone of contention among scholars. On the face of it, though, St John's Gospel does clearly conflict with the argument that Jesus was wrapped after death in one long cloth that is now in Turin. On the other hand, as the Anglican scholar Bishop John Robinson used to argue, might this not support the authenticity of the Turin shroud after all? Would any forger, he asked, really produce something so much at odds with an important New Testament witness?

Calvin did ask another pertinent question about the Gospel evidence and the tradition of a shroud relic: why did no evangelist mention the miraculous imprint? 'How is it possible that those sacred historians, who carefully related all the miracles that took place at Christ's death, should have omitted to mention one so remarkable as the likeness of the body of the Lord remaining on its wrapping-sheet?' he exclaimed. 'St John in his Gospel related even how St Peter, having entered the sepulchre, saw the linen clothes lying to one side, and the napkin that was about his head on the other; but he does not say there was a miraculous impression of our Lord's figure upon these clothes, nor is it to be imagined that he would have omitted to mention such a work of God if there had been anything of this kind.'

The historical existence of the Turin shroud cannot in fact be traced back beyond the fourteenth century, when it appears in the possession of a French knight called Geoffrey de Charny who was killed by the English at the battle of Poitiers in 1356. In 1453 his widowed grandchild, Margaret, gave it to the Dukes of Savoy. The shroud reached Turin in 1578. From the very start some doubted its authenticity. Peter d'Arcis, Bishop of Troyes in 1389 told Pope Clement VII that the shroud was a 'cunningly painted' fake designed to raise money fraudulently from pilgrims. Only the uncanny correspondence of the details of the wounds on the body depicted there with the biblical account of the sufferings of Jesus make it impossible to dismiss the shroud from historical credibility.

So far, then, dispute over the Turin shroud has followed lines common in all attempts to determine the authenticity of a relic since the time of the Reformation. The questions to be asked are: Where did it come from? How does its supposed history fit in with other evidence (in this case the evidence of the New Testament)? Who might have an interest in faking a relic? But the shroud of Turin fascinates us today because it also offers the possibility that modern science might also serve to authenticate or else disprove the claims made for this great relic. Already some remarkable tests have been made. In the 1970s Dr Max Frei, a former director of the police laboratory in Zurich, was allowed to take dust samples from the shroud. He found there pollen grains from plants which can survive only in the conditions prevailing around the Dead Sea. Clearly then the cloth of this shroud, which made its first historical appearance in Europe in the fourteenth century, must also at some time have been in the region of Palestine, the home of Jesus.

So far a further technique of twentieth-century science has not been applied to the shroud – though scientists vie with one another to be given permission for this. New carbon-dating techniques measure the decrease in radioactivity over time in very small samples of material. Since radioactivity in all organic remains decreases at a known rate, a tiny sample of the shroud – no more than a few milligrams – would be enough, it is said, to determine its age. Of course the research could never produce a positive identification of the shroud of Turin with Jesus's winding-sheet. Scientists could determine only whether the cloth was around at the right time or not. More: caution by the Turin authorities is understandable. Suppose the technique were faulty and even misled the faithful. Yet the prospect is too exciting and the outcome too important for such tests to be postponed for ever.

From the point of view of the historian rather than the believer, whatever the outcome of testing the shroud, the result would be fascinating. A relic does not lose its interest when proved false. In Bettiscombe Manor, a private house in Dorset, England, is a famous screaming skull. According to one account the skull belonged to one of Oliver Cromwell's supporters named Theophilus Brome, who – alarmed at what had happened to the Lord Protector's head – directed that at his death he should be beheaded and his own skull kept permanently in the manor. Another story insists that the skull belonged to an eighteenth century black slave, who was buried against his wish in the local churchyard and not in his homeland. Horrid screams from the grave forced the owners of Bettiscombe Manor to dig up the skull again. And when in the nineteenth century the tenants tried to get rid of it, again they were deterred by hideous shrieks.

Carbon-dating techniques can tell us nothing of such shrieks and their source. What they have done with the Bettiscombe skull is prove that neither original theory about its origin is correct. Far more interestingly, the screaming skull is about 2,000 years old. It also happens to be that of a woman in her twenties. And almost certainly it came from Pilsdon Pen, a sanctuary built by the Celts on Bettiscombe land.

Perhaps a screaming Celtic skull does not raise so many hackles as a disputed Christian relic. Ian R. Grant in the early 1930s recorded (with approval) the extreme reluctance of the Neapolitans to have any scientist come near their phials of holy blood: 'Long before unanimity could be reached by Men of Science,' they believed, 'the Relic would be demolished.' Ian Grant also was impressed by the reaction of a London cockney whom he met at the church of San Pantaleone, Ravello, whose holy blood liquefies (though not invariably) on the novena preceding 27 July each year. The cockney explained that this particular year he had come to see the relic in its solid state as well as after its liquefaction, having heard 'a Bloke in 'Ighgate preachin' in the street that the miracle was all a put-up job, all bloomin' rot, in fact, because the Relic was *always liquid* and there warn't no blinkin' miracle abaht it. But now,' the cockney continued, 'I've seen it solid, and I've seen it liquid, and I'm goin' 'ome to find that Bloke.' When Grant asked what he proposed to do having found the bloke, '"*Give 'im bloomin' 'ell!*" was the emphatic reply of my outraged upholder of the miraculous.'

Now the reaction of this cockney to the question of a relic's authenticity is far closer to that of the medievals than might appear at first sight. A long tradition of local worship as well as apparently attested miracles was usually enough to guarantee that the faithful were not being duped. This does not mean that doubts were never entertained. On the contrary: men of the stature of Pope Gregory the Great insisted that relics venerated by Christians under his sway must be genuine. Earlier, the fifth Council of Carthage (A.D. 398) ordered the bishops to pull down altars that had been built over relics that could not be proved authentic. The problem was to devise accurate proofs. One such was ordeal by fire. A relic would be thrown on a charcoal fire. If the relic was consumed, then (people concluded) it had been inauthentic. If the fire went out, the relic was no fake. The extreme hazard involved here – for once burned, a relic was gone for ever – indicates the serious attitude towards the question of authenticity. Gregory of Tours was prepared to risk losing part of the body of the Virgin Mary in such a test. William, abbot of Cluny in 1161, incensed that many doubted that he possessed the head of St Genevieve, tested it by fire and was proved right. In 1377 it is recorded that the Bishop of Ferma was even prepared to test two spines from the crown of thorns in this way.

But the business was risky. It seemed often easier to force one's theological opponents to undergo the anxiety of having *their* relics so tested than risk losing one's own. Thus the Spanish council of Caesar Augustus in 592 decided that relics discovered in the churches of the Arian heretics should be tested by fire. Soon crafty clerics realised that there was no need to put the whole of a precious relic at risk. In 979 Bishop Egbert of Trier tested by fire the body of St Celsus by throwing only the relic's finger into a burning thurible. (It remained intact.)

Even this test could be circumvented by cunning fakers. By the early ninth century so many traders in relics were selling counterfeit pieces of the true cross made either of asbestos or amianthus that in 816 the Emperor Louis the Debonair forbade testing by fire as virtually useless.

Some approximation to modern historical methods can certainly be seen in the attempts of medieval churchmen to authenticate their relics. Many such men and women were after all avid readers of church histories and sometimes also historians themselves. Even where such sources failed, the churchmen were not always credulous believers in the authenticity of the relics in question. St Martin of Tours, for example, was deeply troubled by the relics of a man honoured as a supposed martyr in his diocese. He enquired of the oldest clergymen he could find, but could learn nothing of the true facts from them. Then St Martin had a dream, which revealed not that the relic was authentic but that it belonged to a brigand who had been executed for his crimes. The bones were flung out of Tours cathedral.

Great store too was laid on documentary evidence as well as oral tradition and local memories. This documentary evidence included written attestations that certain bones belonged to specific saints or martyrs. As bishops saw that their power might be increased by issuing these attestations, many such documents were issued and sealed by them as the middle ages developed ecclesiastical bureaucracies. Even so, some took the task lightly: it was one thing to exercise power, quite another to take trouble to exercise it responsibly. So when St Firmin was placed in a new shrine in the early twelfth century Bishop Godefroid of Amiens could find no document identifying the relic. Undeterred, he had the words FIRMINUS MARTYR AMBIANORUM EPISCOPUS inscribed on a lead plaque, and stuck it on the new reliquary.

Inscriptions on tombs were even more important than documentary identification in the early days of the relic cult. In fact, the first recorded use of the word 'relic' to describe a martyr's bones occurs on a tomb inscription at Sétif dated 452 A.D.:

IN HOC LOCO SANCTO DEPOSI
TAE SUNT RELIQVIAE SANCTI
LAURENTI MARTIRIS . . . AMEN

('In this holy place are laid the relics of St Laurence, Martyr . . . Amen.')

Many such epigraphs survive from the sixth century A.D., most in Latin but a good number too in Greek. They often were accurate.

In addition to all this, some certainty was needed that the relics venerated belonged to a person who had in truth been a saint. Here matters were and remain enormously complicated, above all by the fact that concepts of sanctity change alarmingly over the Christian centuries. Not till the seventeenth century does heroic virtue become a *sine qua non* of sanctity. Before then martyrdom alone was a sure route to canonisation, at least by popular acclaim. Thomas Fuller observed in 1732, 'He that will not live a saint can never die a martyr.' Earlier generations would not have agreed.

Perceptions of sanctity varied also from region to region. Professors Donald Weinstein and Rudolph Bell have analysed, for instance how the Tuscan hill towns in the later middle ages 'tended to provide the setting for guilt-ridden conversions of adolescent girls, while Rhinelanders seem to have been inclined to venerate great bishops who had been pious and obedient boys.' They instance St Umiliana of Florence, who was born in 1219 and 'was unusual in that she displayed no special piety or distaste for married life until after she had taken a husband at the age of sixteen (according to some accounts she was only twelve). Within a month of her marriage she began to spurn facial make-up and ornate clothes and to attend mass daily "for her sins". Umiliana spent her money on alms for the poor, visited the sick, and even cut off parts of her own garments to clothe the naked.' After her husband's death her life became happier; she fasted days on end, prayed to be made blind and deaf, flagellated herself, levitated, worked miracles and gave off a divine fragrance. On her death in 1246 she was instantly venerated in Florence as a saint and her corpse was eagerly cut up for relics.

Would the relics of such a saint have been so much sought

after in earlier times or later? Almost certainly not. When you choose a saint or hero, you say quite as much about yourself as about the object of your veneration. As the centuries pass, not all, but certainly many of the needs served by saints and their relics – needs psychological more than physical – vary widely. Even when the papacy finally took control of canonisation in the western church (and the first such affair, initiated and controlled from beginning to end by the Holy See, was that of Gilbert of Sempringham, as late as 1202), perceptions of sanctity continued to change with successive generations of Popes.

To take control of canonisation leads reasonably enough to wishing to have charge of authenticating relics. In the seventeenth century new rules for canonisation were drawn up, insisting that all candidates (except martyrs) had worked miracles since their deaths. In the same century Pope Clement IX created the 'Sacred Congregation for Indulgences and Relics' as part of a similar process of regularising what had once been a spontaneous, at times almost anarchic expression of church life. The Vatican since then has not relinquished control. In the nineteenth century Clement IX's Sacred Congregation was suppressed, but all questions concerning relics were now to be the concern of the Congregation of Rites. The Canon Law Code of 1917 declared that local vicar-generals were not to authenticate relics without special authorisation from the Vatican, and ordinaries were instructed prudently to withdraw relics whose authenticity they doubted. The second Vatican Council deemed it acceptable to give honour and reverence, but only to authentic relics.

Yet the mere exercise of ecclesiastical authority simply cannot be enough to authenticate a relic or declare one spurious. Pope Pius XII seems tacitly to have acknowledged this in 1949, when he spoke at last about the excavations which for many years had been carried out under St Peter's, Rome. To the question, 'Has the tomb of St Peter really been found?' he answered: 'Beyond all doubt, yes.' Then he added: 'A second question, subordinate to the first, refers to the relics of St Peter.

Have they been found? At the side of the tomb human bones have been discovered. However, it is impossible to prove with certainty that they belong to the body of the apostle.'

The Pope's admirable caution respects modern scientific archaeology. As Jocelyn Toynbee (Professor of Classical Archaeology at Cambridge) and John Ward Perkins (Director of the British School at Rome) concluded in 1956, the pile of bones that was reburied in the second century under what is now the greatest church in Rome may or may not be the relics of the apostle Peter himself. 'We must be content to leave all these questions unanswered . . . But at least since the second century, the belief that his body reposed on that spot has been, and always will be, a well-spring of devotion; and of that devotion the great church remains the living monument.'

Does this mean that today any approach to the question of authenticating a long venerated relic can only be one of reverent agnosticism? Must one always respect pious devotion and ancient beliefs when judging whether or not that devotion is due to the relic in question?

Christians have not always done so. An example lies in the ancient Périgord village of Cadouin. For over eight centuries the abbey of Cadouin boasted a sudary said to have wrapped the head of Jesus in the tomb. Unlike the shroud of Turin, this claim did not contradict the evidence about Jesus's burial in the fourth Gospel. Cadouin's 'sweat cloth' was made of linen 2.81 metres long and 1.13 metres wide, lined completely with red velvet and decorated on each side by ornamental bands, as well as six ribbons 16 or 17 millimetres wide.

This particular sudary made its first appearance, as far as western historical records go, in Liège in the mid-twelfth century. It reached Cadouin in 1217. Throughout the Hundred Years' War the sudary of Cadouin increased in renown. Popes soon competed to grant it indulgences. In 1344 Clement VI accorded a whole year's indulgence off purgatory to those who in the weeks after Passion Sunday venerated this sweat cloth 'which St Joseph of Arimathea wrapped around the dead body of Jesus after his descent from the cross.' In 1368 Pope Urban V decreed that for the next ten years anyone who gave alms at Cadouin and prayed before the sudary on certain great feasts would be granted five years off purgatory. Next, Pope Gregory IX extended the term of indulgence to twenty years.

Not surprisingly, the English tried to steal the sudary of Cadouin, but abbot Bertrand de Moulins foiled them in 1392 by taking it to Toulouse. The Archbishop of Toulouse and nine other prelates welcomed the monks and the relic with joy. The people of Périgord complained; but the sudary did not return to Cadouin until 1456, meanwhile touring as far as Paris, working countless miracles, increasingly venerated, increasingly coveted. Pope Nicholas V had by now taken the abbey of Cadouin under his protection, and the monks managed to resist any attempt to take away their precious relic – which continued to bring them gifts of land and money, as well as attracting crowds of pilgrims.

Veneration of the sudary declined somewhat during the eighteenth century, and at the Revolution the church authorities managed to hide it without difficulty until the risks of that era had passed. The abbey church was opened again and the famous relic continued once more to bless the faithful. All was well until 1934, when a scholar visiting Cadouin thought he recognised not Hebrew but Coptic letters embroidered on the ribbons of the holy sudary.

Suspicion dawned that the famous relic, which after all had no surviving history dating beyond the twelfth century, might be Egyptian, even a fake, brought to France after the first Crusade. Help was requested of the Director of the Arab Museum in Cairo. Without any difficulty he read on one of the ornamental ribbons first the usual Islamic invocation of Allah, followed by the name of Musta-Ali, Caliph in Egypt from 1094 to 1101. At the beginning of September the newspaper *Cross of Périgord*, followed by other regional journals, sadly announced that the feast of the Holy Sudary of Cadouin, usually celebrated on the Tuesday after the fourteenth of that month, would no longer take place.

This study of relics has illustrated *inter alia* their close connection with the miraculous. The shrine of the sweat cloth at Cadouin was certainly no exception. Today the lovely apse of Cadouin church, with its softly painted capitals and its fresco of the resurrection, still bears twenty-three plaques thanking the relic for its help. Movingly, parents offer their gratitude for the survival of their sons in the First World War. The latest date on these plaques is 1923 – with a simple thank you:

+

Merci

S. Suaire de Cadouin

1923

Are the fears and hopes that lie behind these plaques no longer part of the human condition? In Cadouin church is a fifteenth-century woodcarving of the Virgin Mary, damaged at the end of the sixteenth century, but restored by the priest of Paleyrac in 1865. When I was last there, early in September, exactly fifty years after the church authorities announced that their holy relic was a sham, I counted fifteen candles burning before this statue. Some human needs do not change.

Bibliography

ANDERSON, M. D., *History and Imagery in Parish Churches*, John Murray, London, 1971.

ANDERSSON, ARON, *The Art of Scandinavia*, vol. 2, Paul Hamlyn, London, 1970.

ATTWATER, DONALD, *The Penguin Dictionary of Saints*, Penguin Books, London, 1965.

BAINTON, R. H., *Here I Stand: A Life of Martin Luther*, Abingdon Press, Nashville, Tennessee, 1950.

BAYNES, N. H., 'The Supernatural Defenders of Constantinople,' in *Analecta Bollandiana*, tôme 67, Société des Bollandistes, Brussels, 1949, pp. 165–177.

BENTLEY, J., *A Guide to the Dordogne*, Penguin Books, London, 1985.

— *Oberammergau and the Passion Play*, Penguin Books, London, 1984.

— *Secrets of Mount Sinai*, Orbis Publications, London, 1985.

— and RODWELL, WARWICK, *Our Christian Heritage*, George Philip, London, 1984.

BENTHAM, J., *Auto-Icon or Further Uses of the Dead to the Living*, privately printed, 1842.

BETHEL, D., 'The lives of St Osyth of Essex and St Osyth of

Aylesbury,' in *Analecta Bollandiana*, tôme 88, fasc. 1–2, 1970, pp. 75–127.

— 'The Miracles of St Ithamar,' *Ibid.*, tôme 89, fasc. 2–4, 1971, pp. 421–437.

BLOCH, M., 'La Vie de S. Edouard le Confesseur par Osbert de Clare,' *Analecta Bollandiana*, tôme 41, 1923, pp. 5–131.

BOTTINEAU, Y., *Notre-Dame de Paris and the Sainte-Chapelle*, tr. L. F. Edwards, George Allen and Unwin, London, 1967.

BROOKE, R. and C., *Popular Religion in the Middle Ages*, Thames and Hudson, London, 1984.

BROWN, P. A., *The Development of the Legend of Thomas Becket*, Philadelphia, 1930.

BROWN, P. R. C., *Relics and Social Status in the Age of Gregory of Tours*, University of Reading Press, Reading, 1977.

— *The Cult of Saints*, SCM Press, London, 1981.

CALVIN, J., *A Treatise on Relics*, tr. Count Krosinski, Johnstone and Hunter, Edinburgh, 1864.

CLANCHY, M. T., *England and its Rulers, 1066–1272*, Fontana, London, 1983.

CORMACK, R., *Writing in Gold*, George Philip, London, 1985.

DE GAIFFIER, B., 'La légende de la Sainte Épine de Pise,' in *Analecta Bollandiana*, tôme 70, 1952, pp. 20–34.

DELOOZ, P., *Sociologie et canonisation*, Faculté de Droit, Liège, and Martinus Nijhoff, The Hague, 1969.

DODWELL, C. R., *Anglo-Saxon Art. A New Perspective*, Manchester University Press, Manchester, 1982.

FLETCHER, R., *St James's Catapult*, Oxford University Press, Oxford, 1984.

GEARY, P. J., *Furta Sacra*, Princeton University Press, Princeton, New Jersey, 1978.

GRANT, I. R., *Questioning the Devil's Advocate*, Burns Oates and Washbourne, 1931.

GRAHAM-CAMPBELL, J., and KIDD, D., *The Vikings*, British Museum Publications, London, 1980.

HERMANN-MASCARD, N., *Les Reliques des Saints. Formation coutumière d'un droit*, Éditions Klincksieck, Paris, 1975.

HOUGHTON, B., *Saint Edmund – King and Martyr*, Terence Dalton, Lavenham, Suffolk, 1970.

JEREMIAS, J., *Heiligengraber in Jesu Umwelt*, Vandenhoeck & Ruprecht, Göttingen, 1958.

LASKO, P., *Ars Sacra, 800–1200*, Penguin Books, Harmondsworth, 1972.

LECLERCQ, H. 'Reliques et Reliquaires,' in *Dictionnaire d'Archéologie Chrétienne et de Liturgie*, tôme 14, 2nd part, Librairie Letourzey et Ané, Paris, 1948, pp. 2294–2359.

MAUBOURGET, J., *Le Suaire de Cadouin*, Ribes, Périgueux, 1936.

MOONEY, J., *St Magnus – Earl of Orkney*, W. R. Mackintosh, Kirkwall, 1935.

MÜLLER, A. V., *Die 'hochheilige Vorhaut Christi' im Kult und in der Theologie der Papstkirche*, Berlin, 1907.

OBELKEVICH, J. (ed.), *Religion and the People, 800–1700*, University of North Carolina Press, Chapel Hill, 1979.

OPPENHEIMER, F., *The Legend of the Sainte Ampoule*, Faber and Faber, London, 1953.

OPPERMANN, C. J. A., *English Missionaries in Sweden and Denmark*, SPCK, London, 1937.

PEARSON, K., and MORANT, G. M., *The Portraiture of Oliver Cromwell with Special Reference to the Wilkinson Head*, Cambridge University Press, Cambridge, 1935.

PFISTER, F., *Der Reliquienkult im Altertum*, 2 vols, Giessen, 1909–1912.

QUADIR, F., and DAIG, M. M. (ed.), KHAN, M. I., *Reliques of the Quaid-i-Azam*, Karachi, 1980.

RUNCIMAN, S. C., 'Some Remarks on the Image of Edessa,' in *Cambridge Historical Journal*, vol. 3, Cambridge University Press, 1931, pp. 238–252.

— 'The Holy Lance found at Antioch,' in *Analecta Bollandiana*, tôme 68, 1950, pp. 197–204.

SAINTYVES, P., *Les Reliques et les Images Legendaires*, Mercure de France, Paris, 1912.

SCARFE, N., 'The Body of St Edmund. An Essay in Necrobiography,' in *Proceedings of the Suffolk Institute of Archaeology*, vol. XXXI, part 3, W. E. Harrison and Sons, Ipswich, 1969, pp. 303–317.

SHARP, M., *The Churches of Rome*, Hugh Evelyn, London, 1967.

SHERRARD, P., *Constantinople, Iconography of a Sacred City*, Oxford University Press, London, 1965.

— *Athos the Holy Mountain*, Sidgwick and Jackson, London, 1982.

TOYNBEE, J., and PERKINS, J. W., *The Shrine of St Peter and the Vatican Excavations*, Longmans, Green and Co., London, 1956.

VAUGHAN, R., *Matthew Paris*, Oxford University Press, London, 1958.

WALL, J. C., *Relics of the Passion*, Talbot and Co., Dublin, 1910.
— *Shrines of British Saints*, Methuen and Co., London, 1905.
WALSH, J. E., *The Bones of St Peter*, Victor Gollancz, London, 1983.
WARD, B., *Miracles and the Medieval Mind*, Scolar Press, London, 1983.
WEBER, E., *Peasants into Frenchmen*, Chatto and Windus, London, 1979.
WEINSTEIN, D., and BELL, R., *Saints and Society: The Two Worlds of Western Christendom*, University of Chicago Press, Chicago, 1983.
WHITELOCK, D., 'Fact and Fiction in the Legend of St Edmund,' in *Proceedings of the Suffolk Institute of Archaeology*, vol. XXXI, part 3, 1969, pp. 217–233.
WILSON, B., and IKEDA, D., *Human Values in a Changing World*, Macdonald and Co., London, 1984.
WILSON, D. M., *Anglo-Saxon Art from the Seventh Century to the Norman Conquest*, Thames and Hudson, London, 1984.
WILSON, S. (ed.), *Saints and their Cults: Studies in Religious Sociology, Folklore and History*, Cambridge University Press, Cambridge, 1983.
WILSON, I., *The Turin Shroud*, revised edition, Penguin Books, London, 1979.

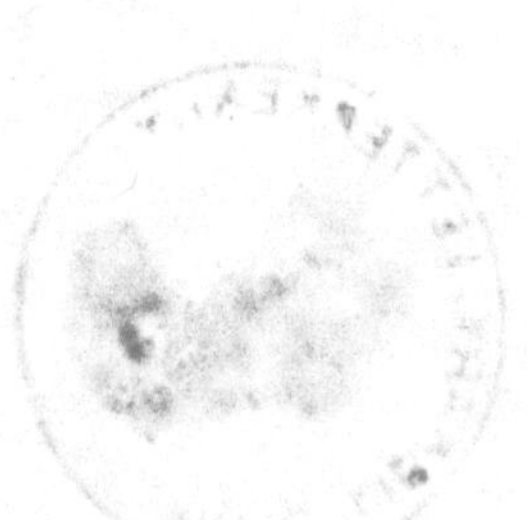

Index

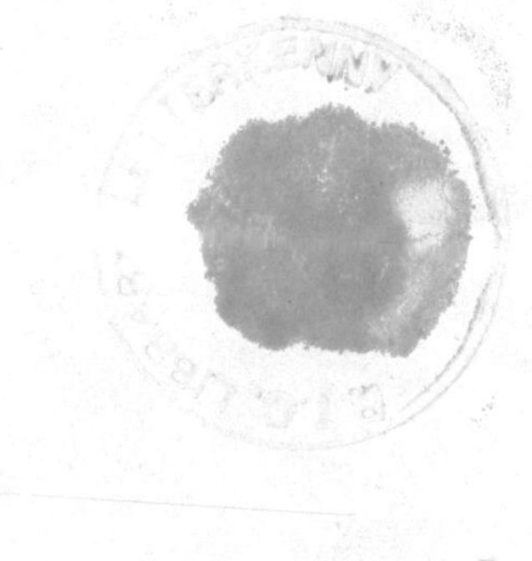